# ESSAYS ON AFRICAN WRITING

## 1 A re-evaluation

Edited by
Abdulrazak Gurnah

**HEINEMANN**

Heinemann Educational
A Division of Heinemann Publishers (Oxford) Ltd
Halley Court, Jordan Hill, Oxford OX2 8EJ

Heinemann: A Division of Reed Publishing (USA) Inc.
361 Hanover Street, Portsmouth, NH 03801-3912, USA

Heinemann Educational Books (Nigeria) Ltd
PMB 5205, Ibadan
Heinemann Educational Boleswa
PO Box 10103, Village Post Office, Gaborone, Botswana

FLORENCE   PRAGUE   PARIS   MADRID
ATHENS   CHICAGO   MELBOURNE   JOHANNESBURG
AUCKLAND   SINGAPORE   TOKYO   SAO PAULO

First published by Heinemann Educational in 1993

Series Editor: Adewale Maja-Pearce

British Library Cataloguing in Publication Data
A catalogue record for this book is available from the British Library.

ISBN 0435 917625

Phototypeset by
Wilmaset Ltd, Birkenhead, Wirral
Printed and bound in Great Britain
by Clay Ltd., Bungay, Suffolk

93 94 95 96 10 9 8 7 6 5 4 3 2 1

# Contents

# Introduction

The essays in this collection set out to re-read texts generally familiar to readers and students of African writing and are intended as re-evaluations of those texts established as part of the African 'canon' – that authoritative list of books accepted as 'literature'. The re-readings which surfaced did not usually contradict the excellent scholarship of earlier ones but, on the other hand, they did tend to shift the focus of attention onto aspects of the texts which had not been addressed before.

Perhaps one of the less familiar of the writers whose work is discussed here is Jean-Baptiste Tati-Loutard, the poet from the Congo Republic. His writing is only gradually becoming known in English and other languages, although his first two collections, *Poèmes de la mer* and *Les Racines congolaise* were published as long ago as 1968. As with many other African poets writing in French, Tati-Loutard's work has been overshadowed by Leopold Sedar Senghor's capacity of functioning as the focus of attention on African poetry in French. Senghor's poetic achievement is, of course, immense – but what has made him such a central figure in African poetry and African writing is his involvement with *négritude*. Despite repeated scares, rumours of the death of *négritude* continually turn out to be exaggerated, and the essentialist proposition at its heart reappears in only marginally less reductive forms.

At its simplest and in its earliest form – and perhaps in its most glorious manifestation – *négritude* was an expression of resistance to the 'assimilation' of Africans and African descendants in the Caribbean into French culture. In 1929, the stalwarts of *négritude*, Senghor from Senegal, Léon Damas from French Guiana, and Aimé Césaire from Martinique seemed, with their aggressive rejection, to be proving conclusively that 'assimiliation' had not worked. With time, matters have looked less conclusive, especially as the movement grew into an orthodoxy of cultural and racial fantasy, and after critics had effectively demonstrated its essentialist fallacy. At the heart of the discourse of *négritude* is an Africanness in direct and precise defiance of the imperial metaphors of African savagery, ugliness and stupidity. Thus Africa is warm and nurturing, often portrayed as a woman longingly remembered in European exile, as in Senghor's 'You Held the Black Face':

> When shall I see my land again, the pure horizon of your face?
> When shall I sit at the table of your dark breasts?[1]

In response to the jibe of stupidity, *négritude* saw the African as instinctual and spontaneous, conceding to the European the high ground of rationality and intellectual sophistication. Senghor again:

> This is not to say that the Negro is traditionally devoid of reason . . . But this reason is not discursive . . . It is not antagonistic but sympathetic. This is another path to knowledge. Negro reason does not impoverish things. It does not mold them into rigid categories, eliminating the juices and the sap; it flows into the arteries of things, espouses all their contours and comes to rest in the living core of the real. White reason is analytical through use, Negro reason is intuitive through participation.[2]

Despite the seductive metaphors of sinuosity and movement, Senghor's proposition remains unpersuasive. For instead of challenging the biologizing of race – the basis of European representations of Africans and African cultures – *négritude* sought to put another interpretation on the characteristics that European discourse had allocated to the African. As Soyinka said in one of his many critical comments on the movement:

> *Négritude* trapped itself in what was a defensive role, even though its accents were strident, its syntax hyperbolic and its strategy aggressive.[3]

While Soyinka's criticism is powerful and ultimately unanswerable, it is curious how much negative attention *négritude* has attracted from

African critics and writers who are not French speakers. Curious because the same critics (Soyinka and Achebe, for example, as we shall see later) have at times described their writing ambitions in terms which mark African arts and public culture as unique. This is some way from the Manichean propositions of high *négritude*, but still an argument about originary essence. And such an argument is implicitly a response to the European narrative of Africa, at whose core was the assumption that African cultural achievement was both slight and crude. The significance of *négritude*, despite the defensive hyperbole, is that it was an urgent attempt to engage with Europe's representations of Africa. A similar kind of urgency and hyperbole is strikingly present today in the debate on the languages African writers use in their work.

When Ngũgĩ wa Thiong'o asserted in *Decolonizing the Mind* (1986)[4] that he would no longer write fiction in English, it appeared that the debate about the implications of African texts using European languages had reached a radical and critical phase. His essays on 'The Politics of Language' were not only lucid and precise, but they also generated a lively and important discussion of the choices open to writers from Africa. If there were good reasons for them to write, why not in African languages, since most Africans would be unable to read them otherwise. But, rather than reaching a critical phase, it was clear that the debate had acquired a new language of its own and was still engaged with the same concerns iterated by Obiajunwa Wali in his 'The Dead-End of African Literature?'[5] For what is crucial about the language question is not just a matter of cultural nationalism – the most basic strand of the argument – or even of loyally serving a mass *African* audience, despite the entreating voices of concerned commentators.[6] It is the degree to which this act of possessing another's language so intimately implicates the text into dependency. The discussion has a long and impressive theoretical pedigree, given new energy not only by Ngũgĩ but by wide-ranging studies in post-colonial theory.[7] Nor has it only exercised African writers and intellectuals. As Anthony Kwame Appiah demonstrates so lucidly in his *In My Father's House*, it is also to be found at the core of national-cultural discourse.[8] In our case, European languages became available to Africans as a result of an imperialist project initiated and sustained by arrogance and contempt towards its victims. The narrative of this project, which is also the narrative of being European, is finely intermeshed with the language that delivers it and by which it is given substance and dimension. It is to this that Fanon was referring when he wrote: 'To speak means to be in a position to use a certain syntax, to grasp the morphology of this or that language, but it means above all to assume a culture, to support the weight of a civilization.'[9] How can this same language now serve the dissident needs of the African without infiltrating his or her discourse with its valencies?

Chinua Achebe, among others, has been writing for years that it is possible for an African to use an English that reflects his or her experience:

> The African writer should aim to use English in a way that brings out his message best without altering the language to the extent that its value as a medium of international exchange will be lost. He should aim at fashioning out an English which is at once universal and able to carry his peculiar experience.[10]

Although Achebe's language is directive here, it is nonetheless apparent that he thinks such 'fashioning' is possible. This process of indigenizing the language diminishes the more serious dimensions of the charge of self-treachery implicit in the argument against the use of English. An alternative answer is offered in more recent post-colonial theory which sees such use of European languages as a 'subaltern' activity, the outcome of which is to destabilize the native's representation in European discourse. This position is exemplified by Ashcroft, Griffiths and Tiffin, in their influential book, *The Empire Writes Back*.[11] The chapter on language opens with:

> The crucial function of language as a medium of power demands that post-colonial writing define itself by seizing the language of the centre and re-placing it in discourse fully adapted to the colonized place. There are two distinct processes by which it does this. The first, abrogation or denial of the privilege of 'English' involves a rejection of the metropolitan power over the means of communication. The second, the appropriation and reconstitution of the language of the centre, the process of capturing and remoulding the language to new usages, marks a separation from the site of colonial privilege. (p. 38)

So, far from describing dependence, the native's use of English displaces the relationship of the post-colonial subject to the colonial language and the colonizing culture. Because by its very nature the substance of the native's account will challenge the imperialist narrative, it inevitably subverts and resists Europe's misrepresenting discourse. Furthermore, by bringing their own narrative traditions to the texts, non-European writers infiltrate and deconstruct the fictional and dramatic forms themselves – what Ashcroft et al. refer to as 'the process of capturing and remoulding language to new usages' – and arrive at something new and hybrid. A striking example of this in African writing is the recent work of the Nigerian novelist Ben Okri, especially in his novels *The Famished Road* and *Songs of Enchantment*.[12] For it is clear that Okri has an intimate and complex understanding of the 'usages' of the novel form in English, and that he is also using narrative forms familiar to us from the writings of Fagunwa and Amos Tutuola, which derive closely from Yoruba oral narrative forms. Descriptions of his work as 'magic realism' – and therefore derivative of South-American writing in Spanish – miss the extent to which this style of writing fiction has been naturalized as an English-novel form.

The debate on the use of European languages is a necessary and important one, opening up complex issues of understanding and affiliation which have only been touched upon here. That its rhetoric is so heated demonstrates its complexity and the profound political and cultural concerns which underlie it, as demonstrated effectively by Ngũgĩ in his *Decolonizing the Mind*. In any case, the use of these languages made it possible for the category 'African literature' to come into being almost as soon as a text existed to be inserted into it, despite the contradictions and differences which made other continental generalizations problematic. The metaphor of independence as African rebirth was not only necessary – as well as gloriously apt – in the discourse of cultural nationalism, but was also a powerful pedagogic paradigm. This paradigm could be summarized as: ignorant accounts of Africa written by arrogant Europeans were followed by insider accounts that wrote back at them.

The 'before and after' shape of the discourse of 'African literature' is not, of course, an invention of academic critics, but the desire of many of the texts themselves. The texts self-consciously spoke above differences, to other 'Africans' whose languages they did not share and whose cultures they did not fully grasp. They were able to do this when they did because they were written in European languages and were therefore capable of generalization as texts whose subject was the African condition. Chinua Achebe's Igbo village in *Things Fall Apart* (1958) could effectively stand as a paradigm for rural Africa at the moment of the colonial tragedy.[13] Camara Laye's *L'Enfant Noir* (1954) could both celebrate, and probably idealize, the ways of old Africa and also suggest how a young African can become alienated from those ways through colonial education.[14] The same theme – colonial education – has echoes in a remarkable number of African works of the immediate post-colonial period, and expresses those anxieties which surface in the language debate – about incorporation, cultural treachery and self-fulfilment. In both Ngũgĩ's and Achebe's writing, for example, colonial education figures as both a dynamic space for individual growth, and also as a means of infiltrating the rooted culture through the unavoidable complicity of the divided convert. For instance, Nwoye in *Things Fall Apart* actively subverts sacred Umuofia customs both to express his rejection of the toleration of such cruelties as the murder of Ikemefuna, and to affiliate himself with his new mentors who have promised him individual fulfilment. In Ngũgĩ's early novels, *Weep Not, Child* (1964) and *The River Between* (1965), Njoroge and Waiyaki paradoxically valorize colonial education into a redeeming ideology in which they play Messianic roles at the very moment when their communities are dispossessed and divided by the same European invasion.[15]

It is all too likely that many among the first group of post-colonial African writers themselves had similar experiences of ambivalence towards colonial education, or in any case understood the divisiveness of exposure. This is expressed most clearly in the way the texts of this immediate post-independence period focus on colonial history. The history they were responding to was the self-righteous narrative of imperial advance into a passive and largely oblivious Africa. While industrious and resourceful Europeans built railways and opened up waterways, despite the often fatal harshness of conditions, ignorant Africans slumbered on in their 'night of the first ages' until shaken awake and forced into the light by European intervention. The European writing on Africa which they would have been required to read during their colonial education was, at best, benignly condescending about childish Africans, and at worst racist. So in addition to the unity which language gave to these texts, there was also considerable agreement in the desire to write back to the 'denigration' (to use Achebe's word) of Africans by Europeans. In his essay 'The Novelist as Teacher' (*Hopes and Impediments*, pp. 27–31) Achebe writes these now famous words: 'Here then is an adequate revolution for me to espouse – to help my society regain belief in itself and put away the complexes of the years of denigration and self-abasement. And it is essentially a question of education, in the best sense of that word'. (p. 30) The education referred to is one whose aim is self-retrieval and 'self-apprehension', the phrase used by Soyinka to describe the ambition behind his book *Myth, Literature, and the African World* (1976). Yet it is remarkable that in his first major play, *A Dance of the Forest*, first performed in 1960,[16] Soyinka is already warning against the self-flattery implicit in such defensiveness about history. It is clear from this play and his other texts that Soyinka sees history both as time past and as dynamic myth contextualizing the present and the future. In other words, history here is not just a matter of putting the record straight, but of locating social paradigms that are essentially African. This is the interesting paradox in Soyinka's writing, namely that it rejects the essentialist position of 'a detailed uniqueness of the African world' (*Myth* p. xii), and asserts its special viability as a social paradigm in such texts as *The Interpreters* (1965), and *Death and the King's Horsemen* (1975).[17]

Under cover of such engagement with social and artistic issues, questions of patriarchy and racism did not seriously arise in this writing. Where they did, they were fudged or handled with a degree of righteousness which justified the later criticism. In respect of patriarchy, the African text was engaged in establishing the potency of African thought and culture to itself and to the world and, at best, it spoke for women without giving them voice. The striking exception to this was Nuruddin Farah's *From a Crooked Rib* (1970).[18] Hence when writing by women emerged this appeared to be quite deliberately writing back to earlier African texts in the same way that Achebe and Ngũgĩ had done to European texts.[19] More importantly, African women's writing scrutinized the metaphors which described the unified self, and which had been encoded in images of potency, strength and self-absorption. For example, by focusing on marriage, as so many women texts did, issues of individual motivation and justification were foregrounded, and the way marriage serves patriarchal social structures was exposed. These issues did not only concern personal choices, but those contextualized in social and historical structures. Instead of women stereotyped as courtesans, or representative of the fecund African earth or as twittering village extras, they become central figures in the narrative, engaged in a profound social critique, as in Marima Bâ's writing and the work of Ama Ata Aidoo.

If African writing was neglectful of women, its commentators were also neglectful of its racisms – evident in the exclusion of South African and North African writers from 'African literature' because of 'race'. This collection includes essays on Doris Lessing and Nadine Gordimer, and J. M. Coetzee as well as Dennis Brutus. The work of each of these writers has focused on the reality of Southern Africa – its racism, cruelties, and the choices open to individuals who are implicated by their history and culture. In a different sense, it is remarkable that writing such as Armah's *Why Are We So Blest?* (1972) and his grotesque novel *Two Thousand Seasons* (1973), as well as Ngũgĩ's *The Trial of Dedan Kimathi* (1976), should have been able to speak with such racist reductiveness, and yet so self-righteously, without any serious protest being made.[20] It is therefore timely that this collection has one essay which addresses itself to Armah's novel.

There are many writers whose work has not been discussed in these essays. Some will be included in a collection which is underway. What has concerned us as much as ideas of cultural space and forms of writing has been to commentate on writers whose work is well-known and due for reappraisal.

Abdulrazak Gurnah

1993

## Notes

1. 'You Held the Black Face (for Khalam)', *The Penguin Book of Modern African Poetry*, ed. Gerald Moore and Ulli Beier, Harmondsworth, Middlesex: Penguin, 1984 (Third edition), p. 237.

2. L. S. Senghor, 'African Negro Aesthetics,' translated by Elaine P. Halperin, *Diogenes*, No 16 (Winter 1956), p. 24.

3. Wole Soyinka, *Myth, Literature and the African World*, Cambridge: Cambridge University Press, 1976.

4. Ngũgĩ wa Thiong'o, *Decolonizing the Mind*, London: James Currey Ltd, 1986. In his introductory remarks to this text Ngũgĩ writes: 'This book . . . is my farewell to English as a vehicle for any of my writings. From now on it is Gikuyu and Kiswahili all the way' p. xiv.

5. Obiajunwa Wali, 'The Dead-End of African Literature?' *Transition* 10 (1963), pp. 13–15. Wali's essay provoked an extended correspondence in *Transition*, and it is significant that in re-opening the language question, Ngũgĩ cites his debt to David Diop the Senegalese poet, 'and to Obi Wali of Nigeria who made the historic intervention in 1964' p. xi.

6. In his intelligent and entertaining essay, Femi Ojo-Ade sees that African writers using European languages are dupes of colonial cynicism: 'Not surprisingly the colonial master, the symbolic Prospero has given the magic of language to only a few chosen Calibans . . .'. Femi Ojo-Ade, 'Of Culture, Commitment and Construction: Reflections on African Literature,' *Transition*, No. 53, 1991, pp. 4–24.

7. It would be impossible to cite a representative list, so the examples below are only to be seen as important introductory texts: *Nation and Narration*, ed. Homi K. Bhabha (London: Routledge) 1990; Bill Ashcroft, Gareth Griffiths and Helen Tiffin, *The Empire Writes Back: theory and practice in post-colonial literatures*, London: Routledge, 1989; and *Past the Last Post: theorizing post-colonialism and post-modernism*, edited by Ian Adam and Helen Tiffin, Hemel Hempstead: Harvester Wheatsheaf, 1991.

8. Anthony Kwame Appiah, *In My Father's House*, London: Methuen, 1992.

9. Frantz Fanon, *Black Skin, White Masks*, trans. Charles Lam Markmann, New York: Grove Press, 1967. Originally published in France as *Peau Noire, Masques Blancs* (1952).

10. This is from an early essay by Achebe, 'The Role of the Writer in a New Nation,' *Nigeria Magazine*, No. 81 (June 1964) p. 16. In a later essay: 'The Writer and His Community' (*Hopes and Impediments*, London: Heinemann, 1988), Achebe champions his right to English in this way: 'I can see no situation in which I will be presented with a Draconian choice between . . . English and Igbo. For me, no either/or; I insist on both' p. 41.

11. See 7.

12. Ben Okri, *The Famished Road*, London: Cape, 1991; *Songs of Enchantment*, London: Cape, 1993.

13. Chinua Achebe, *Things Fall Apart*, London: Heinemann, 1958.

14. Camara Laye, *L'Enfant Noir*, Paris: Librarie Plon, 1954. First published in English as *The Dark Child*, 1955; published by Fontana as *The African Child*, 1959.

15. Ngũgĩ wa Thiong'o, *Weep Not, Child*, London: Heinemann, 1964; *The River Between*, London: Heinemann, 1965.

16. Wole Soyinka, *A Dance of the Forest*, London and Ibadan: Oxford University Press, first published 1963.

17. Wole Soyinka, *The Interpreters*, London: André Deutsch, 1965; *Death and the King's Horseman*, London: Methuen, 1975.

18. Nuruddin Farah, *From A Crooked Rib*, London: Heinemann, 1970.

19. See C. L. Innes, 'Mothers or Sisters? Identity, Discourse and Audience in the Writing of Ama Ata Aidoo and Mariama Bâ'; and Caroline Rooney, ' "Dangerous Knowledge" and the Poetics of Survival: A Reading of *Our Sister Killjoy* and *A Question of Power*'. Both essays are in *Motherlands*, ed. Susheila Nasta, London: The Women's Press, 1991.

20. Ayi Kwei Armah, *Why Are We So Blest?*, New York: Doubleday, 1972; London: Heinemann, 1974; *Two Thousand Seasons*, Nairobi: East African Publishing House, 1973.

Ngũgĩ wa Thiong'o and Micere Githae Mugo, *The Trial of Dedan Kimathi*, Nairobi: Heinemann, 1976; London: Heinemann. 1977.

# Chinua Achebe and the Poetics of Location: The Uses of Space in *Things Fall Apart* and *No Longer at Ease*

## SIMON GIKANDI

It is not an exaggeration to say that the works of Chinua Achebe have up to now been read almost exclusively in terms of time and historicity. But this privileging of temporal terms has not arisen because of critical oversight or theoretical blindness: Achebe seems to have written his works so close to the axis of temporality that his whole oeuvre has an uncanny way of forcing us to read it not so much in the sequence in which his novels were written, but in the progressive historical relation these texts have established *vis à vis* the African experience. In the circumstances, even when our critical paradigms are generated by the desire to trace the formal and ideological relations between Achebe's texts – as I have tried to do in *Reading Chinua Achebe*[1] – we are more likely to follow a trajectory from *Things Fall Apart*, through *Arrow of God*, to *No Longer at Ease*, than one which reads these novels in the order in which they appeared. It is indeed difficult to promote a programme of reading Achebe's novels that will seek their cultural and symbolic value in the genetic relation between *Things Fall Apart* and *No Longer at Ease*, although the latter is considered to be a sequel to the former.

Why does it seem easier to insert *Arrow of God* in the temporal space that separates Achebe's first and second novels even when the three works are not related in any fundamental sense? Or, to put the question another way, why has *Arrow of God* become a *supplement* for the Nwoye Okonkwo story that Achebe, by his own admission, could not write? The most obvious answer to these questions has to do with our own engagement with the novel as a genre: we are still imprisoned in a critical tradition – whose most fervent advocate has been Georg Lukács – in which the history and development of the novel is explicated in strictly temporal terms.[2] In addition, the peculiar condition in which

1

Achebe's novels have been produced – the history of colonialism and nationalism – has affirmed the centrality of the temporal axis in our theoretical and critical reflections. There is, in other words, such a close affinity between Achebe's narratives and his subject – the African historical experience – that it is difficult, if not impossible, not to read these texts as both representations of this experience and a metacommentary on their condition of possibility. The temporal axis offers readers a secure framework for reading Achebe's novels.

My essay seeks to propose a different approach to the epistemology of narrative in Achebe's first two novels, to pose the question of location and space and its relation to the development of meaning in both *Things Fall Apart* and *No Longer at Ease*. Can a methodical interpretation of spatial relations and what Foucault has called 'the fatal intersection of time and space' cast new insights into the epistemology that drives Achebe's works?[3] Can an interpretation of the numerous spatial and geographical metaphors that have such a palpable presence in Achebe's texts proffer us new ways of reconvening the central problems in these texts – problems about identity and location, power and knowledge, and the topography of the nation? Surely, a reconsideration of the poetics of location – and the politics of space – is warranted by the current reconfiguration of global cultures. It is warranted by the simple fact that the present period, a period in which the postcolonial cultures of formerly colonised areas are challenging older, temporal organisations of power and knowledge, has come to be defined, in the words of Foucault, as 'the epoch of space . . . when our experience of the world is less that of a long life developing through time than that of a network that connects points and intersections with its own skein' (p. 22). If this is so, how is a poetics of location exemplified in Achebe's texts, and what is its relation to the inherited nineteenth-century (colonial) discourse on the place and space of the African in the taxonomy of world cultures?

It is important to begin with the question of inherited spaces, and the geopolitics surrounding African cultures, because if metaphors of location seem to play a more prominent role in Achebe's earlier works than they do in the later ones, this has to do with his proximity to the colonial text which had deployed colonised spaces as a key element in the debate on Englishness and its domain. For Englishness, as I have argued elsewhere, defines itself through gestures of situatedness:

English identity, especially in the period of high imperialism, is enacted against the backdrop of the spaces of the Other which function as what Foucault has aptly called *heterotopias*.[4] If utopias are sites that have no real places and present society in perfected form, says Foucault, heterotopias are the real spaces in which the central meanings of a culture 'are simultaneously represented, contested and inverted' (p. 24). Heterotopias are hence spaces of representation and interpretation. Such spaces, according to Foucault, are mirrors that exert 'a sort of counteraction' on the positions occupied by the writing subject; from the standpoint of this mirror, this subject, counteracting itself against the Other, comes back towards itself (p. 24). It is not by accident, then, that some of the most important colonial texts on Africa in the modern period, texts such as Conrad's *Heart of Darkness*, Cary's *Mister Johnson*, and Greene's *Journey without Maps*, are dominated by the problematic of location, of spaces, of maps and roads. As numerous critics have observed, these texts provide the English with mirrors in which to gaze at themselves; but the African is absent from such works except as a projection of European desire.[5]

Now in writing against this tradition in *Things Fall Apart*, Achebe provides us with an ingenious, but paradoxical, deployment of space: he wants, on one hand, to counter the heterotopic representation of the African in the colonial text by making Umuofia an epistemological presence, one defined not only by the process of time, but also by an ensemble of spaces; the African space hence functions as a Foucauldian 'space of emplacement' (p. 22). On the other hand, however, Achebe's narrative does not seek to represent the African space as a utopian counter to European heterotopias; if he were to do so, he would merely be valorising the romantic image of Africa to counter the western projection of the continent as a savage space. To avoid these two traps – that is, the image of Africa as the place of the savage or as the cradle of human values – Achebe invokes a double image of Umuofia: the village is shown to be both an autonomous geographical entity, and a place torn by contending social and historical forces. This doubleness accounts for the chronotopic disjuncture that leads to the triumph of colonialism at the end of the novel.

Moreover, when we consider the tension between time and space in the novel, we realise how Okonkwo's narrative is both progressive and retrogressive. From a temporal perspective, the structure of the novel, especially in the first part, encourages us to see Okonkwo's story as a progressive struggle in which he ultimately triumphs over the process of time. The wrestling match that opens the novel is the quintessential space of emplacement and empowerment because it makes Okonkwo's subjectivity parallel the character of his community and culture: his triumph takes place in 'a fight which the old men agreed was one of the fiercest since the founder of their town engaged a spirit of the wild for seven days and seven nights'.[6] Okonkwo's victory in the wrestling ring has become, over the years, one of the founding stories of the village: 'That was many years ago, twenty years or more, and during this time Okonkwo's fame had grown like a bush-fire in the harmattan' (p. 3).

But if the first part of the novel promotes a progressive narrative in which time brings fame and prosperity to the cultural hero, the second and final parts negate the temporal process. In exile, Okonkwo is forced into a historical hiatus; on his return to Umuofia, he realises that his life (and hence his story) has been reduced to zero ground. Moreover, the ending of the novel appears to be a void in which the hero is silenced and, in his abomination, is cut off from the spirit of his community. As the District Commissioner notes, Okonkwo's story, which opened the novel by being compared to the mythical narratives of Umuofia's founding father, can only be confined to 'a reasonable paragraph' (p. 148). And although it is possible to argue that the compression of the hero's story to only a paragraph in the colonial text arises from the coloniser's ethnocentric negation of the African narrative, we also need to remember that by the time Okonkwo returns to Umuofia after his exile, his story has become marginal even in his own community.

The relation between the space of emplacement and that of negation is, however, more complicated than the structure of the novel suggests. We can discern this complication if we refuse to follow the linear plotting of the novel and focus our attention on the constant juxtaposition of different spatial configurations and the uncanny ways in which the hierarchy of social spaces that emplaces Okonkwo in Umuofia is also responsible for his displacement. We need, in effect, to reconsider Okonkwo's troubled relation with his communal territory, a relation that is defined in the narrative by the tension between space and time in his engenderment. Consider, for example, how the incipient moment of the novel derives its power from the subtle evocation of the metaphorical identity between Okonkwo and Umuofia and his metonymic displacement from it; the novel surrounds the heroic character with innumerable spaces in which his relation with his community is affirmed and his hierarchy within it is denoted. In the wrestling arena of his youth, Okonkwo's identity as a powerful man is realised (p. 3); in the market place where 'the normal course of action' (p. 8) is a connotation of the norms by which the community lives, Okonkwo is recognised as Umuofia's representative man and is 'asked on behalf of the clan' to look after Ikemefuna 'in the interim' (p. 9).

In all these instances, Okonkwo's authority as the protector of the Umuofian doxa is closely related to the character of his household space: 'Okonkwo's prosperity was visible in his household. He had a large compound enclosed by a thick wall of red earth . . . The barn was built against one end of the red walls, and long stacks of yams stood out prosperously in it' (p. 10). This household is, in effect, represented as a replica of the larger social spaces that sustain a cosmos which, in turn, provides natural ground and cultural stability to the larger community. In this household, celestial power becomes symbolised in material terms (Okonkwo's prosperity is written on his household) and also functions as a spatial mirror for both idealised social production and the localisation of the communal doxa. In other words, when we gaze at Okonkwo's social space (his household), we witness not only the materiality of 'his personal god and ancestral spirits', but also the gods that have 'built' Umuofia. Moreover, the novel provides us with a crucial juxtaposition between this individualised space and the communal space (*ilo*) that it replicates. Both function as crucial symbols of the organic community.

But even as we trace Okonkwo's advancement along the temporal axis that elevates him from the son of a pauper to one of the strongest men in Umuofia, we cannot fail to notice how his temporal progression is constantly being challenged by what would appear to be the undialectical force of space.[7] In the first part of *Things Fall Apart*, as most readers will recall, Okonkwo's struggle to succeed is a manifest struggle against the process of time, a struggle that is commented on retrospectively (p. 17). On the temporal axis, the subject has transcended his past; his suffering and penury are narrated in the past tense (Chapter 2) as a qualifying appendix to his present prosperity (Chapter 1). But in spatial terms, the present doesn't have any primacy over the past: Okonkwo remembers his first 'tragic' year as a farmer 'with a cold shiver throughout the rest of his life' (p. 17). In Okonkwo's body and psyche, the very forces he thought he had transcended rule his life, for in this internal landscape his selfhood is mapped by a repressed past association with his father.

So if in the visible space of his household we read Okonkwo's material and temporal advancement from the regime of his father, his internal landscape is defined by Unoka: his 'whole life was dominated by fear, the fear of failure and of weakness . . . It was fear of himself, lest he should be found to resemble his father'; 'he was possessed by the fear of his father's contemptible life and shameful death' (pp. 9, 13). If his household is an affirmation of masculinist power ('Okonkwo ruled his household with a heavy hand'), his masculine aggression arises in his attempt to deny the feminine forces he associates with his father (pp. 30–2).[8]

Moreover, if Okonkwo's masculine ideologies are predicated on the belief that the household (and *natio*) ruled by men is a natural entity, the Ikemefuna subtext both affirms masculinity and carefully questions the intrinsic value of the male-dominated space. Consider, for example, the process by which Ikemefuna is temporarily incorporated into Umuofia: 'For three years Ikemefuna lived in Okonkwo's household and the elders of Umuofia seemed to have forgotten about him. He grew rapidly like a yam tendril in the rainy season, and was full of the sap of life. He had become wholly absorbed in his new family' (p. 37). The images of vegetation and growth are important here: they suggest that Umuofia is an organic community with the natural capacity to absorb and assimilate those who enter it. And yet we know that Ikemefuna does not have natal rights within this community; he can only inscribe himself within it by appealing to Umuofia's implied discourse of what is 'right', especially through the evocation of masculinity (and hence homosociality). In other words, Ikemefuna becomes part of Umuofia by establishing the 'deep, horizontal comradeship' that Benedict Anderson has isolated as a key facet of nationness.[9]

It is through Ikemefuna that Nwoye is masculinised, at least temporarily, thus allowing Okonkwo to sustain his fantasy of an overarching male hegemony that will reproduce itself through his son: 'Okonkwo was inwardly pleased at his son's development, and he knew it was due to Ikemefuna. He wanted Nwoye to grow into a tough young man capable of ruling his father's household when he was dead and gone to join the ancestors' (p. 37). But no sooner has this desire been asserted than it is negated: in the Obi, the male domain, the men bond through 'masculine stories of violence and bloodshed', but in his inner space, Nwoye, eager to please his father and to conduct himself as a man, 'feigned that he no longer cared for women's stories' (p. 38). Masculine stories are hence not able to transform Nwoye's 'essential' character.

In addition, masculine ideologies are exposed as inverted – rather than natural and organic entities – at that crucial junction in the novel when Ikemefuna is 'cut down' by Okonkwo, in spite of his unconditional identification with male hegemony and masculinist spaces. We are told that Ikemefuna could 'hardly imagine that Okonkwo was not his real father', but his evocation of the name of the imagined father does not save him in the end (pp. 42, 43). Indeed, soon after Ikemefuna dies, we are left to witness the collapse of the 'deep, horizontal comradeship' that held the household together: a 'snapping' takes place inside Nwoye (p. 43) and a cold shiver descends on Okonkwo (p. 44). So, if Okonkwo seems to have reached the height of success (in temporal terms), his spaces of empowerment are shown to be in a state of crisis because they were founded on unstable male relationships.

It is in this context that Okonkwo's subsequent exile acquires several important resonances. Okonkwo's exile, it must be emphasised, is not merely the opposite of belonging, nor does it simply denote the hero's displacement from the masculine space he has dominated; it is, above all, the process that compels the hero to confront his repressed feminine space. Although exile displaces Okonkwo from his space of emplacement – 'everything had been broken' (p. 92) – the maternal space, as his uncle reminds him, provides him a sanctuary in moments of distress (p. 94). The motherland, then, functions as an example of what Foucault calls a 'crisis heterotopia', a place 'reserved for individuals who are, in relation to society and to the human environment in which they live, in a state of crisis' (p. 24).

But in this part of the novel we notice, once again, a crucial tension between temporality and spatiality. On one hand, from the perspective of time and historicity, Okonkwo's life in exile is denoted either by temporal suspense (he has to wait seven years before he resumes his place in Umuofia), or by his marginalisation in relation to the grand narrative of colonisation (he hears of the great historical events of his time second hand). In both cases, however, the narrative sustains the illusion that the hero will, in time, return to his proper place. On the other hand, Okonkwo (in exile) inhabits a heterotopic space that is at once privileged (because it is a sanctuary), but is not very different from the desecrated space occupied by the missionaries (the evil forest), or the marginal social spaces inhabited by outcasts. Indeed, when Okonkwo returns to Umuofia in the last section of the book, the narrative constantly calls attention to his loss of place in Umuofia: 'Seven years was a long time to be away from one's clan. A man's place was not always there waiting for him' (p. 121); the hero returns to a community that no longer recognises him ('Umuofia did not appear to have taken any special notice of the warrior's return'); he is forced to mourn for 'the clan, which he saw breaking up and falling apart' (p. 129).

If the novel opened with a symmetrical relationship between the hero and his communal space, they are now placed in opposition. Hence we can say that Okonkwo's exile from his natal space constitutes a radical break with his space of emplacement. In fact, the only reason why we don't read his exile as a radical form of marginalisation is because the narrative promotes the illusion that Okonkwo will be rehabilitated (in time); until the end, the narrative sustains the false belief that the space of exile is really not one of absolute loss. If we ignore this illusion, however, we can see why Okonkwo's exile is both a negation of the progressive narrative promised at the beginning of the novel and an ironic retour to the space inhabited by his father, the space from which he sought to escape.

Let us recall that Okonkwo, by killing a kinsman, has 'polluted' the earth, the source of his masculine power; his act is hence an abomination that recalls Unoka's death; the father's fatal sickness 'was an abomination to the earth, and so the victim could not be buried in her bowels' (p. 13); by committing suicide, Okonkwo, too, has committed 'an offence against the Earth' (p. 147). We may quibble about ostensible differences in the two men's deaths, but we cannot escape the similitude. Above all, we cannot escape the fact that Okonkwo, the great defender of the Umuofian doxa, has in his death (and possibly his life) gone, in Obierika's words, 'against our custom' (p. 147). But one of the questions the novel has raised at the same time is this: now that

Umuofia is being challenged and transformed by the forces of colonialism, what exactly is the authority of custom and what spaces sustain it?

This is the question taken up by the asymmetrical spaces in *No Longer at Ease*. In this novel, Achebe uses as his epigraph a verse from T. S. Eliot's 'Journey of the Magi' to foreshadow the unstable places and spaces in which the poetics of identity formation are played out: 'We returned to our places, these Kingdoms,/But no longer at ease here, in the old dispensation.'[10] The theme of dislocation is also underscored by an Igbo proverb that appears strategically in the novel's moment of closure, a moment that is haunted by the dialectical tension between Obi's desire for identity and the reality of displacement: 'Wherever something stands, another thing stands beside it' (p. 145).

Now, because critical attention has often been focused on the temporal progression of this novel, that is, Obi's transformation from an idealistic young man to a corrupt bureaucrat, we have not paid enough attention to how this crisis of selfhood is generated by the contending loyalties between inherited and designated locations. Obi's inherited location is Umuofia, but far from being a place with a stable space, a natural ground that sustains a tradition, the ancestral home is a schizophrenic and transplanted locale, which is under the hegemony of colonialism, the designated space. In the circumstances Obi has to define himself in relation to, or even against, two contending spaces.

There is, first of all, an Umuofia space that exists as a marginal space in Lagos: this is a small village that subsists on 'its past when it was the terror' of its neighbours (p. 4), but it neither has the authority of the original nor can it sustain its traditions. This space speaks a deracinated language as it tries to negotiate its mythical past and its colonised present (pp. 5, 6). Obi's position, in relation to this space, is one of liminality: he belongs to a nationalistic generation that has rediscovered the value of tradition as a discursive formation, but cannot appropriate the spaces in which this tradition first emerged.

Then there is the Umuofia of colonial desires, the community that had sent Obi to England. This is not the community associated with his legendary grandfather; it does not proffer him a space in which he can fulfil his desire for the past. Indeed, this Umuofia expects him not to be a representative of its mythical history, but a custodian of its communal desire for Englishness (pp. 28–30). For the 'modern' Umuofians, power is vested in the fantasmic image of England which Obi embodies: he is praised as 'Obi who had been to the land of the whites. The refrain said over and over again that the power of the leopard resided in its claws' (p. 29). But Obi cannot identify with this given image either, because once he has lived in England for some time, he becomes convinced that if the notion of Nigeria is to have value, it has to negate the eromania associated with England and Englishness – hence his craving for 'things Nigerian' (p. 31).

And yet, Obi cannot escape from his colonial heritage because his identity is mapped, as it were, by England and Englishness in ironic ways. First, it is only in an oppositional relation to England that Nigeria 'first became more than just a name to him' (p. 11): the realities of English life ('the miseries of winter') necessitated a counteracting value that would, in turn, be imagined as the Nigerian national space; and it is around this space that memories and desires can be reorganised. In the sense of Obi's discovery of it, there would be no Nigeria if England did not exist as its geographic and cultural Other. There is even a second, more pervasive irony: even as he decries the colonial mentality, the cultural spaces that Obi inhabits are exclusively English. His technology of identity formation is English literature, which connects him to the colonial chairman of the civil service commission in ways he cannot be linked with his Umuofian kinsmen and women.[11] Above all, Englishness realises the cultural geography of England in ways that are more definitive than the Nigeria Obi wants to imagine: Housman's poetry hence seems to have a palpability which Obi's poem on Nigeria does not have (pp. 136–7).

In the end, Obi has to negotiate three spaces with contradictory claims and cultural contours: an Umuofia that is displaced from its traditions and is in a perpetual state of cultural crisis; a Nigeria that he had earlier hoped would be an erotic space of fulfilment but has become corrupted in its genesis; and an England whose cultural transcripts have shaped his character but whose function as a colonial power is a negation of the most important ingredients in his Africanity – history, home, language. All these spaces and their problems crystallise in Obi's relation with Clara and the failure of the marriage plot which, in traditional fiction, provides an ideal place for resolving problems of cultural and national identity. In quite unexpected ways, Clara confronts Obi with the problem of abomination that had plagued his ancestors. As an *osu* she inhabits what Foucault would call the 'heterotopia of deviation' (p. 25); she inhabits a place that is part of Igbo culture, but outside its norms.

Obi's intention to marry Clara forces him, in effect, to reflect on what his Umuofian compatriots consider to be his estrangement from the Igbo norm. For example, when Joseph asks him whether he knows what an *osu* is, we are told, he was saying 'in effect that Obi's mission-house upbringing and European education had made him a stranger in his country – the most painful thing one could say to Obi' (pp. 64–5). And yet there is a sense in which marrying Clara would have been the apotheosis of Obi's desire for a Nigerian space. It would have been a willed entry into the desired nationalist space, a space transcending ethnic traditions and family loyalties. At the same time, however, he could not reach his desired space without evoking the (colonial) doctrines of modernity and Christianity.

At the end of the novel, we come to realise that these are not real options: his mother will stand up for tradition and will even commit an abomination to stop her son from marrying an *osu*; his father will not countenance the thought that modernity and Christianity are good enough reasons to defy the inherited norm. So, like his grandfather before him, Obi is left suspended in limbo. His presumed imprisonment at the end of the novel could well be Achebe's way of valorising the split between cultural geographies that have, at the same time, been spatialised by history. For this reason, the way African spaces have been organised and reorganised by Achebe's early novels points towards interesting directions in which the poetics of location can be examined.

## Notes

1. Simon Gikandi, *Reading Chinua Achebe*, London: James Currey, 1991.

2. Georg Lukács, *The Theory of the Novel*, trans. Anna Bostock, Cambridge, Massachusetts: MIT Press, 1971, pp. 120–5.

3. Michel Foucault, 'In Other Spaces', trans. Jay Miskowiec, *Diacritics* 16 (Spring 1986), pp. 22ff. Further references will be included in the text.

4. I am pursuing some of these questions in *Maps of Englishness: Postcolonial Theory and the Politics of Identity*, in progress.

5.  See Abdul JanMohammed, *Manichean Aesthetics: The Politics of Literature in Colonial Africa*, Amherst: University of Massachusetts Press, 1983; and Christopher Miller, *Black Darkness: Africanist Discourse in French*, Chicago: University of Chicago Press, 1985.

6.  Chinua Achebe, *Things Fall Apart*, London: Heinemann, 1958, p. 3.

7.  See Edward Soja, *Postmodern Geographies: The Reassertion of Space in Critical Social Theory*, London: Verso, 1989, p. 11.

8.  An excellent discussion of masculinist ideologies in *Things Fall Apart* can be found in Rhonda Cobham's 'Making Men and History: Achebe and the Politics of Revisionism', in *Approaches to Teaching 'Things Fall Apart'*, ed. Bernth Lindfors, New York: Modern Language Association, 1991, pp. 91–100.

9.  Benedict Anderson, *Imagined Communities: Reflections on the Origins and Spread of Nationalism*, London: NLB, 1983, p. 16.

10.  Chinua Achebe, *No Longer at Ease*, London: Heinemann, 1960.

11.  The relation between space and identity formation is discussed by Caren Kaplan in 'Reconfigurations of Geography and Historical Narrative: A Review Essay', *Public Culture* 3 (Fall 1990), p. 27.

# Ayi Kwei Armah and the Harbingers of Death

## ADEWALE MAJA-PEARCE

To be a writer at a time like this, coming from such a people, such deep destruction, the most criminal. Only one issue is worth our time: how to end the oppression of the African, to kill the European beasts of prey, to remake ourselves, the elected servants of Europe and America. Outside that, all is useless; and I am outside.

AYI KWEI ARMAH: *Why Are We So Blest?*[1]

*Why Are We So Blest?* tells the story of Modin, an African student in the United States, who becomes disillusioned with academia, returns to Africa with his white American lover, Aimée, and stumbles into the desert of mortification and reward in search of the revolution which is certainly not to be found on the campus of a western university:

> The educated Africans, the westernised African successes are contemptible worms . . . Happy to get degrees, then go home and relax on the shoulders of our sold people. The end of a western education is not work but self-indulgence. An education for worms and slugs. (p. 161)

Modin is an idealist; Aimée, the archetype of the perverted westerner, is simply tagging along for the ride: 'What kind of love fires the white-haired American, sucking life that cannot fertilise her dryness, from sources already several times desiccated?' (p. 208), asks Solo, the novel's third narrator, whose own commentary is meant to provide a dispassionate counter-balance to those of Modin and Aimée. But the revolution is elusive. After wandering aimlessly for days in the vast expanse of sand, sand and yet more sand, they happen upon four white men in a jeep. Modin is stripped naked and tied to the back of the vehicle, arms and legs spread-eagled in the manner of a crucifixion;

13

Aimée, who recounts the event, is raped by each of the men in turn; whereupon: 'They held me, legs apart, and rubbed me up and down against Modin. They succeeded in arousing him' (p. 286). Two of the men then tie a thin piece of wire round the base of the tip of Modin's penis and pull hard. For a brief moment nothing happens; then 'the tip of his penis snapped off and hung by just a bit of skin from the bottom':

> Modin started bleeding. The blood curved out in a little stream that jerked outward about every second. I reached him and without thinking of what I was doing I kissed him. His blood filled my mouth. I swallowed it. I wanted him to speak to me. He had groaned a little when I took him and kissed him, but he said nothing.
> I asked him, 'Do you love me?'
> He didn't answer me.
> 'Say you love me, Modin, please.' He wouldn't say a word to me.
> (p. 288)

This is certainly one of the most unpleasant scenes in the entire corpus of modern African literature – and one of the least convincing. But artistic truth is not among Armah's most pressing concerns, as the quotation with which this essay opens makes clear. *Why Are We So Blest?* is written largely to prove a thesis; in the words of Solo: 'Why could he not see his companion? This was an object, destructive, powerfully hurled against him from the barrel of a powerful, destructive culture. Why could he not see that?' (p. 115). The point about Aimée is that she is less a woman in her own right than the representative of an entire civilisation; and it is wholly within the logic of Armah's vision, such as it is, that she is impelled – literally – to suck the lifeblood from the African crucified on the altar of Europe's destructive urge. In a passage from another novel, Armah has written:

> Each single one of them is a carrier of destruction. The spirit of their coming together, the purpose of their existence, is the spread of death over all the earth. An insatiable urge drives them. Wherever there is life, even if it be only a possibility, the harbingers of death must go – to destroy it.[2]

This is taken from *Two Thousand Seasons*, the novel that followed *Why Are We So Blest?* and in which the debilitating history of Africa's bloody encounter with Europe is portrayed on an epic scale that eschews any close examination of the individual sensibilities within the murderous cycle of destruction. History itself is the hero of the novel, the two thousand seasons from conquest through regeneration to the final liberation when Africa throws off the yoke of oppression and reconnects with its own fractured past; in the words of the seer:

> Two thousand seasons: a thousand you will spend descending into abysses that would stop your heart and break your mind merely to contemplate. The climb away from there will be just as heavy. For that alone can you be glad your doors have been so closed, your faculties are now so blunted. You will need them blunter still, to make less perceptible the descent of a thousand seasons. Two thousand seasons: a thousand dry, a thousand moist. (p. 16)

The action of the novel takes place towards the end of the time of overt slavery, 'the open trade in human beings', but at the beginning of 'a cleverer kind of oppression, harder to see as slavery, slavery disguised as freedom itself' (p. 104). Thus speaks the rebel and man of action, who is not fooled by the lies and deceptions of the collaborators in their midst – 'the parasites among us' (p. 59) – through whom the fair-haired destroyers seek to achieve their ultimate ends. The rebel and his fellow sympathisers take up arms in the knowledge that the cycle of destruction will not be finished within their own lifetimes, but that they have a duty to keep alive the flame of their peoples' eventual redemption, whatever the price they themselves are condemned to pay in the process. And in this Armah is nothing if not thorough. He anticipates the charge that to fight guns with guns might itself condemn the African to the same degenerate universe as that inhabited by the destroyers themselves, but argues that such a course of action is justified both in its awareness of what it is doing, and the end to which it is dedicated:

> It is not things we praise in our utterance, not arms we praise but the living relationship itself of those united in the use of all things against the white sway of death, for creation's life . . . Whatever thing, whatever relationship, whatever consciousness takes us along paths closer to our

way, whatever goes against the white destroyers' empire, that thing is
beautiful, that relationship only is truthful . . . (pp. 205–6)

The end in this case – 'the way' – is what Armah understands to be the
genuinely humanistic alternative which was present in African society
before the coming of the destroyers, and which will exist again after the
destroyers have themselves been destroyed. The point is to retrieve
what has been stolen, not to bear arms for its own sake:

> Our way is reciprocity. The way is wholeness. Our way knows no
> oppression. The way destroys oppression. Our way is hospitable to
> guests. The way repels destroyers. Our way produces before it
> consumes. The way produces far more than it consumes. Our way
> creates. *The way destroys only destruction* [my italics]. (p. 39)

That the destroyers will in turn be destroyed is not in doubt, their
destruction being the nemesis of their own inhuman philosophy:

> Their reign is surely bound within the two thousand seasons of our
> oppression. For their greed is preparing deep graves for them; it will
> raise against them the torrential wrath of all things in the universe, all
> bodies, all souls still with the seed of life unkilled in them. (p. 205)

Those who maintain intimate knowledge of 'the way', who keep faith
with the humanistic vision through the centuries of destruction, are
known as the healers, the title of Armah's fifth and last published novel
to date.[3] The healers are those within the community who 'set great
value on seeing truly, hearing truly, understanding truly, and acting
truly'.[4] This function, we are told, necessarily precludes them from
exercising power over others, but then the need to manipulate temporal
power is itself a betrayal of 'the way'. In Armah's universe, we can judge
how far Africa has travelled from its indigenous base by the very
existence of kings and chiefs, which in turn is the result of false divisions
within a society that was once previously whole but which has allowed
itself to become fractured:

> The disease – the breaking up of that community – has taken centuries,
> thousands of years. Most of our people do not even wish to imagine any

such possibility of wholeness . . . The healers are also confused, not about the aim of our work, but about the medicines we may use and about what may look like medicine but may end up being poison.

Often, our confusion comes merely from impatience. The disease has run unchecked through centuries. Yet sometimes we dream of ending it in our little lifetimes, and despair seizes us if we do not see the end in sight . . . A healer needs to see beyond the present and tomorrow. He needs to see years and decades ahead. (p. 84)

Armah is a visionary writer in the strict sense.[5] This much at least must be conceded, even if the details of what is effectively promoted as a blueprint for a social and political arrangement are far too vague and simplistic to be convincing at any but the most hopeful level. It is also a racist vision, his admirers notwithstanding, and racist in the sense that his vision is exclusive *in human terms*: black people, African people, are different from white people, European people, and this difference is not merely one of colour but a profounder difference of sensibility, of which colour is the outward symbol.

Part of the black, African sensibility includes an ability to live in harmony with one's fellows in a genuinely egalitarian society which is only undermined by the presence of the alien destroyers, who are themselves spiritually incapable of achieving such a state of nirvana. Quite how this differs from the equally 'imaginary, fanciful, unpractical' notion of the happy native in a state of primordial innocence until the arrival of 'white' civilisation is not entirely clear. What *is* clear is that it was the same argument in reverse which underpinned the 'cleverer kind of oppression' that Armah himself understands to be the condition of slavery – however subtle – and which necessitates the bearing of arms in the first place. But to fight guns with guns is, indeed, to partake of the same sickness, at least for those who insist on seeing *all* human beings, *irrespective of colour*, as partaking of the same humanity. In other words, it is only by subscribing to the myth of racial exclusivity that Armah is able to judge the same conduct by different criteria.

In this Armah is not alone, merely the most comprehensive; and if his work has so far escaped the charge of racism, it is because the depth of the African humiliation to the fact of their enslavement has blinded African commentators, along with their western apologists, from seeing the thing for what it is.[6] Even Wole Soyinka, admitting 'discomfort over the actual language of confrontation',[7] nevertheless manages to absolve Armah from the charge which he himself has already – and rightly – anticipated:

> *Two Thousand Seasons* is not a racist tract; the central theme is far too positive and dedicated and its ferocious onslaught on alien contamination soon falls into place as a preparatory exercise for the liberation of the mind. A clean receptive mind is a prerequisite for its ideological message, and there is no question that this work is designed for the particular audience of Armah's own race. What he offers them now is 'the way', 'our way'. (pp. 11–12)

Obviously, Soyinka is guilty here of a straightforward confusion over nomenclature, since to talk of 'Armah's own race' is to partake of the same categories which make Armah a racist. In any case, to argue, as Soyinka does, that castigating 'all aliens as inhuman exploiters' (p. 111) is permissible on the grounds that 'the central theme [of the novel] is far too positive and dedicated' might, after all, be used to excuse any number of racist tracts which set out to prove the exact opposite; to prove, in other words, the inferiority of blacks in the slave societies to which they were transported in the wake of the European onslaught, in itself the *raison d'être* of Armah's ire. Soyinka further tells us that Armah's 'unusual vehemence' must be understood in context; that is, 'The quest for and the consequent assertion of the black cultural psyche began as a result of the deliberate propagation of untruths by others, both for racist motives and to disguise their incapacity to penetrate the complex verities of black existence' (p. 107), which is all very well, except that Armah himself, by the same token, fails to penetrate the complex verities of 'white' existence. This is nowhere more evident than in *Why Are We So Blest?*, where the lofty abstractions of the opposing human conditions – one black and humane; the other white and destructive – are embodied in terms of the individuals who proceed to act out their preordained roles.

Why, for instance, does Modin allow himself to have a relationship with Aimée in the first place, much less carry her all the way across the Atlantic in order to participate in an event for which she herself is indirectly responsible, but which is justification enough for the dramatic course he has embarked upon? To say that they are in love is clearly ridiculous, since Aimée, 'daughter of a race of destroyers' (p. 149), is obviously incapable of such exalted passion; conversely, Modin must willingly debase himself in order that he might generate a spurious passion which must end with his destruction.

The telling incident occurs even before they leave America when he discovers, in the heat of love-making, that Aimée can climax only by concocting an elaborate fantasy involving an unnamed African colony, a servant called Mwangi, and a settler husband who is about to discover them *in flagrante delicto*:

> 'Kansa. The rebellion, my period. My husband is coming home. He's a settler. I don't know when. It's dangerous. You're the boy.'
> 'And Mwangi is my name.'
> 'Yes, yes, yes, yes dooon't stop! Yes!' (p. 199)

Naturally, Modin is somewhat upset by this less than wholesome revelation, but which she blurts out despite herself: 'That was a foolish thing I did, going all guilty and making a confession to him' (p. 203); but the author nevertheless conspires to have him forgive her for the insult to his sense of worth, to say nothing of his manhood, in order that the thesis he needs to ram home should reach its own perverted climax in the desert to which they are heading:

> The disgust I began to feel with Aimée is gone. A tenderness I cannot explain has replaced it. I thought I would put her out but in the end I just talked to her. I asked her if she really knew what she'd been doing. She cried and said she had always been told she was bad. She kept using the word monster. Her tears disturbed me. She is not someone I expect to cry easily, and I am always taken by surprise in such situations anyway. (p. 213)

The problem here isn't so much that Modin finds it in himself to overcome the disgust he reasonably feels, but that he continues to believe that love is still possible within the terms of his diminished status. And it isn't enough to say that Modin is able to internalise his oppression, which is what his forgiveness amounts to, on the grounds that he is '[a] pure slave, with the heart of a slave, with the spirit of a slave' (p. 255), but that he himself has already understood the true nature of the beast. We have it on the author's own evidence that Modin is exceptionally bright, bright enough, at least, to win a scholarship to an Ivy League university – 'All your confidential reports say you are a most unusually intelligent African – the most intelligent as a matter of fact' (p. 120), according to his professor – and bright enough, therefore, to draw the obvious conclusions, which is precisely what he does. He sees through the educational system clearly enough to reject his studies in favour of the revolution at home – 'What a farce, scholarships! That blood money never went to any of us for our intelligence. It was always payment for obedience' (p. 160) – just as he sees through the motives of the white women who fasten on to him in order to satisfy their perverted desires:

> These women I have known have had deep needs to wound their men. I have been an instrument in their hands. The men have reacted to me with a fear difficult to hide, and I should have known my annihilation would be a cure for part of their disease. (p. 162)

It is not only Aimée who has opened his eyes to the truth of his condition. He has already had one disastrous affair with another white woman, the wife of his professor:

> Her love-making made it hard for me to think she was a woman, a mature one. I saw her face. She meant well and her body had some shape, but the way she made love, it was a friendly frenzy, and I could not help it if a part of me stood outside of us, watching her joy that had the motions of agony. (p. 130)

That affair almost costs him his life when her husband discovers them in the throes of love-making; but the point is further underscored by Naita, a black woman with whom he also has an affair, and who confirms his suspicions when he confesses his distaste for the professor's wife:

> Why you talk so dumb all of a sudden? You need sex, take it. But this talk about love and sincerity is just foolishness. I thought you were smart enough so white folks couldn't get you sick, but you ain't. That's just too bad. Their men box you in so you feel all tight and lonely. Then their

women move in and pick you clean and you too dumb to know it's got nothing to do with love and sincerity. (p. 134)

Naturally enough, Naita, the inheritor of the humanistic tradition in the New World by the mere fact of her blackness, does to him what no white woman can possibly do: 'We moved together. Each motion told me she felt what I felt. Our end was unforced, natural' (p. 123). And yet Modin manages to make an exception in Aimée's case, even after she confirms what he already knows about the mortal danger inherent in the debilitating racial encounter. 'You're the boy,' she tells him, whereupon he takes her all the way to Africa, there to find the annihilation he had already foreseen.

Armah, in short, attempts to have it both ways. Modin must be at once slavish enough to overlook the insult to his person, and intelligent enough to act as the author's mouthpiece during his sojourn in the heartland of white depravity. This is the novel's central flaw, and inevitable given the task the author has set himself: 'to end the oppression of the African, to kill the European beasts of prey, to remake ourselves, the elected servants of Europe and America'. The method is not fiction but polemic disguised as fiction. To this end, Modin is the fall guy, because in order to have a relationship with 'a daughter of a race of destroyers', then he, too, must be destroyed – and never mind Soyinka's insistence that Armah's vision is 'secular and humane'. Secular possibly, but hardly humane.

On the other hand, *Why Are We So Blest?* might be nothing more than a rape fantasy in which the author, realising the futility of violence to achieve his desired end, that is, the defeat of the civilisation which continues to enslave him, invites his own castration as the only logical end in a nihilistic universe. Modin, certainly, has already been deprived of his manhood even before he leaves the land of the free and the brave, just as the snivelling Solo, the otherwise dispassionate narrator, was himself rendered impotent – his word – following his own (inevitably) disastrous relationship with yet another 'daughter of a race of destroyers':

My impotence simulates omnipotence. Often, what seems a reasonable arrangement I know is false. It is not understanding I am researching for, I have time to kill – an infinity ahead of me, and these notes are reduced to something to help a defeated man survive empty time. I arrange them, rearrange them. Out of all this destruction my aim is no longer to search for sense. My goal is littleness itself: to fill time, to survive emptiness. (p. 232)

Nothing is left but 'What is ordained for us . . . the fate of the *évolué*, the turning of the assimilated African, not into something creating its own life, but into an eater of crumbs in the house of slavery' (p. 84).

Unfortunately for Armah, it probably doesn't matter what happens to men who – à la Naipaul – allow themselves to be reduced to nothingness: 'The world is as it is; men who are nothing, who allow themselves to become nothing, have no place in it.'[8] It is easy enough to dismiss such a sentiment on the grounds that – à la Armah – the place of the African in the world was already defined by those who insisted on constructing the ideology of race in the first place. But this is a conclusion, not a reason, since one's humanity was never a negotiable commodity. Simply to abdicate one's birthright at someone else's insistence is not merely to embrace a death far worse than Modin's otherwise straightforward (if rather dramatic) crucifixion in the desert; it is also to debase the 'other' in order that they might then drink the sacrificial blood – 'Say you love me, Modin, please' – willingly offered by the victim who invites his own destruction. The men in the jeep would be more convincing – artistically, at any rate – as the fantastic creations of Modin's victimhood the better that they might do what it is that the white man must do, that is, rape his woman and seize his manhood, the one inevitably following on the other; but in denying Aimée *her* humanity, it is inevitable, after all, that Modin – and, by extension, Solo – should also be denied theirs. This is inescapable, since any racialist 'vision' is necessarily reductive, whatever its ostensible justification. The pity of it is that the man who was sufficiently privileged to write *Why Are We So Blest?*, who, in other words, was himself caught in the contradictions of two competing civilisations, might have told us something about our common humanity, which ought to have been the novel's real theme. The fact that he was unable to do so must be measured in terms of his failure to transcend the same sickness that demanded of him a true vision.

## Notes

1. Ayi Kwei Armah, *Why Are We So Blest?*, London: Heinemann Educational Books, 1972, p. 230. Page references will be to the 1984 edition.

2. Ayi Kwei Armah, *Two Thousand Seasons*, Nairobi: EAPH, 1973, p. 6; also published by Heinemann (London, 1979).

3. Armah has continued writing, but refuses to publish with non-African publishing houses. Unfortunately, he hasn't been able to find a suitable African publisher; as he explained to Femi Osofisan, the Nigerian dramatist and novelist:

> 'No, I have not fallen silent. I'm writing all the time. It's just that I have not been publishing. In fact I have three completed novels, but I've not been able to find a publisher . . .
>
> 'It's true . . . Or would you have me continue to give my works to multinational companies? If we as writers denounce our politicians for their links with these foreign parasites, how can we in all honesty continue ourselves to patronise them?'
>
> He shakes his head emphatically. 'No, my friend, I'll keep my books in my drawer until I can find an African or black publisher who's capable of handling them. Or until we writers can get together and organise our own publishing houses.'
>
> Femi Osofisan, 'Reflections on a fading breed', *Sunday Times* (Lagos), 26 November 1989, p. 5.

4. Ayi Kwei Armah, *The Healers*, Nairobi: EAPH, 1978; London: HEB, 1979, p. 81.

5. 'Given to seeing visions or to indulging in fanciful theories; existing only in a vision or the imagination; imaginary, fanciful, unpractical' (OED).

6. See, for example, *Ayi Kwei Armah's Africa: The Sources of His Fiction* by Derek Wright (London: Hans Zell, 1989), a work which, the author tells us, 'carried [Armah's] fiction into a broader cultural and anthropological ambience and considers it in terms of a more complex series of determinants'. What this amounts to, in plain English, is a strategy for evading the moral dimensions posed by a novel such as *Why Are We So Blest?* in favour of academic theories about form and structure. We see how the engine is assembled, in other words, but haven't been told what it's *for*. A more readable, because less pretentious, critical study is Robert Fraser's *The Novels of Ayi Kwei Armah* (London: Heinemann Educational Books, 1980).

7. Wole Soyinka, *Myth, Literature and the African World*, Cambridge: Cambridge UP, 1975, p. 110.

8. V. S. Naipaul, *A Bend in the River*, London: André Deutsch, 1979; London: Penguin Books, 1986, p. 9.

# The Emergence of Mariama Bâ

## RASHIDAH ISMAILI ABUBAKR

Mariama Bâ emerges from a society that is both African and Islamic. She was born in Senegal in 1929, and died in 1981. Her writing takes women out of the parenthesis, and offers a direct and clear account to replace the variations which imply the pitiable position of African women in general and Islamic women in particular. The subject of *So Long a Letter* is a Senegalese marriage, while *Scarlet Song* is about a racially mixed one.[1] Decline of personal and public morals, and betrayal of dreams and love echo in both. In her first novel betrayal leads to divorce and abandonment. The second novel has loss of self and culture, leading finally to madness and violence.

Mariama Bâ centres her work on individual figures whose lives are then elaborated with references which place their chronologies and histories. Both novels focus on women figures and their marriages as the means of opening up a wider debate on social and religious structures. Ramatoulaye in *So Long a Letter* is constantly aware that she is an African and Muslim woman, and is self-conscious about these aspects of her identity. Mireille in *Scarlet Song* suffers the consequences of her alienation and exclusion from her husband's Muslim African community. As Senegambian scholar Mbye B. Cham has said: 'In few other places in the creative traditions of sub-Saharan Africa is the factor of Islam more prominent and influential than in Senegal.'[2] Clearly Islam is central and forms a core around and through which Mariama Bâ 'tells her story'.

*So Long a Letter* takes the form of a 'long letter' from Ramatoulaye to her 'milk sister', Aissatou. The two women both married for love and were both later abandoned by their husbands. Ramatoulaye's letter

carefully establishes her relationship to Aissatou as well as context-
ualising the events which befall them:

> I conjure you up. The past is reborn, along with its procession of
> emotions. I close my eyes. Ebb and tide of feeling: heat and dazzlement,
> the woodfires, the sharp green mango, bitten into in turns, a delicacy in
> our greedy mouths. I close my eyes. Ebb and tide of images: drops of
> sweat beading your mother's ochre-coloured face as she emerges from
> the kitchen, the procession of young wet girls chattering on their way
> back from the spring. (p. 2)

Ramatoulaye begins her letter after the death of her estranged husband,
Modou Fall. Through it we come to understand the power of definition
of place and gender. Her rootedness in her culture enables
Ramatoulaye to sit out the wearying funeral rituals with dignity despite
the presence of the young co-wife and a greedy new mother-in-law:
'Comforting words from the Koran fill the air; divine words, divine
instructions, impressive promises of punishment or joy, exhortations to
virtue, warnings against evil, exaltations of humility, and faith' (p. 5).
This rootedness is significant in the contextualisation of her criticism. It
asserts both allegiance and the right to speak strongly, and also enables
Ramatoulaye to settle into the monotony of the expected four-month
retreat:

> I hope to carry out my duties fully. My heart concurs with demands of
> religions. Reared since childhood on their precepts, I expect not to fail.
> The walls that limit my horizon for four months and ten days do not
> bother me. I have enough memories for me to ruminate upon. And these
> are what I am afraid of, for they smack of bitterness.
>     May their evocation not soil the state of purity in which I must lie.
> (pp. 8–9)

The burden of her letter is these 'memories', evoked in a searchingly
introspective manner: memories of the marriages of Ramatoulaye and
Modou Fall, and Aissatou and Mawdo Bâ. Aissatou's and
Ramatoulaye's lives parallel each other in their long marriages, each
over twenty years. Both women fulfil what has become an overworked

appellation of definition: 'mother'. Ramatoulaye becomes the mother of twelve children, Aissatou four – and Aissatou's are all males!

Each woman is undone by the trickery of a mother-in-law. In Aissatou's case, her mother-in-law accepts her only reluctantly, despite her intellectual brilliance and beauty. Her father is a goldsmith and she is marrying into a noble family. She leaves her husband after he takes a second wife. Ramatoulaye elects to stay with her husband when *he* takes a second wife, despite the protests of her children. The young wife Modou marries is a school friend of his daughter Daba, a fact which disgusts his children. Daba says to Ramatoulaye: 'Break with him, mother . . . He has respected neither you nor me. Do what Aunty Aissatou did, break with him' (p. 39). But Ramatoulaye does not break with him, and in her letter reflects on and analyses her decision:

> I told myself what every betrayed woman says: if Modou was milk, it was I who had had all the cream – the rest, well, nothing but water with a vague smell of milk. But the final decision lay with me . . . Leave? Start again at zero, after living twenty-five years with one man after having borne twelve children? . . . Did I have enough energy to bear alone the weight of this responsibility which was both moral and material? Leave? Draw a clean line through the past – turn over a page on which not everything was bright, certainly, but at least all was clear. (pp. 39–40)

Ramatoulaye debates the options available to women in her circumstances: she chooses to stay, Aissatou to leave, and the outcome of Jacqueline's marriage (another friend) remains uncertain. Modou's action is defended as the right of a Muslim man – by the Imam, by his brother Tamsir and by his friend Mawdo Bâ. Ramatoulaye argues that this action is not Islamic. Many suras were written to clarify the point of privilege men claimed at the expense of women, and the specific conditions which allow for multiple wives.[3] The usual reasons for a new wife are barrenness on the part of the woman and 'protection' of the second wife. All of this has to be negotiated openly, and win the first wife's consent.

There are restrictions placed on the man. He must be able to provide for the second wife and he must be *fair* and equal in his affection and treatment of each woman. If he fails to keep his part of the bargain, the wives can seek redress and even divorce. Both Mawdo Bâ, Aissatou's husband, and Ramatoulaye's husband Modou Fall transgress these dictates by marrying without the consent of their first wives. That they were each aided by their mothers or, as in the case of Modou, also by an older woman's plot to insert her young daughter as his wife, is an example of women's complicity in their oppression.

As we have seen, Aissatou divorces Mawdo for his betrayal. She denies Mawdo excuses by reminding him of his former words of endearment:

> You want to draw a line between heartfelt love and physical love. I say there can be no union of bodies without the heart's acceptance, however little that may be . . .
>
> I am stripping myself of your love, your name. Clothed in my dignity, the only worthy garment, I go my way. (pp. 31–2)

The disrobing in the 'stripping myself' is encoded. Aissatou becomes herself by disrobing. She takes off Mawdo's honour and refuses his reasons as hypocritical and dishonest. On his part, Mawdo is left 'completely disoriented' (p. 33). His justification for his action is that in addition to obeying his mother's wish that he should marry again, 'the force of instincts in man' cannot be resisted. Ramatoulaye, the old friend to whom he offers these excuses, rejects them contemptuously.

In the brief tale of Jacqueline from Côte d'Ivoire, Ramatoulaye reflects on yet another response to abandonment. Jacqueline marries a Muslim. His family refuse her as their daughter because she remains faithful to her Protestant religion. This is even though Muslim law allows men to marry women of the Books (Jews and Christians), while forbidding women from doing the same. The pressure for Jacqueline to conform is enormous. Her estrangement, when it comes, is too much for her and leads to a nervous breakdown. With the help of a kind doctor, she faces her illness and that becomes the key to recovery and to knowledge.

Ramatoulaye gradually 'becomes' her own self too after Modou's marriage. She is still 'clothed' in her husband's honour but assumes all responsibility. She finds a way back to herself, and is reborn taking small baby steps:

I was surviving. In addition to my former duties, I took over Modou's as well . . . I survived. I overcame my shyness at going alone to cinemas; I would take a seat with less and less embarrassment as the months went by – people stared at the middle-aged lady without a partner. I would feign indifference, while anger hammered against my nerves and the tears I held back welled up behind my eyes.

From the surprised looks, I gauged the slender liberty granted to women . . . What a great distraction from distress is the cinema! I survived. (pp. 51–2)

However, as Ramatoulaye re-creates her self ('disrobes' her self), she realises she was not 'divorced' but 'abandoned': 'a fluttering leaf that no hand dares to pick up' (p. 53). In her self-analysis she comes to understand her complicity in her own oppression and finds ample examples:

I gave freely, gave more than I received. I am one of those who can realise themselves fully and bloom only when they form part of a couple . . . I have never conceived of happiness outside marriage . . . I mobilised day and night in his service, I anticipated his slightest desire. (p. 56)

These are the virtues of both an African and a Muslim wife, elaborated as the sanctions of patriarchal society.

No less emphatic as an expression of patriarchal authority is Tamsir's announcement of his right to marry his brother's widow, Ramatoulaye, but she defies him: 'My voice has known thirty years of silence, thirty years of harassment. It burst out, violent, sometimes sarcastic, sometimes contemptuous' (pp. 57–8). Her denial subverts Tamsir's plan to acquire her and her inheritance. She shames him with his inability to provide even for his current wives, and mocks him for his greed. Her denial of Tamsir is a disgusted refusal to be treated as property for men to dispose of. In finding her voice, she liberates herself from the burden of obedience which had kept her silent for decades, and also finds the strength to refuse Daouda Dieng as well: 'My heart does not love Daouda Dieng. My mind appreciates the man. But heart and mind often disagree' (p. 66). Ramatoulaye denies him marriage but offers her friendship. She refuses to inflict the same betrayal she had suffered on Dieng's wife Aminata.

Ramatoulaye's daughters are offered as a vision of the future. Not only are they allies to their mother as she comes to grips with her new existence, but the possibilities in their lives reflect on what had been possible for Ramatoulaye and Aissatou in their generation. Daba, the eldest, and her husband manage her legal affairs and are able to retrieve money and property that Modou had given to his second wife illegally. But Daba and her husband also live as 'equals', in a kind of relationship unavailable to Ramatoulaye and Aissatou, even with their own 'love' marriages. Young Aissatou, another of Ramatoulaye's daughters, becomes pregnant, and though Ramatoulaye is appalled by this, she forces herself to respond calmly and helpfully, and is rewarded by the responsible behaviour of the young people.

*So Long a Letter* shows Ramatoulaye slowly emerging through her tunnel of custom, tradition and gender stratification with the realisation that 'all women have almost the same fate, which religions or unjust legislation have sealed' – yet, she remains 'persuaded of the inevitable and necessary complementarity of men and women' (p. 88). She argues for fairness and harmony, 'as the harmony of multiple instruments creates a pleasant symphony'. Her final prediction is 'The success of a nation therefore depends inevitably on the family' (p. 89). Finally she expresses a simple and profound faith: 'hope still lives on within me. The word "happiness" does indeed have meaning, doesn't it? I shall go out in search of it. Too bad for me if once again I have to write you so long a letter . . .' (p. 89)

When Mariama Bâ was writing *Scarlet Song*, a novel which deals with the consequences of an inter-racial marriage, she knew that she was dying. The novel begins with Ousmane being woken by his mother, Yaye Khady, on the morning he is to start university. His father, Djibril Gueye, a devout man, is on his way to the mosque. These details are established precisely and early, and will become significant later. The family live in a suburb of Dakar, respectable and not too poor. Ousmane is the archetypal male child-hero, the pride of his parents, industrious, ambitious. He is a 'continuation' of his father, who in the context of his time achieved more than many others. The father has been 'delivered' from the yoke of a religious teacher when he joined the French colonial army. The war he went to fight 'broadened his horizons' – Djibril Gueye 'had seen Paris', and, more importantly, married a 'beautiful young wife'.

The father is an inspiration to Ousmane, who loves and respects his parents, and 'was grateful to his father for having resisted the temptation to take more wives'. Djibril tries to live his life as the Koran dictates – 'like an evenly balanced scale'. Ousmane is pleased to be from his family: 'Yaye Khady's heart is like a pitcher of fresh water from which, for as long as I can remember, only father and I have drunk.' Ousmane is 'her arms and legs' – he fetches water and coal for her. The father makes comments that reflect typical gender responses of men to their first-born son – 'you'll turn the lad into a sissy' – but otherwise our attention is drawn firmly to his obedience of the law.

This warm and sustaining family huddle contains discords, but they are muted at this stage. The mother works hard all day while the father plays the noble patriarch. Even the image of the mother as a pitcher is an ambivalent one. It is an object of use, in service to others, belonging only to father and son. The high but unspecified ambitions of the parents for their son invite disappointment. Ousmane's glowing 'idealism' about education, hard work and achievement appears naive. In time all these warning murmurs come to be significant.

The heart of the novel is the story of Mireille, the daughter of a French official serving in Dakar. Ousmane meets her at the university and they are attracted to each other:

> They were enriched by their differences. Each worried about the other over the smallest thing: a slight temperature, a scratched pimple, a bad cold. Low marks for a test, failure to understand a lecture upset their serenity. They wanted their happiness to be perfect. (p. 18)

The portrayal of their relationship does not progress far beyond these chaste expressions at this stage, but in the process cultural nuances are exposed. For example Mireille shows Ousmane a pictorial history of herself when she was four: 'I'd just finished reading that book I'm holding. I could read when I was four. What about you? . . . Look at me in my ballet tutu. Here I'm playing the piano . . . These are my paternal grandparents . . . That's a picture of our family home' (p. 19). She has a grasp of the rich complexity of her circumstances and their sources, and an openness which hints at generosity.

Ousmane says in lieu of photographs: 'I will never speak of my family or let you into the secret garden of my origins until I am ready to ask you to be my wife' (p. 19). It is not difficult to see guilt and self-contempt in the evasiveness of this response, and anxious bravado in the proposal of marriage. Mireille marvels at her 'fate': 'I can't explain my feelings. Why should it have to be you?' she asks. The answer is 'fate', but she comes from a culture which has ceased to think of that as an explanation. Mireille's parents, however, discover what is going on and hurriedly pack their daughter off to France.

Ousmane's despair over her absence from school, and the anxiety he cannot hide, causes his mother to take note of his withdrawal without being able to discover the reason. Unlike the French household, the African home is quiet and still apparently locked in its huddle. Ousmane develops ways to camouflage his anguish. By placing her photograph in his textbook he can give the appearance of studiousness while fantasising over his lost romance. While Ousmane grieves, it is Mireille who takes decisive action in her letter to him. She writes:

> I'm not asking you for anything you don't want to tell me. But in order to fight, I must know what I am fighting for.
> Just tell me what to do and nothing else except you will matter. (p. 36)

At the crossroads of decision, Ousmane lets his own history flow through him. For him history is both Yaye Khady and Djibril Gueye, the culture of his Dakar suburb and his religion. Ousmane realises that: 'Yaye Khady's love was echoed in the hearts of all the women of the neighbourhood, all mothers by proxy,' and he cannot imagine a way to extricate himself from their caring. What should he do? Reject Usine Niari Talli, the small impoverished district, with its stench and open ditches?

> No longer heed the pointing finger of his father's respected fellow Muslims, directing him towards God's royal road? Never more to be moved to meditation at the sound of the muezzin, under the minaret of a mosque bathed in the purple glow of dawn? Shred the thousand pages of

his ancestral heritage? Decry pride in one's birth? Die for love and not
for honour? (p. 37)

The debate is rendered in the familiar, polarised form of the 'culture
clash', and in this case 'love' triumphs. He decides to write back, but
obviously 'love' here carries the seeds of profounder implications,
symbolised in the looming opposition of entrenched fathers. Over the
next years there is a semblance of order. The young people write to each
other, acquire education and degrees, solidifying their relationship
through disclosures in their letters.

Much of Mireille's years seem focused on her budding sense of
politics. She rebels in 1968 with her classmates. Leading a double life,
she engages in an antagonistic internal dialogue as she listens to her
father. She is in revolt against him, his class and much of her culture.
She sees her mother as a parrot who uses all her father has said
previously to 'inform' her peers the next day at coffee or at the beauty
salon. All the while Mireille documents these events and dispatches
them to Ousmane, detailing the nihilism of her society. She feels
protected by her secret romance from the pitfalls of a 'good' marriage to
the 'right' type. Mireille can bear this time, waiting for the moment
when life will really begin.

Ousmane also takes part in the student revolt in Dakar, where the
issues at stake and the responses of the authority are brutally simpler.
He is arrested and released, finishes university and responds to
Mireille's weekly reportage. But, unlike her, Ousmane has not been
able to loosen himself from his parents and culture. His success is
shared with his family. With his first pay cheque he purchases his
father's ticket to Mecca, paying the traditional tribute of the prodigal.
But he avoids local girls, keeping his romance sacred. His deception
deepens as pictures and letters from France accumulate and he is
forced to avoid conversation which would lead him into lying.

Finally, Ousmane decides it is time to make his move. He announces
one day that he is going to Paris. His mother warns him: 'white women
are on the look out for black men. Be on your guard. Don't bring us
back one of them' (p. 59). Laden with gifts, Ousmane sets off to Paris to
his 'fairy princess', and in their brief moment of re-encounter, he
concludes: 'His fairy princess was more bewitching than ever, here in

her own environment.' Mireille finds: 'She had left an adolescent. She discovered a man.'

The narrative does not dwell on their reunion, whisking them off to a small mosque where Mireille takes her most important first step away from her culture: the Shahadah – converting to Islam. After this Mireille hurriedly seals an episode in her life by becoming the wife of an African Muslim, and the narrative locks her into the tragedy which has been prepared for her. The directness of the narrative also describes the innocence of the young people, who themselves apparently act with an uncomplicated openness. They have, in reality, been deceiving everyone for years, and it will soon be clear that they have been deceiving themselves as well.

Once again, as in describing the growth of the relationship between Mireille and Ousmane, and in portraying Ramatoulaye's introspection in *So Long a Letter*, letter-writing as a form of disclosure at a moment of crisis becomes a useful tool. Both Ousmane and Mireille write letters to their respective parents to announce their marriage, and it is interesting to compare the parents' separate responses to the news. Ousmane's letter to his father is written in 'foreign' words, an act of affiliation which adequately explains itself. It falls to his younger brother, Babacar, to read this letter. He, of 'constant chatter' as he describes himself, hesitates and falters because: 'My brother's French is too difficult for me.' In other words, he refuses to accept the role of intermediary in an act of self-betrayal. Another interpreter is called. He is a school teacher and through his lips comes the awful truth. Ousmane describes the years of longing, the desire for free choice in love, his inescapable destiny:

> She loves me for myself and has renounced her own religion to become my wife. You have the delicate task of informing my Mother. When you do so, lay stress on the fact that she is not 'losing me'. When you do so, think of the destiny of every creature that is in the hands of Allah, the All-Powerful.
>
> Nothing can alter the deep feeling that I have for you. We shall be seeing you soon. (p. 65)

When the father arrives home with his difficult news, Yaye Khady 'was in tears already, without knowing what she was weeping for'. The couple go back and forth, inside and outside images, reproach themselves for not reading the signs properly. In the end they arrive at an explanation which makes the matter bearable: 'Since this woman has embraced Islam, we must simply accept her into the bosom of our family. In the framework of Morality, he has the right to do what he pleases with his own life' (p. 66). That is the father. The mother has other disappointments:

> A *Toubab* can't be a proper daughter-in-law. She'll only have eyes for her man. We'll mean nothing to her. And I who dreamt of a daughter-in-law who'd live here and relieve me of the domestic work by taking over the management of the house, and now I'm faced with a woman who's going to take my son away from me. I shall die on my feet, in the kitchen. (p. 66)

While the young people have their own naive satisfactions in mind, the old feel a more uncomplicated anguish and some practical regrets.

Mireille's letter to her parents opens with confrontation: 'When you receive this letter, posted just before my departure, I shall already be far away from you starting my new life with my Senegalese family' (p. 75). M de La Vallée, her father, hears the echo of his own words about Africans and we are invited to share the daughter's delectable revenge: 'Primitive, hideous half-wits'. His nightmare image of the gentle daughter in rough black hands has found fulfilment as a means of her rejection of him and the ethos he lives by. Reading her plea for understanding and forgiveness, which we can only read as gloating for the sake of observing the form, predictably only serves to harden his heart against her. Mireille sends the letter to his office, and he leaves for home in a rage to break the news to his wife. His wife's entire morning is spent making 'paella for lunch', another criticism of the empty hedonism of bourgeois life. M de La Vallée's incoherent rage and his wife's sudden despair contrast vividly with the African family's response. Despite the latter's feeling of loss, they find a form of words which will enable compromise while the European family succumbs to a self-indulgent sense of tragedy.

When Mireille and Ousmane return to Senegal, they are met by a proud father bedecked with war medals, but Yaye Khady quietly begins a campaign to get rid of Mireille. Ousmane reassures Mireille with calm self-importance: 'She feels frustrated. You must forgive her. She feels she has lost me. That I now belong to you' (p. 81).

Slowly, they begin to grow apart. Once again the conflict takes the form of 'culture clash' polarities. Ousmane attacks a loyal friend and cousin, Lamine, for abondoning his culture to live in the western world of his wife. Mireille, on the other hand, finds Lamine's marriage enviable. Both parents approve of their daughter Pierrett's choice, and come every winter to visit them. The more Mireille points out how Lamine seems more at ease than him, the more Ousmane parades his Africanity. One one occasion he says to Lamine:

> You don't realise that you are betraying your true self. You live like a *Toubab*, you think like a *Toubab*. If it weren't for your skin you wouldn't be an African anymore. You know you're deserting our ranks, just when we need trained men. (p. 99)

It is at this time of accelerating crises of identity that an old friendship plays an important role.

On the first morning we meet him, at the beginning of the novel, Ousmane is reflecting on his first friendship with a girl, and how disastrously it turned out. Her name was Ouleymatou, the sister of his 'hut-brother'. He helped her with her French grammar but she seemed more interested in another boy. When he spoke to Ousseynou, his 'hut-brother', about her, the latter said: 'My sister doesn't want a boy who sweeps the house, fetches buckets of water and smells of dried fish.' Now this old friendship with Ousseynou is revived. Ousmane's new Peugeot and elegant clothes make quite an impression on the family as Ouleymatou, his old love, serves drinks. Though many years older and divorced, she is still beautiful, and upon seeing Ousmane she plots his seduction. She is on hand at her younger brother's when Ousmane visits. She visits Yaye Khady at washing time and offers to be her hands. Everyone knows Yaye Khady and her son's 'white wife' are not on good terms. Finally her campaign works and Ousmane succumbs. Later she becomes pregnant and Ousmane marries her without telling Mireille.

Mireille finds out soon enough, though, and now the crisis for her has reached the critical moment. By now she is thoroughly alienated from her surroundings, of course, but the possibility of returning to France also seems unattractive. There is her son. The de La Vallées will never accept this brown-skinned grandchild. In the earlier response of her parents, which also represented that of their sub-culture, lies a criticism of European racism and its ungenerous individualism.

Ousmane, on his part, feels guilt for Mireille, and goes to see a *bilodja* for medicine which would cool his passion for Ouleymatou. The man tells him: 'A woman is bringing you bad luck,' and 'bathes' him in water. However, the bath does not cool his desire for Ouleymatou but drives him further into his own sense of being connected to Africa.

When he arrives home he finds Mireille dishevelled and naked. She has killed their son – 'The Gnouloule Khessoul is dead' ('The *neither-black-nor-white* is dead') – and stabs Ousmane twice before he escapes. Mireille makes the tragic journey from the courageous and generous young lover to the alienated and rejected outsider, in the process losing her own sense of identity. The culture she marries into rejects her, and she herself has already rejected her own. Her story shows that it is the woman who has to sacrifice in such marriages, for while she concedes to her new circumstances, Ousmane does not. In fact, his marriage has only left him with a greater need to assert his affiliations to Africa, in case his 'love' of a European woman should seem like self-contempt. As in *So Long a Letter*, it is through the exploration of marriages that Mariama Bâ demonstrates the patriarchal indulgences of Senegalese society. In both novels, the taking of a second wife is the fullest expression of the inequality between men and women, and the point of crisis beyond which her protagonists cannot acquiesce. Ramatoulaye chooses to stay with Modou, of course, but as a result is forced to reappraise herself and her society. Mireille's circumstances are already more dramatic in the first place, and her alienation, when it comes, unhinges her completely.

## Notes

1. Mariama Bâ, *So Long a Letter*, London: Heinemann, 1981. First published in French 1980, translated by Modupe Bode-Thomas. *Scarlet Song*, Longman: Harlow, 1986, p. iv. First published by Les Nouvelles Editions Africaines, 1981, translated by Dorothy S. Blair.

2. Mbye B. Cham, 'Islam in Senegalese Literature and Film', *Faces of Islam in African Literature*, ed. Kenneth W. Harrow, New Haven: HEB Inc; London: James Currey, 1991, pp. 163–86.

3. See for example Sura IV, 'Nusaa', the Koran.

# A Terrible Trajectory: The Impact of Apartheid, Prison and Exile on Dennis Brutus's Poetry

FRANK M. CHIPASULA

In contemporary African literature very few poets have attracted as much international attention for their extra-literary efforts as the exiled South African activist–poet, Dennis Brutus. Having been nurtured on a 'diet of eloquent delectable accolades',[1] he has grown into somewhat of a sacred bull one approaches with great trepidation. However, our reverence for Brutus has less to do with his poetic achievement than his stand against apartheid. Awestruck by the presence of this heroic 'fighter' who survived eighteen months of incarceration on Robben Island and has valiantly lived with the scar of a bullet wound, we have tended to place him constantly among the 'world's finest poets'.[2] A veteran of a life-and-death battle against injustice, Brutus has thus garnered rewards for an art that might not have attracted a stare had it been otherwise.

With eleven volumes currently to his credit, Brutus's poetic career appears impressive.[3] However, a reassessment based on three of his poetry collections, *Sirens, Knuckles, Boots* (1963), *Letters to Martha and Other Poems from a South African Prison* (1968) and *Stubborn Hope* (1978), reveals the terrible trajectory of his poetic performance, which can be attributed to apartheid's restrictive and reductive definition of human beings, and to imprisonment and exile. All the same, Dennis Brutus's career is remarkable, considering that he lived and functioned for many years under immense constraints, risking his very life when he challenged the apartheid system in sport (not in poetry, which came later). Although he has produced the bulk of his poetry in exile, in his work he has nevertheless focused on the South African landscape which he has always imagined as a lover's body.

Several factors encourage a reassessment of Dennis Brutus's poetic career and output. Firstly, the presence of younger poets in South Africa necessitates a revaluation not only of Brutus's poetic oeuvre but also his stature as a black South African poet. Unfortunately, a great deal of Brutus's poetry not only lacks the 'amazing suppleness and subtlety', and perhaps the ingenuity with which urban music confronts black people's experiences in the townships, but it also exhibits what Lewis Nkosi further describes as the 'cracks and tension of language working under severe strain'.[4] In terms of technical refinement, thematic development and poetic verve, Brutus's poems do not approximate the dexterity and linguistic innovativeness of the prematurely plucked Arthur Nortje, Brutus's own erstwhile student whom he himself has called not only the 'beautiful singer', but also 'the finest poet to come out of South Africa and probably out of Africa'.[5]

A recontextualisation of Brutus's poetry within the scheme of anti-apartheid poetry reveals the stunting impact of racial segregation, imprisonment and exile on his creativity. Yet unlike his disadvantaged compatriots within the country, Brutus, as poet and sports politician, has been nurtured and groomed by a group of dedicated and sympathetic critics willing to suspend negative observations on the shortcomings of his work, and he has thus found himself effortlessly in print abroad.[6] Apparently, as long as the poetry exhibited some elements of protest against apartheid and commitment to the cause for the restoration of justice in South Africa, it was worth publishing.

Should we expect or even demand more than protest and political commitment from a black South African poet? In the case of Dennis Brutus, we are justified in our expectation of aesthetic beauty in his poetry because of what his early verse had shown. Further, in a poetry such as Brutus's we expect something profound, what Pablo Neruda, in his essay 'The Poet Is Not a Rolling Stone' terms the 'essences' of his native country. According to Neruda, the 'first stage of a poet's life must be devoted to absorbing the essences of his native land: later, he must return them . . . His poetry and his actions must contribute to the maturity and growth of his people.'[7] However, unless such poetic maturity occurs in the poet, we cannot expect the contribution towards 'maturity and growth' of his people.

Apartheid's worst impact on Brutus's life was to create psychological barriers that apparently engendered a complex and deep-seated identity crisis during his early years, a consequence of his having been reductively classified as 'Coloured', that is, neither 'European' nor 'African', in a racially stratified society. Brutus's description of the racial divisions in Port Elizabeth during his childhood is illuminating, for it indicates the deep chasms the Group Areas Act created among the various 'races':

> Certainly we were not white, and *out there* were the white people who controlled our destiny . . . There were also the Africans, the 'natives' who lived even *further out on the edge of the city* and who passed through *our area*, or the outskirts of it, on the way to *their area*, each morning going to work and each evening coming from work. (*TriQ 69*, p. 366)

The implicit distance and lack of contact among the three groups, with the 'natives' occupying the marginal or peripheral spaces, indicate the degree of cultural isolation the young Brutus experienced.[8] The resultant psychic distortion and fragmentation are revealed in his subsequent doubts about his African identity when he expressed his 'misgivings' about his 'right to be called an "African Voice"; how far were my ideas and opinions and art peculiarly African?' (*Poems from Algiers*, p. 21).

Brutus's doubts and questions concerning his true identity are genuine, and they are a consequence of a breach between his individual imagination and the complex traditions within which it might have functioned had apartheid laws not closed off from him certain *essential* cultural experiences. This identity crisis is also apparent in the implicit discomfort and ambivalence with which Brutus recalls part of his family history:

> My mother talked of the days of slavery, of how her mother had in fact known slavery, may have been a slave herself. She was of African descent, but of mixed heritage: an English family called Webb, apparently. (*TriQ 69*, p. 366)

His grandmother's strong traditions of orature might have empowered Brutus to experiment with the many genres of poetry such as the Izibongo praise poetry, proverbs, riddles, tales, curses, initiation chants and dirges as well as war-songs, wedding and hunters' songs that are prevalent in southern Africa. Apartheid's fragmenting laws must be held responsible for Brutus's apparent lack of exposure to the region's rich oral traditions whose metaphors, symbols, images, and other poetic devices might have authenticated and anchored his work in genuine South *African* traditions.

Although he began writing poetry in the mid-1940s, Brutus's emergence in the early 1960s as the major Coloured South African poet coincides simultaneously with the intensification of the struggles for freedom in the region as well as the alliances among the colonial powers and the apartheid regime. Constantly persecuted by the South African political police, he was arrested, and in 1963 banned for his anti-apartheid activities in the field of international sport. In a bid to escape from the country, he was caught in Mozambique, detained and then handed back to the South African authorities. In another attempt to escape he was shot in the stomach, hospitalised and then tried for subversion. While incarcerated on the notorious Robben Island prison off Cape Town, his manuscript of poems, which had won the Mbari Poetry Prize in 1962 (although he returned the prize money because the award was racially based), was published as *Sirens, Knuckles, Boots* in 1963, in Nigeria.

Ironically, the Mbari Creative Society, in a gesture meant to encourage indigenous creativity, placed the rejected laurels on a poet who declared in a sonnet, 'A troubadour, I traverse all my land.' Within the coupled quatrains followed by the two tercets, Brutus's rhyming of 'land' with his probing 'hand', alternating 'zest' with 'rest', expressed his intense, urgent and passionate love for South Africa. This is all in order, except that Brutus, with all his love for the land, adopts an alien persona, a troubadour, perhaps to convince us of his knowledge of Mediterranean poetic traditions and aesthetics. Couldn't Brutus find, in African, or southern African traditions, an equivalent for this 'quixoting' troubadour? Did he really have to borrow an alien tongue to express his love for his native land? Perhaps we can condone this as merely apprentice poetry, and yet, even then couldn't he have apprenticed himself to such local poets as Vilakazi, Dhlomo and Mqayi and other Imbongi whose works must have crossed his eyes as he stealthily 'traversed' his land during his underground years?

This question becomes critical when one recalls Brutus's own assertion that he functions within the African poetic tradition,[9] which invites comparisons with such traditionalists as Okot p'Bitek, the late

Acoli poet, and Mazisi Kunene who not only composes in the Zulu language and then renders his works into English, but also consciously operates within the Imbongi tradition of Zulu court poetry. Since African traditions are diverse and various it is perhaps not unjustified to ask: To which African tradition does Brutus's poetry belong?

A subtle process of self-definition and hence empowerment is implicit in his early poems that reflect a mind intensely at work, a burgeoning artist trying to wring meanings out of the complex, chaotic, and hostile yet beautiful landscape of his country. *Sirens, Knuckles, Boots* demonstrates a mind busily meditating on mastering anger by channelling it into forceful similes and metaphors. Brutus's economy of means creates a terse zestful line that attempts to link soul to soil, to fuse woman to land, and to project his double love of both, as in 'Nightsong: City' (*A Simple Lust*, p. 18). Poems such as these, which express his love for land in startlingly erotic images of passionate and intimate sexual embrace, also cryptically reference his relationship with a white woman, in defiance of the Immorality Act.[10] A simple lust, for Brutus, metaphorically conjures a man's intimate contact with his beloved country. In the most powerful of these poems Brutus distils multiple meanings into single words, phrases and lines loaded with intense emotion, generating great tensions in the poems.

Nowhere in Brutus's exile poetry is the imagery as vivid and forceful as it is in these early poems. The volume's terse and richly imaged verse, endowed with lavish figurative language, perhaps more than the fact of Brutus's wounding and incarceration, may have impressed the jurors about the poet's now largely unrealised potential. Notice his vivid and harrowing description of the wastelands called the Transkei homeland in 'Erosion: Transkei':

> Under green drapes the scars scream,
> red wounds wail soundlessly,
> beg for assuaging, satiation;
> warm life dribbles seawards with streams. (*A Simple Lust*, p. 16)

Here is a forceful verbal portrait of a wounded, eroded land that becomes more poignant as the poet fuses implicitly the land's physical wounds with the people's psychic wounds. Yet there is always a possibility of 'warm life', new horizons, even as the streams that will be created by 'the quickening rains' carry the rich soil to the sea.

Curiously, the same poet who could deftly conjure up such an apt simile as 'violence like a bug-infested rug is tossed', or the metaphorical 'long day's anger pants from sand and rocks' ('Nightsong: City', p. 18), could degenerate to such flatness as contained in:

> Bruised though we must be
> some easement we require
> unarguably, though we argue against desire

> ('This sun on this rubble after rain', p. 9)

The initial immediacy of 'This sun on this rubble' is totally diminished from a poem that has such powerfully defeatist imagery as 'under jackboots our bones and spirits crunch/forced into sweat-tear-sodden slush'. Alternating pessimism with optimism, the poet may be excused for understating the possibility of regeneration, of something new being born out of this rubble and debris of humanity spiritually crushed under the brutal boots of apartheid.

This defeatist rhetoric takes on an intense preoccupation with the self, becomes almost solipsistic in 'Off the Campus: Wits', a poem which recalls and recreates an aspect of his student days at the University of Witwatersrand where he experienced segregation on the sports field. His bitterness attains the heights of irrationality when he describes white students, who are unjustly implicated in a policy of victimisation, as 'obscene albinos'.[11] What is strangely curious though is the sudden shift from the collective 'we look', 'we cower' to 'I crouch' – from 'us' to the solitary 'I', the oppressed community to the lone 'fighter' poet writing these venomed lines:

> to pierce deaf eardrums waxed by fear
> or spy, a Strandloper, these obscene albinos
> and from the corner of my eye
> catch a glimpse of a glinting spear. (*A Simple Lust*, p. 12)

There is a hint of the cult of the lone poet figure characteristic of the early Soyinka or Okigbo as well as intimations of an impending liberation struggle in the 'glinting spear' which the persona merely glimpses but does not wield. The cyclic nature of this oppression is quite clearly portrayed in the following twelve lines:

> The sounds begin again:
> the siren in the night
> the thunder at the door
> the shriek of nerves in pain.
>
> Then the keening crescendo
> of faces split by pain
> the wordless, endless wail
> only the unfree know.
>
> Importunate as rain
> the wraiths exhale their woe
> over the sirens, knuckles, boots;
> my sounds begin again.
>
> ('The sounds begin again', *A Simple Lust*, p. 19)

Three simple nouns – 'siren', 'thunder' and 'shriek' – effectively conjure the violence that black South Africans had to endure nightly. However, the vicious cycle of these oppressive sounds implied in the rhyming of 'again' with 'pain' is mysteriously broken by the intruding natural force of rain. Thus one caught in the repetitive, odious cycle finds redemptive respite in the rain that presages a rebirth and regeneration.

'The sounds begin again' fairly succeeds with its terse, end-stopped lines, its intricate rhyme–scheme which weaves not only words but stanzas into a neat, coherent whole though again one wishes Brutus had heeded T. S. Eliot's advice to poets to find an 'objective correlative' to emotions in a poem. John Pepper Clark asserts as much when he comments that Brutus is a 'man battering his head against the bars of a cage', yet it is difficult to hear the 'shouting' that Clark hears.[12] The tragedy in Brutus's poem does not become mere melodrama. The poem does vividly project the incessant nature of oppression in apartheid South Africa, and the acceptance in the last line, which is no mere variation on the opening line, might imply the speaker's stoical response to this reality.

Brutus's early volume remains his strongest to date and worth one more word if only to speculate on what manner of poet he might have become had apartheid's prison and exile not stunted his growth. His post-Robben Island poetry is marked by a simplicity and directness quite unlike the earlier poems. But his conscious decision to reach a much wider audience than before meant a great sacrifice in technical virtuosity. Upon his release from prison he was placed under house arrest for twelve hours of each day, and he was served with a new set of bans that made it a crime to draft or write anything, except letters, that might be published. As a result Brutus adopted the epistle form for his poems addressed to Martha, his sister-in-law, whose husband was himself a prisoner on Robben Island. Though not intended for publication, the poems were gathered together into *Letters to Martha and Other Poems from a South African Prison* (1968), a volume that remains the most tangible testament to the adverse effects of apartheid censorship restrictions and prison on this intrepid fighter for justice. The poems belong to the genre of prison poetry, all written under house arrest but exploring the meaning and implications of his prison experiences.

Although the poems lack in both power and craftsmanship, such an otherwise perceptive critic as Adrian Roscoe accredits the prison experience with having enabled Brutus to produce some of the most refined poems he had hitherto written, as he so articulately claims:

> Imprisonment not only pushed the poet to explore the deepest recesses of mind and soul, but also demanded, constantly and at their highest pitch, all those imaginative and spiritual resources necessary for his survival as a man of dignity and self-respect.[13]

Contrary to Roscoe's lavish praises, Brutus's own volume contains hardly any evidence to bolster such an eloquent and over-generous defence of the poet. More valid than these accolades are perhaps Es'kia (Ezekiel)Mphahlele and Lewis Nkosi's observations regarding Brutus's over-reliance on flat statement in that very volume.[14] As the poems lack any depth of feeling, they may serve to demonstrate just how thoroughly prison experience has stamped the 'art' out of these prosaic pieces.

Strangely defeatist in tone, these poems rather intimate to us the shrinking and warping impact such extreme conditions can have on a fine artist.

The very first poem in *Letters to Martha* belies Roscoe's contention that this is some of the best verse ever written by Brutus.[15] In that poem, 'Longing', the speaker poses the following rhetorical question:

> Can the heart compute desire's trajectory
> Or logic obfusc with semantic ambiguities
> This simple ache's expletive detonation? (p. 46)

The response, of course, would have been positive had Brutus heeded Eliot's injunction to poets to seek an objective correlative for that 'simple ache' to resolve all the 'semantic ambiguities' which follow. I find it hard to empathise with the speaker whose 'heart knows now such devastation' because he makes no effort at projecting that devastation vividly through emotive language. The letters' major flaws are outright philosophising and over-use of polysyllabic diction which results in such flat and unevocative words as 'ease*ment*', 'lodge*ment*', 'intrigued speculation and wonder*ment*' (my emphases); or 'reformation/(which can procure promotion)', 'the impregnation of our air', or 'a pugnacious assertion of discontent/ . . . the boundless opprobrium of life/a desperation: despair', or 'after the entertainment/Beethoven with his sonorous percussive exaltation' (p. 93); or when he is 'transcendentally watching the Irish jigsaw' (p. 95) as he flies from London to New York! And when the racists 'yearn unassuagedly', when the SANROC fighter blasts them 'unforgettably' and 'the diurnal reminders excoriate their souls' (p. 90), what emotions or images do these lines evoke in the reader's mind? It is the language, not the experience, that is at fault here.

Ploughing through the eighteen letters and postscripts (written, apparently, *in two days*),[16] another twenty-seven letters, and 'diary-entry-like' meditative verses, is rather taxing on the reader's patience, for the majority of the work here relies so heavily on prosaic and flat statement that one delights even in the rare sparks of vivid imagery. This is not to say that the movement (which the reader must reconstruct) from the trial, the charge, the journey to Robben Island with its stop-overs in various jails and the speaker's apprehensions about prison as well as the harrowing prison experiences is without value. Where is the depth of feeling one expects in a poem about incarceration? In the poem 'On the Island', we are meant to feel the deathly atmosphere of solitary confinement, but unfortunately the over-repeated compound modifier 'cement-grey' becomes irritatingly monotonous and redundant:

> Cement-grey floors and walls
> cement-grey days
> cement-grey time . . . ('On the Island', *A Simple Lust*, p. 71)

Neither lyrical nor narrative, the poems depend too heavily on flat statements and rhetorical questions: 'who has not joyed in the arbitrary exercise of power'. Lacking emotive or figurative language, the *Letters* are level-headed meditations of a wronged man and a tired artist who is capable of such 'bad stumbling verse' (*Poems from Algiers*, p. 21) as the following:

> the complex aeronautics
> and the birds
> and their exuberant acrobatics
> become matters for intrigued speculation
> and wonderment. (Letter 17, *A Simple Lust*, p. 66)

This, of course, is mere posturing on dangerous verbal stilts not many prisoners can afford. Indeed, one is filled with a sense of 'wonderment' why Brutus couldn't simply lament, 'Oh had I a pair of wings!' Where is the precision and 'intensity of imagery', the 'apt image' that Daniel Abasiekong and Romanus Egudu applauded in Brutus's poetry?[17] Unlike Paul Theroux, I see more total misses from Brutus's wild swinging punches than we have hitherto been willing to acknowledge (Beier, p. 122).

Scribbled at lightning speed, under house arrest – itself a worse form of imprisonment since it alienates one from one's own home – these poems, whose purpose was 'partly to wrench ease' for himself, show the paralysing impact of both apartheid and prison on the poet. There is more moralising, didacticism and rationalisation of actions as well as unwitting revelations about Brutus's own fear that he may have been psychologically tainted by his prison experiences.

In the *Letters*, as in the previous collection, Brutus exposes the injustices the majority suffer in a police state which arbitrarily exercises and displays force through its various 'Special Branches'. Major themes here include the denial of freedom and dehumanisation of both the oppressors and the oppressed who nevertheless retain a measure of their humanity through endurance, tenderness and love. Imprisonment results in further fragmentation of lives and distortion of moral values, as the poems on prison sexuality indicate. The dominator–dominated dichotomy finds its parallel in the homosexual relations between the men and youths in prison. We notice, for instance, the changes and transformations that occur to 'Blue Champagne', a youthful male who plays the role of 'girl' in the sexual embrace, but when he grows older he becomes the dominant 'man' in the unions. Certainly, such 'random pebbles' as Letters 3, 6, 7 and 8 could not console a wife whose husband might not only be driven to such 'desperate limits' as to seek relief from sexual tension in 'this' but also find it 'preferable,/even desirable' (Letter 7, p. 58). Letters 9 and 10 do little to allay her fears, try as the persona may to reassure her.

What then is the real motive for composing these letters, and are the statements Brutus has made over the matter credible and conclusive? Letter 13 reveals more about the letter-writing project itself than Brutus or his critics have acknowledged (*A Simple Lust*, p. 63). Deliberately misplaced in the sequence, the letter recalls the eve of his departure for Robben Island. What begins as a moment of personal illumination:

> "So, for a beginning, I know
> there is no beginning"

becomes suddenly generalised, as is Brutus's wont, to pre-empt any charges of a preoccupation with the self that borders on narcissism:

> So *one* cushions the mind
> with phrases
> aphorisms and quotations

> to blunt the impact
> of this crushing blow. [my emphasis]

The placement of the 'letter' here indicates its function. If these poems are about the human condition, they do less to enlighten us about that condition as it is modified by prison than they do about the poet himself. Brutus's apartheid prison is hardly unique to South Africa and might not particularly enrage sensitive audiences abroad. Rather, the *Letters* project, undertaken after Robben Island, is apparently a futile effort to 'cushion' his own mind and to conceal the psychic scars left by the 'outrages of prison' (p. 63).

Artistically, Brutus does not fare any better in exile, as his later work indicates. Just as chaotic as the other volumes, *Stubborn Hope* (1978) continues in the monotonous vein of his earlier verses, with flat statements, intriguing self-accusations, imagined questions or objections, without thematic linkages or apparent order, save for the sameness of voice.

Characteristically brief, yet more prosaic than before, these poems reveal an anguished heart, sometimes curiously 'remorseful', and a turbulent mind, understandably so considering that the poet is finally recognising the wounds garnered from incarceration in the notorious island prison and under house arrest, as he states in the verbose 'A Comparative Peace':

> One requires
> more
> an intellectual acceptance
> assent
> the erasure of sharp memories. (*Stubborn Hope*, p. 19)

an erasure which is next to impossible as the exile is continually haunted by the fact that other detainees still languish in the country's prisons. Hence:

> One knows
> only an unquiet ease
> only a comparative peace. (p. 19)

The half-rhyme on 'ease' and 'peace' hints at the turmoil beneath, which is clearly discernible in the following poem, 'It is without the overtones': for despite the poet's efforts at concealment of his dis-ease, he cannot 'find (in the Abergavenny hills) some small easement' (p. 19).

Again, over-reliance on flat, sometimes even partially abstract, statement weakens Brutus's work here. And, although the poet is himself aware of this slackness in his verse, he is apparently unable to do anything about it. Brutus himself is his own best critic, as the following poems indicate, both from *Stubbon Hope*, his next substantial volume after *A Simple Lust*. Both poems are framed as crucial questions an artist in Brutus's position might ask, caught in a circumstance where, although he is intensely aware of his artistic failures, his admirers think otherwise. The reference to that 'something beautiful' and the nostalgic tone of 'When Will I Return' force one to re-examine the technical aspects of Brutus's earlier work to which these poems refer. The following claims need to be taken seriously because they are made by Brutus the reader of his own past performance, who simultaneously laments the loss of his artistic dexterity in sadly prosaic lines. 'When will my heart/ever sing again?' the poet prosaically laments in one poem, and in another he nostalgically asks, 'when will I return/to the tightly organised/completely structured/image and expression/rich in flying tangential associations'. (p. 13) Is this also perhaps a case of a poet's over-rating of his own past achievements? For beyond the few poems, such as 'The sounds begin again', which is compact yet in need of Eliot's 'objective correlative', not much in his accumulated work can support such a claim. Indeed, these large claims cannot be substantiated by many of his pre- and post-prison poetry. Besides, one would have to go to great pains to find that rich, complex, and resonant imagery in abundance among those issued during the earliest phase of his exile. The few exceptions are nevertheless marred by their own glaring flaws.

If these poems do not yield much in terms of issues, they nevertheless crack open the door into the poet's pained mind as he grapples with the reality of his continuing exile and the uncertainty of his country's future. They also offer us insights into the exile mind, the poignancy of his memories, as in 'At Odd Moments' which reveals psychic ordeal and torment, as the pain surges without warning:

> At odd moments
> my bullet scars will twinge:
> when I am resting,
> or when fatigue
> is a continuous shriek in my brain. (*Stubborn Hope*, p. 43)

What one encounters over and over in these very personal poems is an acutely lonely man estranged from both his family and perhaps friends, futilely concealing his guilt and bitterness in political (SANROC) work, as revealed in the poems: 'These are times (2)' (p. 17); 'How are the shoots of affection withered at the root?' (p. 17), and all those obviously futile attempts at self-justification for every little move the persona takes, even when he reminisces over prison experiences, as in 'Beyond Sharp Control' (p. 21); 'I would not be thought less than a man' (pp. 21–2) and 'I come and go' (p. 25), for instance.

We encounter here a mind that is constantly groping for the meaning of exile, death of political prisoners, friends and the meaning of friendship, loneliness, the oppressor–oppressed dichotomy and the meaning of the life of a wandering man. Nostalgia, a significant aspect of the external exile, returns him again and again to the island prison as this sequence in which, after many lines of 'tired prose' (as his compatriot Mphahlele once described this verse), we are shown into the image-laden chamber that constitutes the memory of prison. Yet the imagery is often forced, as in 'the bright airy air/lightwoven, seawoven, spraywoven air' (p. 59); or his description of the water as 'rushing wave water/lightgreen or colourless, transparent with a hint of light' (p. 59).

The third, final, section is perhaps the most effective in its vivid portrayal of the tragicomic lot of prisoners lining up 'for hospital', only to receive castor oil (p. 60). However, a good portion of this section remains prosaic; 'Sharpeville' (p. 89) consists of prose lines chopped up into verse. Also there are axioms and aphorisms masquerading as poetry, for instance: 'Perhaps/all/poems/are simply/drafts' (p. 55), or the one tucked towards the end of the South African sequence 'Exile/is the reproach/of beauty/in a landscape,/vaguely familiar/because it echoes/remembered beauty' (p. 94).

Further, the presence of such a prophetic poem as 'On the Coming Victory' (p. 95) which presages the impending victory of the liberation forces and the dawn of a new day raises a very important issue.

Strangely, the declaration he makes in 'I am a rebel and freedom is my cause' recalls Brutus's reticence regarding his relationship to the major liberation movements in South Africa. In this regard comparisons with two other central and southern African poets, Antonio Agostinho Neto, the late combat poet of Angola, and José Craveirinha, the Coloured poet of Mozambique who threw in his lot with the liberation movement in his own country, need to be highlighted. Curiously, finding himself in similar conditions, Brutus did not lend his harp entirely to the principal liberation movement in South Africa, though he claimed that he wrote 'a poetry which sings people to battle' (Alvarez-Pererye p. 137).

Brutus's claim that he wrote poetry that 'sings people to battle' must also be interrogated closely, for while Brutus was having a tryst with his lover-land, his contemporaries in Angola and Mozambique were injecting courage into their fighting arms with songs. While Brutus indulged in highly eroticised fantasies about the 'far flung flesh' of his land, Antonio Agostinho Neto, Antonio Jacinto, Marcelino dos Santos, Jorge Rebelo and José Craveirinha were not only vilifying the colonial masters while chiding and inciting the docile African peasants to revolt, but they were also reinterpreting African values through their poetry and offering a vision of democratic and racially integrated societies after the wars. They were actually engaged in an armed struggle to reclaim their lost lands and to reinstate their cultures. While Rebelo, for instance, saw 'bullets beginning to flower' in Mozambique Brutus was reflecting: 'somehow we survive'.

The most memorable word from this collection is 'stubborn', which is so over-used and worn thin that it ceases to have any impact on the reader. From stubborn hope to stubborn love, one plods through a myriad redundant phrases and words whose unintended effect is to create 'stubborn' verse, a great deal of which saps the reader's energy. One feels drained, not emotionally but physically worn out by this poetry, as if the poet had been wrestling with the reader to try and wring some reaction from him or her.

If aesthetic value is not a strong element in this poetry, its social value cannot be underestimated or denied. Brutus's work, bearing witness to an epoch, a long dark season in South African political and social history, is indispensable. Characterised by the cacophony of violent sounds: thundering boots breaking down doors of Africans suspected of subversion, sirens wailing in the night as police cruisers cart transgressors of apartheid's irrational laws to prisons and concentration camps, the clang of handcuffs on wrists and prison doors slammed shut, vociferations of curses and insults as policemen search black people for passes; separate amenities; hard labour in prisons as innocent men engage in senseless drudgery of breaking stones in quarries; the murders and 'suicides' in prison, the whole image of a police state and its brutality are fairly successfully delineated in these verses. Present also is the tenderness, surprisingly, in victims of this system, moments of respite when even with torn, bleeding lips, blacks and whites caught in immorality acts, exchanged stolen and forbidden kisses before the final raid.

This exposure of an evil system that simultaneously harbours an implicit call for its destruction or total transformation defines the functional nature of this poetry. But it also suggests the beauty that is possible in a post-apartheid society. If, as critics, we have tended to turn a blind eye to Brutus's technical failures, our admiration has often focused on the fact that he has apparently heroically borne his physical and psychic wounds. However, a systematic reading of the work reveals the acute pain, loneliness, and mental anguish that dog him: that is, the work as a whole brings down our hero to a more human level where we are able to appreciate his suffering, whose origins are located in the evil apartheid state currently in the process of being dismantled.

Finally, Brutus has not realised his potential as a result of the disappointments and pain of exile; constant doubts seemed to plague him even when, as in *Poems from Algiers* and *China Poems*, he takes stock of his triumphs in his campaign against apartheid in international sport in cold, factual prosaic lines totally devoid of emotive language and vivid imagery. Anyone looking for memorable lines will not find them in *Airs and Tributes* either. The spectre of apartheid appears to have so paralysed the poets that they found it difficult to transmute the 'social facts' that they most often present to us in their verses into literary art.

## Notes

1. 'No Banyan, Only', *A Simple Lust*, London: Heinemann, 1973, p. 14.

2. Lamont Steptoe, publisher's statement in Dennis Brutus, *Airs and Tributes*, Camden, NJ: Whirlwind Press, 1989, p. iv.

3. Dennis Brutus has published the following collections of poems:

*Sirens, Knuckles, Boots,* Ibadan: Mbari Publications/Evanston: Northwestern University Press, 1963;
   *Letters to Martha and Other Poems from a South African Prison,* London: Heinemann, 1968;
   *Poem from Algiers,* Austin: African and Afro-American Research Institute, University of Texas, 1970;
   *Thoughts Abroad,* Del Valle, Texas: Troubador Press, 1970;
   *A Simple Lust,* 1973 (which collects *Sirens, Knuckles, Boots; Letters to Martha; Poems from Algiers; Thoughts Abroad;* and the Brutus section of *Seven South African Poets,* London: Heinemann, 1971);
   *China Poems,* Austin, Texas: African and Afro-American Research Institute, University of Texas, 1975;
   *The Ordeal,* Austin, Texas: University of Texas Press, 1975;
   *Strains,* Del Valle, Texas: Troubadour Press, 1975;
   *Stubborn Hope,* Washington, DC: Three Continents Press, 1978;
   *Salutes and Censures,* Lagos: Fourth Dimension, 1982.
   *Airs and Tributes,* Austin, Texas: University of Texas Press, 1989.

4. Lewis Nkosi, 'Fiction by Black South Africans', in Ulli Beier, ed., *Introduction to African Literature: An Anthology of Critical Writing,* London: Longman, 1979, p. 221.

5. David Bunn and Jane Taylor, eds, *From South Africa: New Writing, Photographs and Art, TriQuarterly 69* (Spring/Summer 1987), Evanston, Illinois: Northwestern University, p. 366.

6. During the 1974–5 academic year Brutus and Bernth Lindfors published three volumes of Brutus's poetry, as follows: *China Poems* (1975); *Strains* (1975) and *The Ordeal* (1975).

7. Pablo Neruda, *Passions and Impressions,* New York: Farrar Straus Giroux, 1983, p. 331.

8. See Brutus's 'Childhood Reminiscences' in Per Wastberg, ed., *The Writer in Modern Africa,* New York: Africana Publishing Co, 1968, p. 96.

9. Introduction to a new edition of *Salutes and Censures,* published in Bunn and Taylor, eds, *From South Africa* (1987), p. 364.

10. J. Alvarez-Pererye, *The Poetry of Commitment in South Africa,* London: Heinemann, 1984, pp. 133–4.

11. Theroux and Pererye have discussed this issue at length. See Paul Theroux, 'Voices Out of the Skull: A Study of Six African Poets', in Ulli Beier (1979), p. 122; and J. Alvarez-Pererye (1984), p. 139.

12. John Pepper Clark, *The Example of Shakespeare,* Evanston: Northwestern University Press, 1970, p. 50.

13. Adrian Roscoe, *Uhuru's Fire: African Literature from East to South*, Cambridge: Cambridge University Press, 1977, p. 163.

14. Ezekiel Mphahlele, *Voices in the Whirlwind and Other Essays*, New York: Hill and Wang, 1972, p. 92; Lewis Nkosi, *Tasks and Masks: Themes and Styles in African Literature*, Harlow: Longmans, 1981, pp. 166–7.

15. Page references will be to *A Simple Lust* where *Letters to Martha* has been collected and slightly rearranged.

16. See *Letters to Martha*: Letters 1–11 are dated 11 November 1965; he may also have written 'Letter to Basil', 'Presumably' and 'For Bernice' on the same day. On 16 December 1965 he wrote four poems: 'Blood River Day', 'The Impregnation of the Air', 'Their Behaviour' and 'For X. B.'. Letters 12–18 are dated 20 December 1965; although the six postscripts are undated, they may have been composed on the same day as well.

17. Romanus Egudu, *Modern African Poetry and the African Predicament*, London: The Macmillan Press, 1978, p. 64; Daniel Abasiekong, 'Poetry Pure and Applied: Rabearivelo and Brutus', *Transition*, Vol. 23 (1965), p. 46.

# J. M. Coetzee: Writing in the Middle Voice

## TERESA DOVEY

As early as 1972, J. M. Coetzee was addressing the issue of the responsibilities of the South African writer, and asking: 'What is the "correct" mode for a society which, self-divided, swings uneasily from the Geneva of Calvin to the Manchester of 1830 to the Los Angeles of today, in search of an identity it may never find?'[1] The question is a telling one, articulating as it does Coetzee's awareness of the inevitable imbrication of South African novelistic discourse in a set of conflicting international discourses, and the acute sense of a divided self seeking an identity which informs all of his novels to date.

This preoccupation with identity cannot be written off as a modernist obsession with problems of consciousness, nor can it be dismissed as simply another of postmodernism's self-reflexive gestures, serving to endorse the endless deferral of meaning, and, ultimately, a position of extreme relativity.[2] Rather, it arises out of Coetzee's particular historical situation: that of being a white writer in South Africa in the last quarter of the twentieth century, of being a member of the colonising race in a complex situation which demonstrates features of colonialism, postcolonialism and neocolonialism.

The subtleties and complexities of Coetzee's attempts to negotiate a space for his writing in this context are frequently not recognised, and he has suffered a fate common to writers in this situation, which is to be subjected to an obsessive demand for their writing to be politically relevant in an overt, explicit and often simplistic way. Coetzee recognises this, in an interview, when he asks 'whether it isn't simply that vast and wholly ideological superstructure constituted by publishing, reviewing and criticism that is forcing on [him] the fate of being a "South African novelist".'[3] His novels have been read and

56

judged in terms of whether they are on the side of the oppressor or of the oppressed, but the white writer's task in South Africa is not as simple as choosing to represent faithfully the actual conditions of oppression, or of choosing to give a voice to the oppressed. And good intentions alone do not ensure protection against entering unwittingly into complicity with the dominant discourses, as, for example, some novels of Nadine Gordimer do.

Coetzee has described the writer's task as that of 'adapting whatever models and theories lie to hand to make writing possible',[4] and this is what he does: recognising that repetition is inevitable, he wittingly inhabits prior modes of discourse in order to deconstruct them from within. In this sense the novels may be described as postmodern allegories, which undermine the authority of the appropriated discourses. Their self-reflexive gestures are frequently articulated in explicitly Lacanian terms, and reading them as Lacanian allegories allows one to see them as speech acts, which erect an identity in writing on behalf of the speaker. In a short piece titled 'A Note on Writing', Coetzee describes a mode of writing, which is essentially his *own* mode, as writing in the 'middle voice':

> Though modern Indo-European languages retain morphologically distinct forms for only the active–passive opposition, the phantom presence of a middle voice . . . can be felt in some senses of modern verbs if one is alert to the possibility of a threefold opposition active–middle–passive. 'To write' is one of these verbs. To write (active) is to carry out the action without reference to the self, perhaps, though not necessarily, on behalf of someone else. To write (middle) is to carry out the action (or better, to do writing) with reference to the self.[5]

Coetzee's novels, while always making reference to the self of writing, exploit the notion of the *divided* subject of Lacan, the split between text and narration, or utterance and enunciation, in order to gesture towards the possibility of escaping complicity with the dominant discourses. They also exploit the Lacanian definition of the function of language as being 'not to inform but to evoke', with the subject seeking, via speech, 'the response of the other', an 'I' which requires the response of a 'You' in order to achieve identity.[6] In this way the novels are able to locate themselves as specific modes of discourse, each attempting to communicate within a particular historical moment, and are able to express their desire for a response from the victims of colonisation. Furthermore, Lacanian theory concerning the subject's construction in language allows one to posit a material and transformative role for the subject in society, via the *dialectic* between self and language.[7]

The issue of identity is handled differently in each novel, according to the mode of discourse being deconstructed: tracing the modifications it undergoes will allow us to follow Coetzee's analysis of and relation to certain discourses of colonialism and postcolonialism. In the first novel, *Dusklands*, Coetzee adopts and adapts an intersecting set of discourses, ethnographic and historiographic, documentary and fictional, which describe the encounter between European and indigene, usually in the narrative form of the journey of exploration and the frontier encounter.[8] These constitute the earliest forms of writing about southern Africa (or, indeed, any colonial situation), and are modes of discourse that have persisted into the present.[9]

Structurally the novel consists of a series of repetitions which involves a proliferation of voices: there is an historical document, the original 1792 Deposition of Jacobus Coetzee (one of J. M. Coetzee's ancestors); the fictitious contemporary Afterword and 'revised' narrative of Jacobus Coetzee by the historiographer S. J. Coetzee; and a recent version of the frontier narrative in 'The Vietnam Project'. The narrator of this first section is Eugene Dawn, 'mythographer' in the US Department of Defense, rebelling against but nevertheless needing the approval of his enigmatic manager, Coetzee.

Both Jacobus Coetzee and Eugene Dawn are shown engaged in a ruthless attempt to erect the self into being, the former via his Faustian penetration into the southern African interior, the latter via the act of leaving his wife and abducting his son, whom he stabs in an ultimate gesture of self-reflexivity. They both fail in this attempt: Jabobus Coetzee fails because, paradoxically, his all-consuming advance into Africa eliminates everything outside of himself, destroying the limits which would allow the self to distinguish self from Other; Eugene Dawn fails as he is inevitably recaptured by the institutions embodying societal control. Both are nevertheless made to articulate their sense of the possibility of an identity which persists in spite of these failed attempts, Jacobus Coetzee describing how he retreats into 'the blindest alley of the labyrinth of [the] self' (*Dusklands*, p. 103), and Eugene

Dawn referring to the labyrinth of his history which will lead to 'the heart that holds [his] secret' which 'will not die' (p. 50).

The ontological query 'I have high hopes of finding whose fault I am' (p. 51), situated at the centre of the novel and voiced by Eugene Dawn, is clearly a question which also concerns the identity of the writer of *Dusklands*. And, just as clearly, there is no simple answer to the question, which represents a culminating point in the history of western individualism. The novel's structure allows one to read from front to back or back to front in an attempt to find an answer, and in this way deconstructs two opposed views of history, and the concomitant forms of identity established via the historical project. One of these is based on monocausality, and the other on the indeterminacy of a potentially infinite self-reflexivity. The self that is brought into being by the novel cannot extricate itself from these discourses upon which it is dependent for existence, but it seems to escape into the gap between the two, eluding the dominant discourses at the same moment as reproducing them.

Whereas the different sections of *Dusklands* articulate the repeated insistence on the possibility of *achieving* an individual identity, the structure of *In the Heart of the Country* is founded on the repeated *failure* of the single woman narrator to envisage erecting a self into being. Written in numbered segments, her speech does not attain the continuity of narrative at all: the segments function as separate, successive units, and the metaphoric signifying function is made to intrude in the domain of the metonymic function, which *would* allow for continuity. The narrator, Magda, is a woman on a Karoo farm, who spends her time engaged in introspection or railing against her omnipotent father. The mode of discourse adopted here appears to be the anti-pastoral of Olive Schreiner's *The Story of an African Farm* (1883), a seminal novel in the context of white South African writing. In the history of colonisation, this corresponds to the phase of agrarian settlement, when the land has been fenced in, boundaries established, and when the active penetration of the explorer is replaced by the sterility and stasis of rural life in the colony.

Magda says: 'I move through the world not as a knifeblade cutting the wind, or as a tower with eyes, like my father, but as a hole. I am a hole crying to be whole' (*In the Heart of the Country*, p. 41). Unlike the phallic discourse of Jacobus Coetzee, hers is a feminine discourse which cannot anticipate assuming authority: it is as though her speech remains (figuratively, of course) trapped in the realm of the Imaginary, unable to project a response which would release it into the Symbolic, unable to achieve a place in the family constellation which would grant a name, a signifier of self and subjectivity to the speaker. Magda's successive fantasies of killing the father are both attempts to subvert the Symbolic and desperate appeals for a response, as she cries out 'Speak to me! Do I have to call on you in words of blood to make you speak?' (p. 71). In this way the novel seems to repeat Schreiner's failure to anticipate a response, either from a readership in the colonies or 'back home' in England.

Magda is the most explicitly Lacanian of Coetzee's narrators, delivering monologues such as the following:

> To the spur of desire we have only one response: to capture, to enclose, to hold. But how real is our possession? The flowers turn to dust, Hendrik uncouples and leaves, the land knows nothing of fences, the stones will be here when I have crumbled away, the very food I devour passes through me. I am not one of the heroes of desire, what I want is not infinite or unattainable, all I ask myself, faintly, dubiously, querulously, is whether there is not something to do with desire other than striving to possess the desired in a project which must be vain, since its end can only be the annihilation of the desired . . . It is the first condition of life for desire not to be fulfilled, otherwise life ceases. Fulfilment does not fulfil. (pp. 113–14)

Coetzee has described the literature of empty landscape, in which he includes Schreiner's novel, as a literature of 'the failure of the historical imagination',[10] and from this it is evident that Magda's monologue in *In the Heart of the Country* is a deliberate repetition of this kind of failure. Coetzee goes further than this, suggesting that 'the failure of the listening imagination to intuit the true language of Africa, the continued apprehension of silence (by the poet) stands in the place of another failure, by no means inevitable [as is the attempt to elicit a response from the landscape itself]: a failure to imagine a peopled landscape, an inability to conceive a society in South Africa in which there is a place for the self' (*White Writing*, p. 9). This question concerning a place for the self is posed when Magda asks the servant girl, Anna: 'Toe, wie is ek?' (Well, who am I?) (p. 30). Anna refuses to call Magda by her name, and answers simply 'Mies is die Mies' (Miss is the miss) (p. 30), recognising Magda only from her own dependent position as servant, which, in terms of the Hegelian master/slave dialectic (explicity referred to by Magda), is no recognition at all.

At the end, Magda makes a virtue out of her apparent failure to erect a self into identity, preferring 'to die an enigma with a full soul' than 'to die emptied of [her] secrets' (p. 137): like Jacobus Coetzee and Eugene Dawn, she posits the existence of a secret self on the frontier between language and silence. Coetzee's writing erects an identity for itself via these figures, recognising that it is imbricated in their modes of discourse, but, like them, positing a 'secret' place *outside* discourse, from where it might be possible to elude them and undermine them. In so doing, he engages in the apparently paradoxical task of making the self's presence evident by means of an absence, of manifesting the self in the moment of its disappearance, or fading, that Lacan has called *aphanisis*.

The attempt to elicit a response from one of the victims of colonisation becomes more central to the next novel, *Waiting for the Barbarians*. The ageing magistrate of a remote outpost of an unspecified empire embarks on a relationship with a barbarian girl, who, like the servant, Anna, in relation to the mistress, Magda, cannot provide proof of his identity because she cannot return the look of recognition he seeks. Partially blinded by torture, she cannot reciprocate his look, his desire. His question is 'What do I have to do to move you?' and he describes with horror the answer: 'in the image of a face masked by two glassy insect eyes from which there comes no reciprocal gaze but only my doubled image cast back at me' (p. 44). In this novel Coetzee adopts the liberal humanist discourse of novelists such as Alan Paton, Dan Jacobson, Laurens van der Post and the early Gordimer, a mode of discourse which, historically, was impotent in the face of the increasingly bureaucratised and militarised totalitarian control of the South African state. Via the figure of the Magistrate, Coetzee explores the attempts of this discourse to construct an identity for itself via the representation of the suffering victim: the Magistrate's obsessive gesture of massaging the barbarian girl's scarred and damaged feet implies the *fetishistic* and guilt-ridden attachment of South African liberal humanist discourse to the figure of the victim.

The Magistrate does make the gesture of returning the girl to her people, but it is, at the same time, a gesture which he hopes will allow him to erect an identity for himself. Firstly, in restoring her to an originary state of wholeness, he hopes he will be able to achieve reciprocal recognition from an equal, and asks her to return with him, of her 'own choice' (p. 71). That this hope is an illusion, he realises at the moment of handing her over, when he says: 'There is only blankness, and desolation that there has to be such blankness. When I tighten my grip on her hand there is no answer' (p. 71). Secondly, the alliance with the girl becomes the means whereby he sets himself in opposition to 'the guardians of Empire' and so is himself able to assume the identity of persecuted victim.

Crying out against the violence of the state, the Magistrate says:

> I cannot save the prisoners, therefore let me save myself. Let it at the very least be said, if it ever comes to be said . . . that in this farthest outpost of Empire of light there existed one man who in his heart was not a barbarian. (p. 107)

The notion of saving the self works metaphorically to imply the achievement of identity. Magda, in *In the Heart of the Country*, asks: 'How shall I be saved' (p. 16), lamenting her inability, in the absence of an interlocutor, to transcend the endless duality of the intrasubjective imaginary relationship of self to self, expressed in her repeated statement, 'I am I.' The shift in historical context makes the Magistrate's desire to be saved something quite different: it is the desire of liberal humanist discourse to register its distance from a system which has rendered it quite impotent, to 'save' the speaker or writer from being accused of complicity with this sytem.

Unlike Magda, the Magistrate does succeed in producing a continuous narrative, although at the end he regrets that he has failed to produce a *history*. And, unlike the speech of Coetzee's other narrators, his speech is not overtly self-reflexive: only the autodiegetic, present tense mode signals its constructedness. The sense that he is somehow able to operate outside history, along with the absence of self-reflexivity, would seem to suggest the tendency of liberal humanist discourse to see itself as 'natural', would seem to imply its failure to see itself *as* a particular mode of discourse arising out of certain historical conditions and as ineffectual once those conditions no longer pertain. Viewed in this way, the Magistrate's sexual impotence becomes a mark of this loss of discursive power. Similarly, the progression from a position of superior vision or insight in the beginning – he asks of Colonel Joll, who wears dark glasses: 'Is he blind?' (p. 1) – to the admission of failure at the end, as he says 'There has been something staring me in the face, and still I do not see it' (p. 155), signals the loss of authority of this particular mode of discourse.

*Life & Times of Michael K* is even more centrally concerned with the inarticulate victim, as the title itself indicates, but it too, raises the issue of 'salvation'. It is the only one of Coetzee's novels to have a heterodiegetic narrator, and this choice appears to be motivated by the genre adopted here: a self-effacing narrator articulates the experience of the victim, supposedly on his behalf, in order to tell a story which would otherwise not be told, to give a voice to one of the voiceless ones (the most notable example of this genre being Elsa Joubert's *Die Swerfjare van Poppie Nongena*, 1978, translated as *The Long Journey of Poppie Nongena*). This purpose is made explicit in the interposed autodiegetic narrative of the medical officer, who intercedes on behalf of the incarcerated Michael K, saying: 'listen to me, Michael. I am the only one who can save you. I am the only one who sees you for the original soul you are' (p. 207).

At this point the medical officer/narrator does not acknowledge the way in which his own needs are served via the figure of K, but a series of subtle shifts register his attempt to construct a *different* type of relationship between himself and the victim who is Michael K. He progresses from the use of the referential pronoun, *he*, in relation to K, to the pronouns of communication, *I* and *you*. A dialogue is set up between the medical officer/narrator and K; K is given speech, is made to pose the question 'What am I to this man?', a question which the medical officer himself asks in return, articulating, as do the other novels, the fundamental question concerning the identity of the speaker. Following this, the medical officer confesses that what he has wanted from K is his story (p. 204), and that the figure of K has been made to articulate a meaning on his behalf: 'Your stay in the camp was an allegory . . . of how scandalously, how outrageously a meaning can take up residence in a system without becoming a term in it' (p. 288). K's obscurity, his talent for escaping and for surviving without food, make him a figure who can represent the possibility of eluding the meanings inherent in any system, of bypassing the hierarchy of authorities (and authorship). What is significant here is the positive emphasis that this novel places on the ability to *avoid* constructing an identity. It is the equivalent of Magda, Jacobus Coetzee and Eugene Dawn's insistence on a secret self, outside discourse, but the weighting of the previous novels is reversed. Even the meaning which the medical officer wishes to construct via Michael K is, in the end, a snake which swallows its own tail, because it has to do with *evading* the power and authority inherent in the positing of conclusive meanings. The sexlessness of Michael K, too, becomes a way of insisting on the absence of authority. This shift in emphasis may be related to the fact that, from *Life & Times of Michael K* onwards, Coetzee's novels inhabit contemporary discourses of opposition, so that his writing approximates their position more closely than it does the earlier modes of discourse it has inhabited. Coetzee is constrained to make use of their methods for registering both their *opposition* to various systems, and their *affiliation* with the victims of those systems. Because of this proximity, it becomes even more important to avoid the pitfalls of these discourses he inhabits, pitfalls which have to do, precisely, with claims to identity and authority.

Coetzee refers explicitly to this dilemma when he says, in an interview on *Foe*:

> 'Successful author' is a barbed phrase here, a highly barbed phrase. Foe in the book, or Daniel Defoe in 'real' life, is the type of the successful author. Am I being classed with Foe, though my interest clearly lies with Foe's foe, the *un*successful author – worse, author*ess* – Susan Barton? How can one question power ('success') from a position of power? One ought to question it from its antagonist position, namely, the position of weakness. (Morphet, 1987: p. 462)

Short of remaining silent, Coetzee has to find a way of figuring an extreme form of marginality, of weakness, and he does this via the figures of Michael K, Susan Barton and Friday, and Elizabeth Curren and Vercueil.

As with Magda in *In the Heart of the Country*, we have represented in the speech of Susan Barton a feminine discourse attempting to narrate itself into a position of power. With *Foe*, however, Coetzee moves into the contemporary discursive arena of feminism and an international discourse of postcolonialism (as opposed to an earlier South African colonial discourse). Susan Barton's speech takes the form of unanswered letters addressed to Foe, the author in relation to whom she attempts to negotiate a position of authority. While the novel as a whole enacts a rewriting of Daniel Defoe's *Robinson Crusoe* (and also parts of *Roxana*), Susan Barton attempts to write her own story, and then the story of Friday, who has had his tongue cut out, and has also possibly been castrated.

Like Coetzee's other narrators, Susan Barton raises ontological doubts:

> In the beginning I thought I would tell you the story of the island and, being done with that, return to my former life. But now all my life grows to be story and there is nothing of my own left to me. I thought I was myself and this girl a creature from another order speaking words you made up for her. But now I am full of doubt. Nothing is left to me but doubt. I am doubt itself. Who is speaking me? Am I phantom too? To what order do I belong? And you: who are you? (p. 133)

Representing a feminist discourse, she has wanted to establish her radical Otherness from masculine discourse, but recognises at this point that, within discourse, one inevitably expresses the self via the Other which is the word, the third position between two subjects.[11] From this perspective, radical Otherness is not possible as a mode of articulation: it can be figured, but not spoken. Friday, the speechless colonised victim, becomes the means of figuring this Otherness, and she dreams of restoring him, paradoxically, via language, to 'the time before Cruso, the time before he lost his tongue' (p. 60). Her gesture is similar to that of the Magistrate returning the barbarian girl to her people in the hope of restoring her to a pre-colonial wholeness and identity. And, like the efforts of both the Magistrate and the medical officer, the project of 'saving' Friday, of telling his story, is inextricably bound up with the project of 'saving' herself – of constructing an identity for herself in writing, in a book which, as she tells Friday, 'will make us famous throughout the land, and rich too' (p. 58).

It is important to recognise that Friday's speechlessness does not mean that the colonised subject does not have a voice of his/her own. It suggests, rather, that the colonised subject has no discursive authority within the field of western discourses. If Susan Barton's feminine discourse, along with its strategic silences, represents the attempt to speak *as* Other, to evade masculine discourse, Friday's tongueless, castrated body is testimony to this novel's resolve not to speak *for* the Other. The concluding image of the novel gestures towards a future time when an equal exchange will be possible, as Susan Barton lies face to face with Friday underwater, and feels 'a slow stream, without breath, without interruption' (p. 157), coming from inside him and beating against her eyelids, against the skin of her face.

In *Age of Iron* we again have a feminine voice – that of Elizabeth Curren, a woman dying of cancer. This novel returns us unrelentingly to the South African socio-political context as it depicts this age of iron in the late 1980s, an age of extreme violence and of utterly intransigent attitudes. Here, the black people of South Africa do have a voice; there is no need to refuse to speak on their behalf, because they are speaking for themselves. Via Elizabeth Curren, an ex-lecturer of Latin – which she describes as 'a dead language . . . a language spoken by the dead' (p. 176) – Coetzee returns to the discourse of liberal humanism, but, unlike that of the Magistrate, it is a discourse that is truly marginal, hovering as it does between life and death. This is a self-reflexive liberal humanism, aware of its severely circumscribed position in this age of iron, and addressed to a daughter in America, gone into voluntary exile there until 'the softer ages return in their cycle, the age of clay, the age of earth' (p. 46).

While she records the events of her last days with clarity and compassion, and without guilt or self-pity, Elizabeth Curren also wants to be saved. She wants to say 'Save me!' to her daughter (p. 67), who perhaps represents the possibility of a humanist response from readers in the future: 'Come, says this letter: do not cut yourself off from me. My third word' (p. 127). This is the salvation desired by Magda and Susan Barton, the salvation which is the product of an achieved narrative brought to fruition by a receptive readership. But we also find a desire for salvation akin to that of the Magistrate, who imagines he can save himself by publicly setting himself in opposition to the state. Thus this dying woman contemplates setting herself alight in front of the Houses of Parliament, 'the house of shame' (p. 104), explaining to her companion and interlocutor, Vercueil: 'I want to sell myself, redeem myself, but am full of confusion about how to do it' (p. 107). She resists, however, saying: 'The truth is, there was always something false about that impulse, deeply false,' judging this gesture, finally, through the eyes of her domestic worker, Florence, as she asks: 'Will the lies stop because a sick old woman kills herself? Whose life will be changed, and how?' and 'What would count in Florence's eyes as a serious death?' (p. 129).

Elizabeth Curren is preoccupied with the notion of shame, and claims that her cancer is the result of the accumulation of shame. 'That is how cancer comes about: from self-loathing the body turns malignant and begins to eat away at itself' (p. 132), she says, describing the terminal stages of a discourse that has been consumed by guilt. She expresses an ambivalence concerning shame, however, both seeing its value and wanting to reject it as a mode of being. Her words 'are not Yes, they are not No'. She tells Vercueil: 'What is living inside me is something else, another word. And I am fighting for it, in my manner, fighting for it not to be stifled' (p. 133). On the positive side, shame is 'a touchstone, something that would always be there, something you could come back to like a blind person, to touch, to tell you where you were' (p. 150). On the negative side, there seems to be no way of extricating the self from its convoluted, self-fuelling movements, as is implied when she says: 'I did not wallow in it. Shame never became a shameful pleasure; it never ceased to gnaw me. I was not proud of it, I was ashamed of it' (p. 150). This expresses a central problematic for Coetzee in this novel: how to give expression to his shame, without proudly erecting a self into being via the confession of this shame (in the manner of Riaan Malan in *My Traitor's Heart*,[12] for example).

This would, indeed, seem to be the expression of one of the fundamental concerns of Coetzee's writing as a whole: how *not* to sell himself or attempt to redeem himself; how to describe the horrors enacted on black South Africans in the name of white South Africans, without succumbing to the false impulse to construct an identity founded on self-castigation or immolation. In conclusion, then, it is possible to say that the novels are founded on a self-critical awareness of their own processes of construction, and of the material conditions of their production and reception. Despite the predominance of autodiegetic narrators, they are not monologic,[13] but are dialogic in a profound sense, engaging in a discursive confrontation with the discourses they inhabit. While they articulate a strong desire for a reciprocal speech from the victims of colonisation and of apartheid, they do not imagine that they can fabricate, in a facile way, a cross-cultural dialogue within their own structures: they recognise that, if this kind of dialogue does ensue, it will have to be a product of their reception. Finally, they subject themselves to the most rigorous interrogation: in Coetzee's words, always asking the question '*Who writes?* Who takes up the position of power, pen in hand?' (Morphet, 1987: p. 462).

*Notes*

1. J. M. Coetzee, 'Alex la Guma and the Responsibilities of the South African Writer', *Journal of New African Literature and the Arts* (9/10), 1972, pp. 5–11.

2. For a discussion of 'problems of consciousness' in this context see Michael Vaughan, 'Literature and Politics: Currents in South African Writing in the Seventies', *Journal of Southern African Studies* (9/1), 1982, pp. 118–38; and Peter Kohler, 'Freeburghers, the Nama and the Politics of the Frontier Tradition: An Analysis of Social Relations in the Second Narrative of J. M. Coetzee's *Dusklands*. Towards an Historiography of South African Literature', paper presented at a history workshop entitled *The Making of Class*, Univ. of the Witwatersrand, 9–14 February 1987. On postmodernism as self-reflexive gesture see Paul Rich, 'Tradition and Revolt in South African Fiction: The Novels of André Brink, Nadine Gordimer and J. M. Coetzee', *Journal of Southern African Studies* (9/1), 1982, pp. 54–73.

3. Tony Morphet, 'Two Interviews with J. M. Coetzee, 1983 and 1987', *TriQuarterly 69* (Spring/Summer), 1987, p. 460.

4. J. M. Coetzee, 'Blood, Flaw, Taint, Degeneration: The Case of Sarah Gertrude Millin', *White Writing: On the Culture of Letters in South Africa*, Johannesburg: Century Hutchinson; New Haven and London: Yale UP, 1988, p. 162. First published in *English Studies in Africa* (23.1), 1980, pp. 41–58.

5. J. M. Coetzee, 'A Note on Writing', *Momentum: On Recent South African Writing*, ed. M. J. Daymond, J. U. Jacobs and Margaret Lenta, Pietermaritzburg: Natal UP, 1984, p. 11. Citing Roland Barthes, 'To Write: An Intransitive Verb?' in *The Languages of Criticism and the Sciences of Man*, ed. Richard Macksey and Eugenio Donato, Baltimore: Johns Hopkins, 1970, Coetzee continues: 'Or – to follow Barthes in his metaphorical leap from grammar to meaning – "today to write is to make oneself the centre of the action

of *la parole*; it is to effect writing in being affected oneself; it is to leave the writer (*le scripteur*) inside the writing, not as a psychological subject . . . but as the agent of the action." The field of writing, Barthes goes on to suggest, has today become nothing but writing itself, not as art for art's sake, but as the only space there is for the one who writes.'

6. Jacques Lacan, *Ecrits: A Selection*, trans. Alan Sheridan, London: Tavistock Publications, 1977, p. 86.

7. For an extended discussion of the role of Lacanian theory in the novels, see Teresa Dovey, *The Novels of J. M. Coetzee: Lacanian Allegories*, Johannesburg: Ad. Donker, 1988.

8. The novels of J. M. Coetzee:
*Dusklands*, Johannesburg: Ravan, 1974.
*In the Heart of the Country*, London: Secker and Warburg, 1977; Johannesburg: Ravan, 1978.
*Waiting for the Barbarians*, London: Secker and Warburg, 1980; Harmondsworth: Penguin, 1982.
*Life & Times of Michael K*, London: Secker and Warburg; Johannesburg: Ravan, 1983.
*Foe*, London: Secker and Warburg, 1986.
*Age of Iron*, London: Secker and Warburg, 1990; Harmondsworth: Penguin, 1991.

9. Stephen Gray has argued: 'The frontier myth has no clear beginning and no foreseeable end . . . for the European in Southern Africa it starts as an uneasy xenophobia, continues as a social principle, and in South Africa today could be shown to be so deeply entrenched that all of the literature is to some extent explained in terms of the pressures at work within a continuing frontier mentality.' *Southern African Literature: An Introduction*, Cape Town: David Philip, 1979, p. 38.

10. Coetzee, *White Writing*, 1988, p. 9.

11. Anthony Wilden, 'Lacan and the Discourse of the Other' in *The Language of the Self* by Jacques Lacan, trans., Notes and Commentary by Anthony Wilden. Baltimore: Johns Hopkins UP, 1968, p. 269.

12. Riaan Malan, *My Traitor's Heart*, London: Bodley Head, 1990.

13. As claimed by Benita Parry in 'The Hole in the Narrative: Coetzee's Fiction', *Southern African Review of Books* (April/May), 1989, pp. 18–20.

# Fabling the Feminine in Nuruddin Farah's Novels

DEREK WRIGHT

Nuruddin Farah's statement that he sees 'women as the symbol of the subjugated self in everyone of us' has obvious political ramifications.[1] The powerful influence of women over the young in African countries is, arguably, capable of damaging the national psyche and adversely affecting the nation's destiny if it is exercised, as it is in the Somalia of Farah's novels, by a class of people who are continually violated and degraded. To the extent that the specific repression of women by tribal patriarchy is, either by these or other means, instrumental in the political oppression of the whole people, the two can be seen as broadly analogous, and the victimised woman construed as a metaphor for the nation under dictatorship. In the trilogy *Variations on the Theme of an African Dictatorship*, sexual power is but a further manifestation of political power along a continuum of patriarchal authority. A widow is pressed by the government to marry the policeman who murdered her husband, another woman a political dissident who has raped her, and power itself is imaged as a captive mistress who is pandered to, courted and finally seized by the General: his Minister of Police, unwrapping a cigar, '[breaks] its polythene with the same cruelty as a rapist would deflower a virgin'.[2]

What the clannish dictator does to the nation is an extension of what the clan does to women, though it does not follow that freedom from one will spell freedom from the other. Somalia is now rid of the General: whether this will have much effect upon the position of women is yet to be seen. Indeed, Farah has said elsewhere that he has used women as 'a symbol for Somalia' precisely because 'when the women are free, then and only then can we talk about a free Somalia'.[3] No nation can be free when half of its people are still slaves, their

70

identities defined and their positions negotiated by husbands, fathers and brothers; when, as in the case of Misra in *Maps*, they cannot even establish their citizenship without oaths sworn by two male witnesses. These conditions make suspect all feminine genderings of the independent nation, all renditions of a 'free Somalia' or a free Somali Ogaden, through specifically female archetypes. Farah is, in any case, a subtle and elusive writer who treats the problematics of nationality and gender in a very discriminating way and avoids drawing up categoric parallels and oppositions. It is only through a wishful effort of the allegoric imagination that the downtrodden but irrepressible Ebla, in *From a Crooked Rib*, can be translated into an image of the nation groping its way towards independence. Meanwhile if, at the other end of the spectrum, Medina in *Sardines* fails to do service as a symbol of the subjugated national self it is because she is too western–internationalist in her orientation, too privileged and protected a member of the elite, and too little oppressed as a woman: the worst that can happen to her are banning orders and harassment by the kinsman of her abandoned husband Samater. She is described at the outset as the female equivalent of the unbending, self-righteous patriarch, and the freedom and knowledge which she forces prematurely upon her young daughter are at times almost as oppressive and manipulative as the obedience which her tyrannical mother-in-law Idil forces upon Samater. Farah's foreign women are also notoriously unreliable as national typifying agents. Whether he is being wickedly accurate in his political observations, as with the white stooge Sandra and the black American spy Atta in *Sardines*, or playfully and preciously parodic, as in his treatment of the mixed marriages in *A Naked Needle*, his national and racial tropes are passed through a deconstructive sieve which allows the individuals to retain little value as national representatives. The flat, self-debunking literary representations (Colonial Mistress, White Destroyer) thrown up by Koschin's exuberant imagination in the latter novel deliberately disable belief and decline to serve as vehicles for broader political statements, whether about white neo-imperialism or patterns of African subservience and western domination.[4]

The fabling of the feminine in Farah's work is as its most problematic, however, in his recent novel, *Maps*. In this novel the Somali poet unfolds a fable of national identity in which Somalia, portrayed as a beautiful woman, freely accepts the advances of five suitors. In the allegoric scheme, these represent the original five territories of Greater Somalia, and she conceives children by each of them, three of which miscarry: namely, French Djibouti, Kenya's Northeastern province, and the Ogaden region of Ethiopia, each of which continues to lie outside the Somali Republic which was constituted at independence from the former British and Italian Somalilands. The figure in the novel whose personal history approximates closest to the archetype in the fable is, of course, Misra, who, ironically, is not a native Somali though she has done more than enough to earn Somali status: she fosters a Somali child and teaches it its national language and folklore, slaves in a Somali–Ogaden household where she is sexually abused by Somali men, and is, in the end, doubtfully accused of treachery by them in the Ogaden war and murdered. Misra too is pursued by five men, some of them from the disputed homeland territories; only in her case she is the object of their largely unwanted sexual attentions. These are the Amhara warrior who abducts her from the Ethiopian Highlands as a child; the pious Muslim Abdullah who adopts her as his daughter and then forces her to become his wife; the Qotto teacher Aw-Adan who exploits her sexually and finally betrays her to the Western Somali Liberation Front; Askar's despised Ogadenese uncle, Qorrax; and the Ethiopian captain with whom she forms a liaison in the Ogaden war. In Misra's story the miscarriages become the abortions forced upon her by Qorrax and Aw-Adan. In each of these relationships except the last (and even then, we are told of the cruelty of the Ethopian captain), Misra, as the woman Somalia, is the abused, enslaved victim of a brutal patriarchal tyranny, and Farah's point is clearly that this is the most fitting form for the image to take in the modern context. If Misra fails as an image of a free Somalia, it is not because she is a foreigner of mixed Oromo and Amhara descent, but because no woman in the Horn of Africa can serve in a signifying system which indulges in the clichéd gendering of national freedom in falsely heroic and idealised terms. A more appropriately negative metaphor of Woman as Nation is the Camel, the "Mother of Men" who, in Askar's childhood anecdote, is held captive and blindfolded and, when untethered and freed from foreign masters by her men, can only die because when they remove her blindfold they neglect to provide her with any enlightened vision and hope for the future. In the fable of the woman and her five suitors, it is significant that, although the political tenor of the metaphor connotes an expansive, unifying generosity, it is partly eclipsed by its sexual vehicle, which presents the woman as promiscuous, a treacherous whore. This overshadowing is, in fact, more revealing of continuing patriarchal attitudes and prevailing Somali male psychology. The Somali poets, Misra tells Askar, see their country 'as a woman . . . who has made it her habit to betray her man', and the comments of Askar's schoolmates seem to uphold the stereotype: 'Why, if she isn't your mother, your sister or your wife, a woman is a whore.'[5] The nation is disingenuously gendered as an imaginary woman, for whom lives must be laid down, by patriots who in fact despise the real women in their daily lives.

Throughout his fiction Farah is alert to this tendency to unmoor metaphors from their vehicles, particularly in the area of politics and gender. The rape of Amina in *Sardines* is a good example of this dislocative process. Under the dictatorship it becomes impossible to disentangle personal affairs from the General's stranglehold on public life (the hyper-imaginative Sagal even construes her seduction of an ill-treated West Indian visitor as a gesture of political revolt) and in this context it is possible for the victim's father to dismiss her rape as a merely 'political' incident. 'But which rape isn't?' Amina answers him. The choice of rape as a political weapon against the General by the three young rebels is significant because it indicates that they share his sexual politics and that rape, like circumcision, continues to be an instrument of tribal patriarchal power over women. And yet it is, of course, not wholly or solely this. Farah is acutely aware of the danger that the extrapolation of abstract 'significances' from sensitive subjects such as rape and circumcision may blunt the edge of the actual barbarity; that by rendering rape purely in terms of political coercion the writer may end up presenting it to the reader in much the same way as the assailants present it to their victim – as a purely symbolic act. 'We're not doing this to you, but your father,' they tell her: Amina is regarded merely as an attribute of her father and becomes, metonymically, what the attribute stands for.[6] What is disturbing about the fantasy-ridden politics of characters like Koschin, Medina and Sagal is that they partake of the totalitarian state's frightening capacity for making a nominal reality prevail over the actual; for giving the symbolic or representative signifier priority over its referent. 'How I hate what she *represents*,' says Koschin of the American Barbara, and

Medina proliferates metonymic motifs regardless of relevance or occasion, culminating in the gigantic solipsism which indexes her house arrest to the condition of the state and her rearrangement of the furniture in her room to the shaking, 'with seismic determination', of the foundations of the national house of Somalia.[7] The same tendency is present in the wilful official fiction that a sixteen-year-old American-born daughter of Somali expatriates on her first trip, as a tourist, to her ancestral home is really a Somali citizen on whose person the state has licence to perform a brutal circumcision. Things must first be themselves before they can be made into symbols and, perhaps with this in mind, Farah dwells at some length upon the shocking, savage details of both the rape and the forced circumcision.

The attempt to endow gender with political significance and, especially, to read Woman as Nation in the Somali context, finds its *reductio ad absurdum* in the eccentric telescoping of national and biological fates in *Maps*. In this work there is a deliberately puzzling indeterminacy about where metaphor ends and reality starts, and a habitual erosion of topographical into physiological space which allows the narrator Askar to view the political destiny and military fortunes of the nation, analogically, through his adoptive mother's biological rhythms. Specifically, after Misra's vengeful pack-rape by WSLF patriots in the Ogaden war, he sees the deaths of the six hundred Somali soldiers she is accused of betraying in terms of the death-cycle of her own body. Askar's charts are simultaneously military and menstrual maps, historical and contraceptive calendars on which the green-clad Somali troops who march backwards and forwards across the Ogaden correspond, with a perverse ingenuity, to the green-ringed dates for safe (in the sense of non-procreative) sex. The immediate reaction to such lurid conceits – which put the reader in mind of remarks like John S. Mbiti's, in *African Religions and Philosophy*, about the African woman's equation of infertility with genocide[8] – is to protest that, at the level of the psycho-narrative, they are the neurotic fantasies of an alternately mother-fixated and misogynistically self-centred child. Nevertheless, it is Askar's consciousness which is *our* map in the novel, his conceptual space that determines our perception of reality, and in the fantastic distortions of his paranoid male psychology, menstruation is fetishised into something over and above its simple biological function. It is, in Askar's words, 'the cycle of life and death, the circle ending where it began – the flow of menstruation, of death ascertained' (p. 31), and in his pervasive vision the notion of the failure to conceive as a kind of killing is realised with a graphic vengeance. 'Was it true that she had betrayed a trust and set a trap in which a hundred Kallafo warriors lost their lives?' he asks himself, and remembers that 'living with Misra wasn't always full of exhilaration and happiness'; that at the time of her agonised menstruation 'she was short-tempered, beating him often, losing her temper with him. She was depressive, suicidal, no, *homicidal*' (p. 48). In this instance, the metaphoric vehicle seems to have become a reality in its own right, literally investing the woman's monthly trauma with homicidal propensities. The political haemorrhagings of the nation are recast, preposterously, as massacres of the menses; as atrocities inflicted by a vengeful premenstrual terrorism wielded over the lives of men.

The undermining and supplanting of reality by metaphor in *Maps* is not restricted to the woman's menstrual 'illness'. Susan Sontag drew attention, in her seminal essay *Against Interpretation*, to the impoverishment and depletion of the world, and the erosion of sensory sharpness in responses to art, by the construction of shadow worlds of portentous meaning; and in her later work *Illness as Metaphor* she went on to assess the damage done by this over-interpretative process in the literary treatment of serious illnesses such as cancer.[9] In establishing rhetorical proprietorship over an illness, metaphor, Sontag argues, has a pernicious tendency to psychologise physical conditions, turning them into mirrors of mental states or signposts to moral and spiritual subtexts. Thus, Misra's breast cancer, like her menstrual traumas, is invested by Askar with 'evil' elements over and above the level of a merely physiological phenomenon, with the result that she comes to be regarded as an extention of her disease, as malignant as her tumour. In Askar's narrative speculations the tumour acquires the ancient punitive associations of the 'canker of guilt', something which she has both caused and deserved, and which her body, by its own inner logic, has brought upon itself. Cancer, in the mythology of the disease, is the body's 'hidden assassin', and the unknown WSLF executioners who abduct Misra from the hospital are its outward agents, symbolically correlated with the invisible disease that put her there. In particular, cancer, Sontag observes, has its own 'pathology of space', a military topography which draws upon the language of warfare, weaponry and colonisation – all of which is consistent with Askar's idea, when he visits Misra in hospital, that she should exhibit her mutilated breast as if it were a war wound, and his comparison of Misra, who has been unfeminised by her mastectomy, with a veteran in the next bed who has been emasculated by a bomb (pp. 207–8). Cancer cells, moreover, are said to 'spread', 'proliferate' and 'invade'; the patient's body is a besieged citadel infiltrated and insidiously taken over by enemy cells, representing the non-self. Cancer, says Sontag, is therefore 'the disease of the Other', and Askar, despite a physical closeness to Misra that enables him to taste the blood of her death in his mouth, uses the disease frantically to 'other' her into the alien menace, the enemy whose blood is to be vengefully drunk and whose flesh is figuratively devoured (pp. 213–14, 221). In this hysterical metaphoric milieu, Sontag argues, the surgical removal of the unhealthy, infected parts by multilation or amputation may take on the fanatical self-righteous tone of a moral campaign or a crusade to excise evil. The partisans' perverse moralistic reading of Misra's mastectomy and their subsequent removal of her alleged traitor's heart after killing her are of this order. For these men, who are convinced that they need no proof of her guilt, Misra is simply the impure, contaminated part of the Somali heritage, the infiltrative foreign cancer to be rooted out and cut off; whereas a more accurate reading of the amputative imagery is that those who live through a number of cultures as Misra does, always have missing parts of themselves elsewhere, on the other side of some border. What Misra really represents are the truncated parts of cultures and countries in the Ogaden.

In *Maps* the feminine gendering of the nation is problematised by this infestation of physiological phenomena with interpretation and, at a more general level, by the narrator's subsequently obtuse vision of his adoptive Oromo mother as an agent, rather than as a victim, of oppression. Askar, representing the Ogaden in the novel's allegoric scheme, is the orphaned offspring of two Somali patriots martyred in the cause of the region's liberation from Ethiopian occupation. As he grows up his need for independence gets mixed up with an imperative to shoulder the burden of his biological inheritance from his natural mother, by defending his country from the people of his nurturing mother, even though he has only the most theoretical sense of the former, compared with the excruciating intimacy of the latter. After the ritual separation of his circumcision, Askar begins to define his 'specific–Somali' adult maleness against his 'generic–Ethiopian' mother-figure and to measure Somali military progress on his map of the Ogaden in terms of the distance between himself and the woman whose foreign presence within him he feels he must rid himself of. Askar's first steps towards psychological independence thus initiate a fortuitous involvement with his homeland's political independence, and when he meets Misra again in the capital years later he feels that he is now 'weaned' from his 'mother-figure', for 'in the process of looking for a substitute, he had found another – Somalia, his mother country' (p. 96). He thinks that he can espouse one of his rival adoptive mothers only by denying the other, and the ominous words of his childhood, 'To live, I will have to kill you', now take on, in the quite different context of her suspected betrayal of the Somali army, the tone of patriotic duty.

In reality, however, this association of Misra with the foreign occupation of the Ogaden is from the beginning a spurious one: she is, after all, an Amharic-speaking Oromo, not a full-blooded Ethiopian, and she has more natural affinity with the occupied zone than with the occupier. She is herself an occupied possession on Somali as on Ethiopian territory, a slave-girl sexually colonised by a host of avuncular wardens. Like Askar, she is an uprooted orphan and her Oromo culture, like his Somali one, has been historically marginalised by its orality and oppressed by a literate Ethiopia. She is, in fact, doubly displaced: first as an Oromo living in Ethiopia under a dominant Amharic culture, and then as an 'Ethiopian' reviled by Somali ethnocentrism. Ironically, Misra is, much more precisely than Askar, a fitting image of the Ogaden which she is accused of betraying – the Ogaden as herself a motherland abused by patriarchy, raped by her self-professed defenders, and finally, mutilated and dismembered, her heart torn out by war. Moreover, that irretrievable hybridisation of cultural reality which is the real essence of Ogaden life is most keenly represented in the novel by Misra. Misra is the daughter of an Amhara nobleman and an Oromo servant, she lives with a Somali family, and has Qotto and Ethiopian lovers. Accordingly, like the woman in the fable approached by the five suitors/territories, she has access to and concourse with all of the fertile neighbouring micro-cultures and tribal nationalisms by which the Ogaden is hedged around and diversified, in spite of its ethnocentric efforts to resist them. Appropriately, the

Ogaden, which is a collection of border territories, is symbolically entrusted by Askar's biological mother to one such border person, to one of mixed descent and therefore with a choice of identities. This entrustment by a Somali woman to an Oromo servant-girl reaches across artificial boundaries erected by male nationalistic obsessions, and is done in recognition of their common Cushitic heritage and interpenetrating cultures.

Two key motifs in the novel contest this cultural hybridisation: the first is incest, the second maps. Firstly, it is significant that Misra regards the fabric of Somali society as 'basically incestuous', for incest, of which woman is the main target in this novel, is an expression of the inward-looking ethnocentrism of Somali culture, its failure to recognise its kinship with neighbouring peoples in a broader generic family. More particularly, paternal guardians quasi-incestuously abuse the foreign wards entrusted to their care ('uncles' become rapists, fathers husbands) and, in the process, stereotyping the national or ethnic 'other' as a mere object of denigration. Secondly, Askar draws up a politico-linguistic map of Greater Somalia which is really as much a fiction of cultural geography as the colonial maps were figments of political geography; which overrides socio-political divisions as the old western imperial ones overrode ethnic and linguistic barriers. Askar's own coercive cartography claims to unite people who both linguistically and in other respects are becoming more and more diverse, while it artificially sets apart other groups of people who are much more closely bonded. Misra, a non-ethnic though fully acculturated Somali speaker, is automatically mistrusted and is denied a place on her ward's identity papers while honorary citizenship is granted to another non-ethnic Somali, Aw-Adan, for no other reason that that his Arabic input into Somali culture is politically more acceptable than Misra's Amharic one.

The process of cultural interpenetration contested by the motifs of incest and maps is, however, aided by a number of androgynous fusions in the mindscapes of the novel which cut across its divisive political landscapes. Farah has said of *Maps* that 'an intellectual and psychological debate is going on between two selves – the woman's self in the man, the man's self in the woman'.[10] As a result of the physical intimacy of the crucial early years, the motherless male child and the childless surrogate mother are able to reach across national borderlines to live inside each other, accounting for that part of the other being which is least aware and in possession of itself. 'Body is truth,' says Hilaal, and the body seems to be an alternative way of constituting identity and one more reliable than maps. Askar knows his adoptive mother wholly through the body, which operates according to its own instinctive wisdom and logic, and makes 'autonomous decisions' which override the abstract intellectual hatreds of creed and country. His failure lies in his inability to trust to this special knowledge and his sin is his psychological surrender of Misra's reality to the female stereotype of the betrayer, the scapegoat for the misfortunes that men bring upon their own heads. Misra is approachable only through intuitions aroused by her physical presence – to feel her 'truth' Askar must 'touch her in a dark room' – and Askar opposes to this tactual 'truth' the nationality-ridden world of maps, denoting the distancing and distorting control of reality through the imposition of boundaries. The 'notional truths' expressed by Askar's partisan cartography correspond to the political actuality of the Horn of Africa no more than his moral conception of Misra (who has no understanding of maps) coincides with real woman. Misra, like the political map of the territory of which she is the figurative custodian, is a floating signifier, zoned into many stereotyped figures and rival fantasy embodiments: on one side, mother–martyr and victimised nation; on the other, wicked stepmother, betrayer, and national enemy. At one point Askar even thinks of her as 'a creature of his own invention', and it is difficult to say exactly what constitutes her reality or if she is, in any sense, a person in her own right, since she seems to exist solely through the guardians and wards who control her existence in one way or another, from her nobleman father and adoptive father-turned-husband to Askar and her Ethiopian lover. Askar's view of Misra as having no reality of her own to express but being merely a cipher through which others express themselves is consistent with the punitive mythology of cancer, according to which the disease is a failure of expressiveness and the wages of self-repression.[11] For Askar, as the girl in the dream shows him, both Misra and Ogaden are mirrors in which each sees his own image and desire. Maps, similarly, reflect the dispositions of their makers. 'The Ogaden, as Somali, is truth,' says Hilaal. 'To the Ethiopian map-maker, the Ogaden, as Somali, is untruth' (p. 218). The 'truth' of maps, like the deliquescent political realities of the trilogy, is a highly unstable, subjective, ethnocentric kind of truth.

Inevitably, since Askar is one of the map-makers and Misra is, symbolically, a part of the shifting, hybridised reality which is mapped, the nationality categories unsettled by his extreme cartographic relativism have some bearing upon the novel's equally unstable gender categories. Significantly, the trans-sexual spirits of the *mingis* are also instruments for the interpenetration of national and marginal cultures, bringing the Boran language into the Somali heartland, and it is no accident that Farah uses gender confusion to demonstrate that even Somalia's much-vaunted linguistic homogeneity is not unassailable. The peculiar misgenderings of the language once found only in 'non-native' peripheral territories subject to foreign influence are brought back to the urban centre by refugees from the Ogaden and elsewhere, and these all contribute importantly to the broader, interpenetrative matrix of cultural forces which now constitute Somali identity. Of course, the misgendering of people is more problematic than the misgendering of language; and because the categories of nation and gender in the novel appear to be neither wholly independent nor vitally interdependent, it is never certain how far one can be used as an index for the other. Askar's nationalistic aspirations are grounded, problematically, in the stifling intimacy of the one-child-one-parent family, in which the gender-confused male child first identifies with and then seeks to exorcise the oppressively close maternal presence. He feels that he can liberate his male self only by denying his maternal one, but only in retrospect do these 'female' and 'male' identities acquire political meaning in the allegoric scheme as, respectively, 'Somali' and 'Ethiopian'. In the narrative of events, it is a historical accident that, after the loss of the Ogaden, the mother figure and the Ethiopian 'enemy' become, arbitrarily, one and the same, making the surrogate parent a 'false mother' in an additional sense. Askar's misogynistic rejection of Misra when she takes an Ethiopian lover merely receives external reinforcement from his xenophobic Somali ethnocentrism. Moreover, Askar's curiously determined adherence to the idea that there is a 'woman living inside' him and his near-fetishistic treatment of menstruation have little to do directly with the national alien Misra, the woman who is most physically present in his life; they seem rather to be narrowly tied up with a theoretical guilt complex over his dead mother whom he accuses himself of killing at his own birth. Guilt is the means by which Askar wills his biological mother to survive in himself and it is after brooding not over Misra but over this spectral figure ('she who claimed she "lived" in him who had survived her') that he imagines himself to have menstruated (pp. 105, 151). Thus it is specifically the native mother, rather than the foreign woman in him, whom Askar desires by turns to preserve or to kill.

And yet this reductive element in Askar's behaviour which is privileged by a conventional psychological–realist reading of the text is, at the same time, belied by more expansive tendencies of a peculiarly postmodernist kind which are at work in the construction of his character. Askar straddles not only sexual and national but also ontological boundaries. He aspires to be, at once, 'half-man, half-child', male and female, ethnocentric Somali and culturally diverse Ogadenese. He also fancies himself to be both a real child and an epic miracle-child who was present at his own birth and born out of his mother's death (one who has 'met death when not quite a being'), and who is able to argue metaphysics at the age of seven. He claims to hold 'simultaneously multiple citizenships of different kingdoms: that of the living and that of the dead; not to mention that of being an infant and an adult at the same time' (p. 11). Like his prototypes, Grass's Oskar and Rushdie's Saleem, he is a liminal creature, an occupant of the between-worlds space of the zone, that improbable area in postmodernist fiction where these incongruous elements can coexist. Like them, he is a composite imaginative construct put together from diverse sources and finally, as he struggles on the last page of the novel to free himself of blame for Misra's death, fragmenting back into its constituent parts: defendant, plaintiff, juror, witness, judge and audience. There are, admittedly, limits to Askar's indeterminacy. His fantasy that he is one of the race of epic children who kill their mothers is quickly disposed of by uncle Hilaal and was apparently planted in his mind by Misra's oral tales: thus, at the level of psychological explication, his vaunted multi-dimensionality is the fruit of her multicultural nurturing. But the idea of a liminal, indeterminate area of experience, a third space which exists between alternatives and which is neither one thing nor the other but both at once, is one of the great positives of the novel. The Ogaden is hedged around by fertile minority cultures. Creative energy, it seems, lives, liminally, along borders: Askar notes that two-thirds of Somalia's major poets are from its marginal territories and that one such peripheral people, the Boran, provide the Mogadiscio *mingis* with its ceremonial language and trans-sexual spirituality.

Some of this dangerous liminal energy appears to have been discharged to Askar, whose androgynous tendencies coincide with his straddling of the kingdoms of childhood and incipient adulthood. Askar looks to Misra both as a child, for succour, and as a male adult, for her submission to his patriarchal will, and it is in this context that his fascination with her menstruation is best seen. Though he begins, as a child, by wanting to relieve her of some of her periodic pain – 'If I had some of it, then Misra will have less of it, yes?' (p. 49) – his preoccupation turns into the ultimate male fantasy of control, reducing her by his sanguinary stare to the ultra male-dominated object. When Askar, possibly as a result of a urinary infection, imagines himself to have menstruated, he once again collapses options, in this case the ones posed by Misra: 'You prefer being sick to being a woman' (p. 107). In Askar's mind, to be a woman is to be periodically sick and he proceeds to affect a periodic sickness, becoming mysteriously, quasi-menstrually ill, in order to duck out of confrontations, decision-making, and the facing of responsibilities at each of the crisis-points of his life: at the betrayal of the Ogaden; at Misra's subsequent arrival in Mogadiscio; and at her final abduction and death at the hands of an organisation of which he himself is a member. Thus Askar, paradoxically, imaginatively appropriates Misra's 'female illness' in order to express sympathy and solidarity; to indulge in fantasies of power and control; and to dissociate himself from and finally abandon her. At one and the same time, he indulges in a sexual 'othering', in the form of object-making, of the woman – 'By touching me he knows he is there,' says Misra – and he articulates a female self which fails to recognise physical and emotional boundaries between Misra and himself. He seeks at once the cross-gendering capacity to share her suffering and an opportunity to exercise power over her ('I had her whole life in the power of my mouth'). Furthermore, the child's makeshift solidarity with his adoptive mother as a fellow victim of patriarchal brutality is accompanied, during her nocturnal visitations, by a rage not merely at her neglect of him but at her sexual domination by the uncles and Aw-Adan, for whom he feels an incestuous Oedipal envy.

In the early intimacies Askar passes imperceptibly from the status of an infant child in androgynous fusion with its mother – 'a third breast' – to that of a crypto-incestuous lover, lying 'somewhere between her opened legs . . . [like] a third leg' (p. 24). The third leg identifies him explicitly with the wooden leg that Aw-Adan speedily removes before intercourse with Misra and thence, vicariously, with Aw-Adan's penis; and Misra, during her sexual climax, uses the same endearment as the one she uses to Askar ('my man!'). Yet, again, more complex interpretative options are built into the reductive psychological reading, for the choice of a 'third' property is itself significant and leads out into that third space or area of further possibility beyond the binary polarisations of male and female, child and adult, Somali and Ethiopian. The child adopts a female self, and a figurative female part, and at the same time asserts his real male ones. Askar both participates imaginatively in Misra's sexuality and incestuously exploits it, as he both vicariously suffers her menstruation and desires to control it. Not surprisingly, at the level of the psychological narrative, the adolescent Askar is plagued by subconscious guilt over his physical attachment to his stepmother, and his elected psychological ruse for escaping this guilt is to externalise his incestuous desires and alientate them to their object (thus he accuses Misra of murdering her adoptive father/ husband 'during an excessive orgy of copulation' and identifies her Ethiopian lover as a half-brother). In fact Askar is, in this one of his many selves, part of the incestuous abuse of power which in the novel is a symptom of the introverted ethnocentrism that prevents the Somalis from opening up hospitably to neighbouring cultures. In this persona, he represents allegorically a chauvinistic Somali concept of the Ogaden, as his Somali mother represents the dead dream of an ethnic nation, of 'Mother Somalia' as the Ogaden's natural parent, and of 'a getting together of her and the Ogaden/child separated from her' (p. 97). But standing opposite him and also representing part of himself is Misra, who signifies a broader, hybrid, generic concept of the Ogaden, in which mixed ethnicity is metaphorically indexed to sexual indeterminacy. Misra, prophetically, embodies everything in himself that he must destroy to realise his sectarian Somali dreams: 'One day you will identify yourself with your people and identify me out of your community. You might even kill me to make your people's dreams become a tangible reality' (p. 95). What Askar, self-laceratingly, attempts is tantamount to these things. Together with his uncles, he strives to 'other' Misra, misogynistically and xenophobically; as woman and foreigner; as an object of desire and control; and as a colonising, cancerous enemy cell. There is a separative process at work here which struggles to reaffirm both gender lines and divisive nationality categories ('male' Ogaden and 'female' Somalia). And yet Askar, for all this, is still crucially caught up in Misra's uncertainty and torn by conflicting, contradictory impulses which he fails to resolve. His desire to exorcise Misra's presence from himself remains at odds with his desire to be at one with her; his assertive male self grapples with his fears of sexual ambiguity; and these things, translated into the book's allegoric scheme, mean that his desire for the Ogaden to fulfil a specifically Somali destiny remains at war with notions of cultural pluralism and interpenetration. 'So long as I lived, she would too,' Askar notes of his and Misra's interdependent, symbiotic lives and, by extension, of the national groupings with which they are entangled. As presented through Askar's psychology, both the Ogaden's cultural hybridisation and the androgynous interplay with which it is metaphorically correlated in the novel remain a potentially realisable, albeit unrealised, reality.

*Maps* is a novel of multiple possibilities and as such it could be mistakenly regarded as being no great advance upon the self-undermining, deconstructive tendencies of the *Dictatorship* trilogy, in which multiplicity is a largely negative and confusing phenomenon. In *Sardines* the shifting, pluralist oral convention, though it abets Medina in the speculative reconstruction of multiple motives for her actions, is principally a sinister political weapon deployed by an obscurantist dictator to sustain the required atmosphere of suspicion and uncertainty. In *Sweet and Sour Milk* the dictator and his security corps of spies and informers, recruited from illiterates working entirely in the oral medium, maintain a floating, indeterminate order of reality which is infinitely interpretable – and hence fundamentally uninterpretable. The washing away of Soyaan's words from the sand in the Prologue prefigures the dissolution of a stable, expressible reality, the erasure of the written text: predictably, the novel's narrative plot is in the end unable to 'write' the unravellable political–criminal plot to murder and mythologise Soyaan. The proliferation of 'versions' precludes the literary representation of reality as the discovery of indivisible truths and it seems that Farah is undermining the whole idea that a knowable personal reality is still verifiable behind coercive political misinformation. In some respects *Maps*, with its Socratic and Conradian epigraphs about the necessity and inevitability of doubt, seems to be moving in the same territory of existential threat. In *Maps* Farah is not concerned with searching epistemological questions about the seriousness and meaning of the deed performed by the guilty party, and with the gradual revelation of his hidden traumas. Rather, he is breaching ontological barriers by posing the problem of *what* it is that the narrator has done and is now concealing from himself, or, indeed, *whether* he has done anything, and how, if at all, these things can be known. There are, for example at least two passages in *Maps* – where Askar pictures a soldier standing over a wounded woman with a blood-stained knife and then imagines himself a fish feeding from Misra's menstrual blood – which could be interpreted to mean that Askar himself was the initiator, or at least an accomplice, in Misra's murder and dismemberment (pp. 211, 214–15). But as these are presented in the form of dream-sequences, it is difficult to say exactly what is happening, or when, and at what level the images are meant to be read.

Where *Maps* is importantly different, however, is that here doubt is essentially a healthy and creative thing, and ambiguity constructive, if only at the metaphoric and allegorical levels. It is only through the continuation of inner conflict and the interplay of debate between alternatives that there is any hope of emergence from false and constricting divisions. At the end of *Sweet and Sour Milk* what we have been led to believe is an unfolding of meaning turns out to be a deconstructive unstitching of the entire fabric in which meaning should reside. What is being deconstructed in *Maps*, however, is the territory in which categoric oppositions reside, whether national, cultural or sexual. Farah's aim here is not the evaporation of reality but the creative opening out, through positive doubt, into new imaginative regions, into that liminal third space which is neither Somali nor Ethiopian, male nor female, but is constituted from and so combines and transcends both. The area charted by *Maps* is a borderless, genderless, supra-rational reality where the nation is, necessarily, neutered – to be properly *en*gendered, as a viable concept, it must first be *un*gendered. Misra's name is instructive in this respect, existing in both genders and in three languages (its Somali form is an incomplete version of the Ethiopian 'Misrat'). It means 'foundation of the earth', indicating the elemental, non-partisan character of the disputed strip of ground, which does not discriminate between its diverse occupying nationalities and the rival maps that overlay it like the layers of a palimpsest. Interestingly, on the cover of the English edition the desert earth is depicted as covering and almost obscuring the map instead of the other way round. The illustrator's design has caught something of the spirit of Farah's novel. In *Maps* the system of signification does not oppressively determine and delimit a given reality but bursts its own bounds and gestures hopefully towards a new, uncreated one. In this novel Farah fables beyond the feminine, beyond gender itself and gender-based concepts of nationality, into fresh and appropriately ill-defined possibilities.

## Notes

1. Nuruddin Farah, 'Mapping the Psyche' (Interview with Robert Moss), *West Africa*, 1 September 1986, p. 1828.

2. Nuruddin Farah, *Sweet and Sour Milk*, London: Heinemann, 1980, p. 180.

3. Nuruddin Farah, 'Author in Search of an Identity', *New African*, December 1981, p. 61.

4. In fact, the English woman Mildred is not the victimiser in her marriage to Barre but the duped, trapped victim, while the American Barbara, the wife of Mohamed, is the model of adjustment. It is only in the clichéd cameo of Mahed and his graceless Russian mistress that Farah appears to adhere to the Fanonian model of the white dominatrix and black love-slave. See Nuruddin Farah, *A Naked Needle*, London: Heinemann, 1976, pp. 28, 62–4, 167; and Frantz Fanon, *Black Skin, White Masks*, trans. Charles Lam Markmann, New York: Grove Press, 1961, p. 63.

5. Nuruddin Farah, *Maps*, London: Picador, 1986, pp. 52, 98. All further references will be given in the text.

6. Nuruddin Farah, *Sardines*, London: Heinemann, 1982, p. 119.

7. Farah, *A Naked Needle*, p. 58; *Sardines*, p. 250.

8. John S. Mbiti, *African Religions and Philosophy*, London: Heinemann, 1969, p. 110.

9. Susan Sontag, *Against Interpretation*, New York: Laurence Pollinger, 1967; *Illness as Metaphor* and *Aids and Its Metaphors*, Harmondsworth: Penguin, 1991.

For the allusions to Sontag's work in this paragraph, see *Illness as Metaphor*, pp. 15, 41, 47–50, 56–8, 65–9, 85–6.

10. Farah, 'Mapping the Psyche', p. 1828.

11. See Sontag, *Illness as Metaphor*, pp. 22–3, 49.

# Sharp Knowing in Apartheid?: The Shorter Fiction of Nadine Gordimer and Doris Lessing

MARK KINKEAD-WEEKES

White southern Africa is lucky enough to have produced two of the half-dozen outstanding women novelists, in English, of the century. Nadine Gordimer was awarded the Nobel Prize for Literature in 1992. Some years ago on a lecture-tour of Scandinavia, I was asked on three separate occasions how (as an ex-South African) I would 'judge between' her and Doris Lessing. The enquirers, I now realise, were correspondents of the Academy; but the prizegiving does not seem to me by any means to have settled their question. On what basis in any case could such a 'judgement' be made? And what would be its point?

Such awards are sometimes justified on broadly political grounds; and here perhaps something should be said to clear the air of cant. Nadine Gordimer is justly praised and fêted around the world as a courageous and effective opponent of apartheid from within. Two of her novels were banned in South Africa. She has become in many ways the representative voice of white South African literature seen as a cumulative awakening of consciousness and conscience. In one public meeting after another, and in countless private encounters, she has opposed the tyranny and corruption of apartheid and given inspiration and comfort to its opponents. To read her essays and speeches is to increase one's sense of the honour she deserves.[1] Yet, political realist as she is, she would not I think see it as derogatory if one rubbed up the other side of the coin. For many decades she has lived what thousands of white South Africans have found impossible to accept: the life of multiple and radical privilege that comes at the cost of the misery of millions, and cannot be renounced or avoided while one remains within the system. She has lived in Parktown near the Witwatersrand University, in a style possible only to a small minority in South Africa (and the rich elsewhere). She has always been safe enough, because she broke no law, and her reputation in the outer world was sufficient to protect her from brutal arrest and imprisonment without trial. The other decision, to go, to make a relatively harmless life somewhere else, perhaps to boycott the homeland, is very costly. It costs home, family, friendships rooted in childhood; the consciousness that goes with nationality landscape and speech – being saddled instead with the exile's rootlessness and constant questioning of identity in some country to which s/he cannot ever truly belong. If you are a writer – like Dan Jacobson for example, who used always to be paired with Gordimer as the most promising of the younger South Africans – you begin immediately to lose your subject-matter, together with the whole ethos and nuance within which expression came naturally. You are forced to rethink and indeed wholly reshape your art. And then you may find that you have also lost the cachet among the chattering classes and arbiters of publication that comes from being a 'freedom fighter'. Though you write one of the finest of novels about the corruptions of collaboration with tyranny, the fact that it is not identifiably *South African* allows it to be quickly forgotten – while much less compelling *South African* works by others are talked up and kept in print.[2]

I happen to be convinced that Nadine Gordimer made the right choice, for her, and I think it likely that she made it clear-sightedly, knowing that it too had its price, which could only be paid by success in what Steve Biko called conscientising her own people. What I have said is not meant to imply a moral criticism. Indeed my point is just the opposite: that between those who stayed in South Africa, believing that the work they could do would justify the privilege they could not avoid; and those who went, believing that their best work lay outside, and unable to feel that attempting it on South African terms would justify the 'privilege' of remaining, there is no intrinsic moral superiority one way or the other. If the Nobel prizegivers were influenced by such considerations, so much the worse – especially if Doris Lessing were being weighed in the balance as 'the one who went'. For her sense of political commitment came much earlier and more radically, though it took her abroad. Moreover the writer who was denied re-entry to Ian Smith's Rhodesia, but was invited by Robert Mugabe as a guest of honour to the Independence celebrations of Zimbabwe, has no need to fear comparison with any opponent of racism. It is true that Lessing seems altogether a more rebarbative personality, whose dislike and distrust of academics, critics, reviewers and other chatterers is notorious; true also that her political and religious thinking is both unfashionable and uncomfortable in the present climate, most especially when it questions 'progressive' complacencies.

However, my real purpose is to declare that if literary honour be in question, all these considerations are beside the point. What interests me is the quality and process of each imagination, which comparison can help to focus; most economically perhaps in the shorter fictions at which both of them excel.

Beneath obvious similarities of subject and value, which ensure that comparison is fair, essentially different ways of imagining reveal themselves in the opening stories of *Some Monday for Sure* (Gordimer's own selection) and *This Was the Old Chief's Country*.[3] The subject – the awakening of consciousness and conscience in a young white girl – is the same, but the shaping is quite other.

Gordimer's 'Is There Nowhere Else We Can Meet' is a really short story, barely three and a half pages; and (being also one of her earliest) the sureness of its economy is remarkable, as though the essentials of her art had come to her quickly. A girl walks in the early morning across a patch of waste ground. We know, and will know, nothing of character or upbringing. It is enough that all her senses seem vividly alive, while the third-person narrative preserves a little distance. As she walks, one element in her ambience gets seen from her point of view, three times, differently. At a distance there is a red dot in a landscape, something essentially pictorial giving 'balance' by its 'placing'. Nearer, this becomes – she must be white, then – 'a native in a red woollen cap', and in passing him, details register: a trouser leg torn off above the knee, the 'peculiarly dead, powdery black of cold' of his skin, his reddened eyes, a smell (now) of sweat. Her senses 'perceive' these things, but she is actually just as occupied and perhaps more interested in the feel and tangy scent of a pine-needle run against her thumb as she walks on. Then behind her a thudding of feet, the black man bars her way, *swart gevaar* (black danger) grabbing at her, terrifying yet somehow expected, every South African white girl's nightmare come to pass. Yet through the medium of 'absolute' fear comes intenser seeing: his heaving chest, the 'yellowish-red' of the eyes, the torn pyjama jacket instead of a shirt, the cracks in the feet making them look 'like broken wood', the choking smell of him as they struggle, a pink spot on his face where the skin is grazed off. She abandons handbag and parcel, flees in terror, scrambles through a barbed-wire fence, is safe among white houses, but damp-cold with the sweat of fear as she pauses at the first gate. But she doesn't go in, doesn't telephone the police. Instead the story ends with a series of questions:

> Why did I fight, she thought suddenly. What did I fight for? Why didn't I give him the money and let him go? His red eyes, and the smell and those cracks in his feet, fissures, erosion. She shuddered. The cold of the morning flowed into her.
>
> She turned away from the gate and went down the road slowly, like an invalid, beginning to pick the blackjacks from her stockings. (p. 5)

The questions echo into silence; the author is absent from her story; it is for the reader to interpret. Between the lines, however, there is more to 'see' than the girl can, as she only now begins to shudder into what lies below surfaces. The real point of the story lies in the ironic gap between surface and implication; the realisation of what was there all the time unrealised: first the deprivation and suffering embodied in the concrete detail, and then the racist blindness that prevents sight from becoming insight, fully human consciousness, conscience. The title suddenly locks in; those words usually spoken by boys and girls whose relationship is opposed and who cannot meet at home.

Nadine Gordimer's imagination, as she herself says in her introduction to this anthology, seems from the beginning to have been essentially ironic.[4] The point of view from which she writes is not her own, indeed her point is to expose the inadequacy of its vision and perhaps, also, the extent to which a reader may at first have shared it. She works from the outside in, concealing herself. As with all irony there is a double risk: that the reading between the lines may not come through clearly, and that the point of view may be mistaken for the author's. On the other hand, it is a method very useful for an opponent of state racism, since in the actual words on the page there is no actionable offence, what comes up between them being so much a matter of interpretation.

Doris Lessing's 'The Old Chief Mshlanga' is much longer, necessarily. For it is about a process of imaginative growing up, so there has to be a phased development through time. The story begins in the third person, describing a colonial girl whose imagination, conditioned by the English landscape of her childhood reading, cannot lock home on the Africa which surrounds her. She is equally conditioned to take the blacks on the farm for granted as inferior beings; and, later, she walks the land fearlessly with gun and dogs, occasionally letting them chase a black man up a tree. Like Gordimer's girl, she is typical. But the next phase switches to the 'first person', the beginning of an 'I'. The technique beautifully mimes its human point; brings us, too, 'inside'. Aged now about fourteen, she encounters the old chief of the title and his attendants, who do not move from her path, but meet her with a dignity that makes the old man her equal, or 'more than an equal, for he showed courtesy, and I showed none'. As she begins to read about Africa, pioneer accounts of 'the Old Chief's Country' create questioning, a first sense of usurpation, a land and its people seen for the first time apart from herself. But, she thinks, this is her heritage too, she was born here, surely there is room for all, given mutual tolerance and respect? – though these virtues are not apparent in the way her mother relates to the chief's son, cooking in her kitchen. In a new spirit, she sets out to visit the old chief. At the centre of the story, however, lie far deeper awakenings. What she enters is a quite different landscape from her father's farm (a difference of tilth implying a different relation of people with the earth and its resources, though the point is not laboured). But alone in the heat and the silence, she experiences a moment of paralysing fear. She has read about this experience of the white person in Africa:

> how the bigness and silence of Africa, under the ancient sun, grows dense and takes shape in the mind, till even the birds seem to call menacingly, and a deadly spirit comes out of the trees and the rocks. You move warily, as if your very passing disturbs something old and evil, something dark and big and angry that might suddenly rear and strike from behind. (p. 19)

Absurdly, within reach of home and neighbours, she feels lost, panic-stricken; but the evil is not in the landscape. To her fear is added a terrible loneliness. When she reaches the old chief's kraal it is to realise that she has no reason to be there and has nothing to say to him or his people. As she walks home the fear is gone, but she has realised its cause; with the sense of alienation has come an inescapable knowledge: 'you walk here as a destroyer'. The final phase simply fills out the facts of colonialism. She sees the old chief again only once. His people's goats have broken into a maize-field, her father has confiscated them in compensation, the chief cries out that his people will go hungry, he is challenged to go to the police. Mshlanga's son, the cook, has to interpret the reply in a language the whites do not understand: 'My father says: All this land, this land you call yours, is his land, and belongs to our people' (p. 24). But the next time a policeman calls, and hears the story, he remarks that the kraal ought not to be there at all. He mentions it to the Native Commissioner at a tennis party – and Mshlanga and his people are moved 'two hundred miles east, to a proper reserve' so that 'the Government land' can be opened up to further white settlement. The operative language is that of power. Yet the girl, driven to revisit the site where the village had been, is struck by another kind of truth. Her first impression is that 'There was nothing there.' But there is: a complexity of waste, in which devastation of what was human is inseparable from natural fertility gone rank. Any settler lucky enough to be 'allotted' the valley, she muses, will find suddenly, in the middle of a field, the mealies growing fifteen feet tall, 'and wonder what vein of unexpected richness he had struck'. The irony is hers, not directed at her, and it marks the awareness and the conscience she has grown into.

It strikes me that the only judgement required at this point is the full perception of the difference in the modes of imagination, highlighted by the similarity of subject and basic aim. Both seem to me finely concentrated, albeit in very different terms. The superb economy of the Gordimer story, the cleanness and craft of its impact, give one a sharp kind of pleasure. Yet the greater length of the Lessing story is necessary to its kind of focusing, which relates the contemporary to the historical, and man to nature. There too, though in a different way, nothing is superfluous. Gordimer's irony works from the outside, through eyes not her own, to make us measure the gap between the story's surface and a fully human vision, from which the protagonist is still a clear distance at the end. Lessing puts us inside, and makes the vision grow with a growing sense of dimension towards her own. Gordimer sets up a situation, there are three clicks of ironic focus, and then comes the satisfaction of seeing, in sudden sharp relief, something pictured with a kind of finality. Lessing puts us behind the lens, refocusing, refocusing, again and again. One is an art of implication, the other of exploration; one gives the pleasures of exposure, the other those of development. Different tastes and temperaments may give rise to different preferences in readers, but each writer seems highly successful in her kind of art. Other readers may point to a limitation implicit in both stories. Each, by its own definition, ends where true human vision begins; and it is possible for the white world to overvalue the dawnings of its conscience over racism and colonisation.

I have gone into some detail, in distrust of generalisation and ideology (both of which have their place at the end of the day, but not at the beginning); and have begun with short stories to uncover more economically the kinds of shaping through which imaginations reveal their nature. But first impressions need to be checked against other examples in the same genre; and to get closer to the intrinsic nature of the two imaginations, it seems important to enquire into the effect of increasing scale.

Luckily, for a quick check, there are two more stories in which the subject matter is again identical but where the imaginative approaches also seem closer, since Lessing's is more ironic and Gordimer's a phased development. The subject matter in this case is the psychological damage inflicted by the well-meaning pater/maternalism of white liberals. 'Little Tembi' is probably Lessing's most anthologised African story – rather to her annoyance, of which more later. Jane, a good-hearted ex-nurse, runs a clinic on her husband's farm, and against all the odds saves the life of a black child, Tembi. While he is small he remains a favourite, allowed to become a herd-boy ahead of his years. But then Jane gets caught up with her own children, and there is a mini-tragedy when the little herdsman twice falls asleep and lets calves get into the maizefields, so that Willie, Jane's husband, feels he has to be beaten lest it happen yet again. Afterwards Tembi becomes more and more demanding, for more money, for work in the house, and he begins to take things, without concealment. When he is turned away he becomes a criminal. Yet, finally caught in Jane's bedroom, he refuses the chance to escape and breaks down in tears 'like a small child'. The story ends (like 'Is There Nowhere . . .') in agonised questioning:

'There's something horrible about it all,' she said restlessly. 'I can't forget it.' And finally, 'What did he want, Willie? What is it he was wanting, all this time?'

The questions, again, are for the reader: a challenge to measure, in re-reading, the full difference between love and a 'maternal' benevolence which can be withdrawn; but also, to uncover the reason why Jane, for all her good-heartedness, cannot yet answer herself. Love for a black is still unimaginable to her.

In Gordimer's 'Not For Publication' Adelaide Graham-Grigg, adviser to the chief of a British protectorate, finds a black child of the tribe begging on a city pavement, rescues him from abject poverty, begins his education, and discovers an extraordinary intelligence. When the school in the Protectorate can take him no further he passes into the hands of Father Audry who runs a private non-racial school (like that of the Community of the Resurrection in Johannesburg). There he can be brought on, encouraged, coached, in learning and music, till he is ready to take his 'matric' at 16 and open up a glittering career. But there are signs of stress – and suddenly, the boy is gone. When he is sought in the township, two voices in African English bring the story to a close. An old woman, 'in a stylised expression of commiseration' shakes her head into her bosom: 'My-my-my-my! . . . And he spoke so nice, everything was so nice in the school.' A younger one remarks: 'Maybe he's with those boys who sleep in the old empty cars there in town – you know? – there by the beer hall?' (*Some Monday for Sure*, p. 99).

Nobody knows. So we are confronted again by the Gordimer ironic challenge to examine what we know. And there should come welling up between the lines quite another story, one that the boy might have told if he'd ever been asked how he saw things. This would be about what it felt like to be removed from the only background and relationships he had ever had, by a spinsterly woman whose benevolence cannot conceal that she doesn't have any real feeling for him, and that he is a kind of experiment and justification for her. Then, just as he has won acceptance from his peer-group and is about to undergo the initiation that will seal it, he is removed again. Finally there is the increasing pressure, and gradually the terror, of the priest's demanding expectation that Praise should deserve (as it were) his name, until he can bear it no longer and flees. If he is to become a prime minister, as an early hint suggests, it will be out of a distorted and suffering childhood with no reason to praise his white 'benefactors'. The final voices ironically pose the only life-choices he apparently had.

Summarised thus, the two stories look interchangeable. Yet the closer the imaginations seem to come in method and structure, the more one sees how essentially different they – and therefore the experiences and responses they create – actually remain. For the thrust of the Gordimer story is to expose the attitudes of the liberals through the ironic story of the child; hence the often cutting detail in the portraits of the do-gooding spinster and the authoritative priest, edging close to satire; hence also the fully maintained distance of the narrative voice. The Lessing story is more generous to the genuine kindness and affection in Jane; to the natural reasons for getting caught up with her own children; to the worry of the white couple about how to handle the childish importunities and failures; to Jane's grief at the end. Lessing is also more interested in the psychology of the child which, though still done largely between the lines, can nevertheless be seen to build up step by step into a convincing syndrome. She creates complexity of 'character' in both the white couple and the child. This in turn lessens the distance, involves the reader with conflicting sympathies, complicates response. On the other hand, the Gordimer story is more satirically effective, and its sharpness and punch depend on the acuteness of the angling, so that to complicate it would have been to diffuse the impact.

One reaches the point at which judgement, or rather a deep kind of critical disagreement, may begin to take shape. D. H. Lawrence said of Jane Austen, the finest of British ironists, that she typified a 'sharp knowing in apartness instead of knowing in togetherness' which he found 'thoroughly unpleasant'.[5] Such knowing is predominantly intellectual, as opposed to 'religious and poetic', and creates fixed personalities. For Lawrence, it is only in 'togetherness' that the relationships of forces within the psyche, of men with women, and of the human to the living universe – all intimately connected – can become healthy, vital, capable of change and growth. Is there not something too coldly clinical, too selective and exclusive, in the sharpness of Gordimer's kind of knowing:[6] the ironic distance, the author so detached and concealed, the fixed attitudes so ruthlessly pinned down from a carefully chosen angle? On the other hand, might not the attempt to know in depth and complexity, involving so many dimensions, create a kind of messiness, over-elaboration, mixed perspectives – especially when there is conscientising work to be done in conditions of political crisis? Yet, interestingly, Jane Austen partly bore out Lawrence's critique by herself developing beyond the tendencies to whose human limitations he was to point;[7] and his own art had to struggle to create rather than state such three-dimensionality, to avoid over-involvement of the author, to struggle to clarify and contain. If, instead of seeking very similar stories for fair comparison one were to choose stories one thought of as among the best, might one find something similar?

In 'A Chip of Glass Ruby', Gordimer's ironic framing and distance still predominate. The reader must measure in stages the ironic gap between the attitudes of the Indian vegetable hawker Bamjee and those of his wife, whose political activities lead to her arrest and imprisonment; must register the 'unpleasantness' of his racism, myopia, self-pity, as opposed to the qualities (more precious than real rubies, according to the Bible) which make the good wife and mother *and* the inter-racial political activist. The author's detachment can indeed reveal a 'sharp knowing in apartness' that brings one up short: those black eyes of the children, 'surrounded by thick lashes like those still, open flowers with hairy tentacles that close on whatever touches them'. There is moreover nothing religious or poetic, and something culturally condescending, when the 'political' roneo machine displaces 'the two pink glass vases filled with plastic carnations and the hand-painted velvet runner with the picture of the Taj Mahal'. The story imagines no deeper sense of Indianness or Islam. However, this is in fact a love-story; and the irony – this time – permits its target to change. A sensitive reading will register the suffering and grief behind Bamjee's apparently angry outcries, and the growth of his understanding of what it is that makes his wife precious to him also. There is a new humanising warmth which, fitting treatment to the theme of caring, keeps warming the irony too. And Gordimer's art is reaching out across the 'apartheid' that makes it so difficult for a white South African to imagine the points of view and the experiences of other races. The limits of this are clear, but in a short story matter far less than they might in a novel. Above all, the nature of the experience, though just as finely economical and contained, is quite different from that of 'Not for Publication', and the protagonists seem on the point of turning from 'attitudes' into more complex characters. Gordimer shows something of Lessing's kind of strength without losing or compromising her own.

Doris Lessing's impatience with the overvaluing of 'Little Tembi' is explained by the stories she herself thinks 'larger'.[8] 'A Sunrise on the Veld' is one of her shortest, but it is 'large' enough to call in question the whole romantic view of man-in-nature of Wordsworth and Coleridge. Yet 'Winter in July', about a woman living with two men on an African farm, needs to be one of her longest, a novella, in order to explore the essential relatedness of its various dimensions. In 'The De Wets Come to Kloof Grange', one's admiration for the density and multi-dimensionality of the fiction is allied with a paradoxical sense of wanting still more, though it can only just contain as much as it does. It would be impossible to deal with the artistic process of this story as it seemed feasible to try to do, however summarily, with Gordimer's. For even summary reading would require one to touch on multiple themes: how the English couple, the Gales, embody colonial attitudes to farming, to black people, to the natural world; how, though their living room puts Augustan elegance into Africa – 'Kloof Nek' renamed a 'Grange' – they live in a past become unreal and are at 'home' nowhere; how they try to keep up 'values' which in fact insulate and conceal reality; how their marriage has never held sexual commitment or fulfilment so that he lives in his work and she in her cultivated privacy. But at the same time we must see how all of these are essentially connected, and embodied together in the 'English' garden that *is* Mrs Gale: her parasitism and disconnection with the landscape, her over-looking of the African ravine, her possessive enclosure; but also her desire for beauty, her affinity with the lonely hills in the distance, her imperilled reserve. For though there is irony, the vision is always complex. It has the togetherness of a *nek* (a ridge which joins) rather than the apartness of a *kloof*, and demands a complicated understanding and some sympathy rather than sardonic distance. Now the arrival of the De Wets, a new Afrikaner manager and his young wife, brings a contrast of cultures, manners, outlook, an invasion of Mrs Gale's privacy, breaking her open. Tensions increase to explosion, bringing the inside of the characters out beyond concealment. There are questions of sexuality and inner balance, of the relations of man and woman, of the relation of the human being to nature; questions of fertility, and also of danger and violence. It is a fine story, stretching a reader's ability to comprehend on many levels and respond complexly. And yet, isn't the portrait of the young Afrikaners too simple? If we are to understand, shouldn't there be *more* about Afrikaner patriarchy and extended families; and puritanism, and colour prejudice; and the socio-economic pressures which brought people like the De Wets to Rhodesia? And what about the black people? Granted, the story is densely complex, crammed, already; our response very complicated. And yet . . . It would seem that Lessing's kind of imagination, fine 'short' story writer though she is, intrinsically puts pressure upon space. Is that also true of Gordimer's?

The novella is a favourite form for Lessing, though on grounds deeper than the ability 'to take one's time, to think aloud, to follow, for a paragraph or two, on a side-trail'.[9] For in 'The Ant-heap', probably the finest of her African fictions, all trails lead to the centre; yet the compression still needed, even for a novella, disciplines her tendency to discourse when really given room. Themes and methods pursued separately in the short stories can now be brought together: the sensitive use of a child's eye to show the corrupt implications of adult behaviour; the exposure of paternalism, and of exploitation both economic and sexual; the essential connection between Lawrence's three dimensions of relationship, within the self, between people, and of man with nature; racist blindness; but also the awakening of imagination and feeling, toughened by conflict.

The story begins with an evocation of the spirit of place, hardly scratched by human greed until now, when Macintosh's voracity lays it waste in a vast open-cast mine, a hole, a devouring of nature and of human life. If that is one aspect of colonialism, another is the settlement of the misfits. So Tommy is born into a world not of relationship but covert mutual exploitation; yet the story turns out to be less interested in exposure than in how the child's sensitive ear and eye begin to discriminate, to sense what can then be grasped, to grow in consciousness and conscience. Lessing proceeds to display Tommy's development in a series of concentrated stages – not a type or an attitude, but a credibly growing boy. At five he begins to know the isolation of the white child, in a house enclosed with mesh like a meat-safe, and forbidden to play with 'dirty kaffirs' like Dirk. All alone, Tommy looks at the mine and sees it as a vast ant-heap. A little duiker, bought from Dirk who killed its mother, dies, and Dirk now calls him 'baas'. In the child's mind, faced with cruelties, questions begin to coil: why? why? Why above all is Dirk yellow-coloured and not dark brown? At seven, Tommy knows, and begins to play with Dirk again, defying his parents and, to their horror, breaking the conspiracy of silence: 'Why shouldn't I play with Mr Macintosh's son?' It is time he went to school. The awakening that in Gordimer comes to the reader, responding between the lines to an inadequate point of view from which one must separate oneself, is done here as a gradual and painful growth from the inside of the child, in which the reader is involved together with him.

Now the story is increasingly 'double'. The more Mr Macintosh reaches out to the white son he never had because of his preference for black women, the more Tommy rebels against the injustice to Dirk; yet the more he tries to help Dirk and teach him what he has learned at school, the stronger and more violent Dirk's reaction to his patronage. At eight and nine there is another ant-heap, on top of which they build a shed to be together, where both lessons and fighting go on, in love and hate, in vicious battles and a growing bond of commitment. The full difficulty and pain of relationship across the colour-bar comes through unsentimentally. At ten Dirk is sent down the mine; but we must also see more deeply than before as the white boy sits miserably alone again.

'The ant-heap' has already become a metaphor both for the capitalist/colonial mine which reduces human beings to insect-like insignificance, and for the human struggle to rebuild relationship. Now Tommy must learn, also, the horror that lay at the heart of 'Sunrise on the Veld', that there are cruelly destructive forces 'felt working in the substance of life as he could hear those ants working away with those busy jaws at the roots of the poles he sat on, to make material for their different forms of life' (p. 363). If one knew the beginnings of Mr Macintosh, too, one would find what termite forces had eaten *his* humanity to the benefit of their lives. 'It was all much deeper than differently coloured skins': the story demonstrates a kind of tragic irony which comes from knowing-into the complexity of human hearts and relationships, forbidding crisp judgements.

Now Tommy wants to understand; so for the first time he insists on seeing Dirk's mother, and sister – and finds that he cannot know them, since he has no entry to their language and experience. Yet out of this comes a whole new vocation that has been growing all the time, for the story is also a portrait of an artist as a young man, and a statement of what art is for. The sequence of Tommy's sculptures is another sensitive register of growth, of 'knowing in togetherness', from the first childlike imitation of outer reality, the model of the mine; and the first expression of inner feeling, the earth-lump that has something of Dirkness. Next come carvings which try to redeem cruel reality: a duiker that is well, a boy 'bent and straining under a heavy load' when Dirk is sent to the mine. Then new human sympathy grows into the shapes of Dirk's yellow sister and black mother; and there is new symbolic 'religious and poetic' vision of evil, in the carving of the mine as hell, presided over by the devil. The last work, convincing proof that Tommy will become a real artist, is the figure of Dirk 'struggling out' of a tree which is still growing in the earth – but Dirk's angry criticism shows that this too is only a stage. Dirk must be realised in his full humanity, and his hatred accepted as part of a fully human relationship:

> 'I get sick of you,' said Dirk. 'I sometimes feel I don't want to see a white face again, not ever. I feel that I hate you all, every one.'
> 'I know,' said Tommy, grinning. Then they laughed . . .

It is Tommy's art which gets under Macintosh's defences. He burns the hut down, but finally they can fight him and open Dirk's gateway towards freedom. There is no happy ending however, indeed no sense of closure at all (as opposed to the good Gordimer story to which no word could be added). The last words are: 'now they had to begin again, in the long and difficult struggle to understand what they had won and how they would use it' (p. 397). That would take another story to explore; but though we know now that it would have to deal with civil war, so that 'what they had won' was more preliminary than it might have seemed in 1953, the 'ending' is not invalidated, since it was always open to the future. We merely know more clearly, now, but still 'in togetherness', how much further they both will have to go.

Gordimer seems not to be attracted to the novella,[10] though her title story 'Some Monday for Sure' somehow feels longer than usual because of the development within its protagonist. It also marks a new step across the imaginative colour-bar, seemingly in the direction of a novel of character freed from irony, since it is spoken in the first person by a black youth with whom we are clearly meant to sympathise, and done 'from the inside' with some maturing of consciousness through time. The title also suggests affirmation rather than ironic exposure, a future freedom looked forward to with confidence. Its first movement of armed resistance begins on a Monday, and some Monday, for sure . . . Yet it is still a *short* – that is, carefully selective and angled – story, only a little longer than 'Not for Publication'; and it remains a work of irony concealed until the end. At the beginning there is one obvious and nicely ironic point: Josias has been (like South Africa itself) sitting on dynamite for years, giving warning without realising what that might mean. Now however the time for passive resistance – those meetings and demonstrations that he used to attend – has gone by. The ANC has gone underground, Mandela and other leaders are in jail, but the 'Spear of the Nation' is organising for sabotage and guerilla war and the moment for dynamite has come. (Whereas knowing the date of a Lessing story is rarely important – and she gets irritated when asked – each of Gordimer's stories is very much of its time, and tellingly so. To read a selection of them is to experience an accurate history of developing consciousness decade by decade;[11] as our four stories – about first awakening, about the disillusion with liberalism, about the post-Sharpeville Emergency, and about the beginning of armed struggle – will show.)

So, Josias has been asked to help hijack the dynamite-lorry; and young Willie, the narrator, picks up the signs of unusual excitement and nervousness in the big, slow man. The Gordimer 'sharp knowing in apartness' is still visible in the description of 'those brown chipped teeth' of Josias, like 'the big ape' at the zoo. We are still asked to decipher between the lines the 'signal' that Emma 'couldn't know', that is like catching a rope (why men, particularly, feel the sense of imprisonment, unable to climb up and out) – whereas Emma's intense feeling for another, her man, leaps in imagination past the action and sees him already dead. Willie responds to both, but the major current of the narrative is his determination to join the struggle.

However, he does have something of his sister's need to see further and her practicality; discovering by going to look, that 'the road' is not just a spot on a map, an idea, a stretch between turnings, but a physical place with real people. This is also growing up, not taking things as they come. Irony however returns. Though the struggle is 'for the nation', there is a huge gap between the snappily dressed township youth on his bicycle, and the farm labourers in their mud huts. There is comic distance and condescension again (the 'eyes the colour of soapy water' and the aha-ing and *ehê*-ing of the old men) but there is also surprise at the unknown or forgotten: the beauty of Ndebele hut-decoration; the reminder, watching a girl with her little brother, of how he and Emma used to be. So there can be a moment of solidarity when he longs to tell them that, some Monday for sure, 'we' will win. Knowing more of what he is talking about he can talk to Josias as a man not a kid, and convince the others to let him help. What might have seemed the central action however, the hijacking itself, is played down. Gordimer is clearly not concerned with heroics or even drama. But why not? As we find the wavelength of her story, we discover that it is ironic after all, in that the narrator has to keep learning how, underneath, things are never what they seem. Not merely are the best-laid plans subject to accident – and disaster to those arrested – but there was dynamite concealed in the action that they never saw at all: 'Oh, I sent a message to Emma that I was all right; and at that time it didn't seem true that I couldn't go home again' (p. 132). The long walk through three countries to Tanzania is again only touched on, for it is not that which is really significant. At first, though things are different there, they seem all right. There is no job for Josias, but Willie with his Standard Seven education can earn, and Emma can join them because hospitals are being Africanised and there is a demand for trained black nurses. This is a land without apartheid, where Africans can take their full place: 'it was like it had happened already: the time when we are home again and everything is our way' (p. 134).

Three years later, however, there are signs that the South Africans are no longer so welcome, and in their fervent greetings and enquiries for news of 'home' the pain of exile shows. The irony becomes clear now, in two directions. That little word 'home' is the whole of life for Emma. When Josias leaves for guerilla training she becomes terrified of losing Willie, and begins to clutch so hard that she is already losing him before he goes. She cannot adapt to new circumstances at the hospital or anywhere else. The language is 'just a noise', in 'a place where there's no one', because only her own place, language and people are fully real to her. Josias and Willie in the two-room township house made everything else real, and it was in caring for them that she found her identity, not in nation or freedom or rights. What the stolen dynamite did, was blow up her whole life. But there is also irony as we listen to

Willie. He is still eager for the future, but his living for it dislocates him as much from the present, as does Emma's living in the past. The technicality of present-tense narrative is itself ironic. (It will be even more so, differently, in *The Conservationist* [1974].) 'I don't take much notice. I'll be sent off one of these days' (p. 134); 'Well, I'll be going off soon' (p. 136). Not only has he grown away from his sister, but there is also a growing unease and frustration as he waits for the call, and tells himself he hasn't been forgotten. This mustn't be overplayed; the story still points ahead. Yet the apparently confident emphasis of the title has become more ambiguous. Some Monday, surely, he will stop being a walker in the night, only seeing other people at home, in glimpses through cracks of light.

It is a good story, and a brave attempt for a white writer. Yet the move towards greater inwardness underlines how the intrinsic nature of the imagining remains unchanged, for here again as strongly as ever are the 'Gordimer' characteristics: the clear structure defining attitudes and their implications, and the challenge to detect what is concealed between the lines. The ironic artistry still has a subtle joining of author and reader at the end in a knowing sharper than the protagonist's, thus necessarily apart. Moreover, the more the fiction appears to invite the reading we give to fictions of character, the clearer the sense of what would be limitations if that were really what the imagination was up to. For Gordimer's real concern is not with individuality, the inward depth or complexity that makes each human being unique. She is still interested in situation, and response to situation. Even when we are allowed to get more 'inside', we experience consciousness as a process of exploring and defining attitudes whose significance is representative rather than particular.[12] A danger then comes in sight. Willie and Emma's attitudes are worryingly close to typecasting, 'male' and 'female', which would be damaging in a novel unless counterpointed as powerfully by the other kind of woman, who has played such a part in the history of the ANC.[13] 'Some Monday' may escape the criticism, because of the short story's necessary economy, but the danger is there and appears in other Gordimer fictions.[14] Also, while Willie may function successfully enough (just) as a young African within the bounds of a short story, to attempt more ambitious exploration and inwardness would expose – as Gordimer's novels do when set against Achebe, Soyinka, Ngugi, Bessie Head – how difficult it is for even the best white writers, brought up in apartheid, to know with enough *togetherness* what 'black' and 'coloured' people's experience, first-language, culture, and consciousness feel like. Also, Josias vanishes into an unknown where Gordimer cannot follow. This hardly registers in a short story, whose selective angle is concerned to focus the opposed 'tenses' of Emma and Willie; but it would matter if we imagined an expansion into a novel of character and relationship. On the contrary, 'Some Monday' is kept precisely to its most effective angling, focus, and scale – and I believe it is in her short stories that Nadine Gordimer generally gives the most unalloyed pleasure and satisfaction, maximising the artistry appropriate to her kind of imagination, and minimising what might prove limitations if she tried 'to know in togetherness'.

It would require another essay to argue the effects of the bigger scale of the novel. To compare *The Grass Is Singing* (1950) and *July's People* (1981) for instance – both about a white couple incapable of fully human relationship, with each other or the land or black people – would show that even on this scale Gordimer's success is still essentially ironic. The exposure of how Bam and Maureen's 'liberalism', sexuality, even their sense of identity, depended on possessing power and technology, is 'sharp' indeed, and the 'distancing' increases to the end. When Maureen 'runs' at the last, her solipsism is not liberation but final proof of her inability to relate. Nor can 'July' escape the irony which questions his relation with his own people as well as with the Smaleses. Like *The Late Bourgeois World* (1966) this is a 'play unpleasant', effectively corrosive.

Lessing's novel, by contrast, must discover why Dick and Mary are what they are and behave as they do. Marston thinks 'what really mattered . . . was to understand the background, the circumstances, the characters of Dick and Mary, the pattern of their lives' with 'impersonal pity', but the novel does what he funks and more.[15] Moreover 'knowing in togetherness' becomes available even to Mary at the end, though Dick is driven mad by seeing what he has been blind to. Though it seemed atrophied, Mary's imagination awakens on the last day of her life, even to the certain knowledge that what she has done to her black lover will make him kill her, and to a final perception of guilt. But Moses's point of view remains untold, presumably because Lessing is aware she cannot summon for a black man the kind of 'knowing in togetherness' she can give to Mary. Yet the final sentences challenge us to re-read and imagine what we can. Gordimer exposes, pins down, defines. Lessing's people are complex, so can always change, though this can come too late for new life. The novels contrast as strongly as the stories.

Yet such an essay would also have to explore the significance of the two books within the oeuvres as a whole. Lessing's was her first novel, and its successors began from the question of how and why it was not 'large' or complex enough to satisfy her need to know in full – but also to investigate what it is to 'know'. Southern Africa was the source of the challenge, but in the *Children of Violence* sequence, and *The Golden Notebook*, the exile learns to distrust her emotions about it. The left-winger must connect it with the great movements of sexual and political challenge in a far wider world; the modernist must look for forms that will satisfy both the need to 'know' connectedly, and a growing scepticism about the pretensions of 'realism' and indeed the patterning of all 'story'. Later, the 'religious and poetic' imagination will turn to space fiction for a deeper sense of more ultimate issues. Not even a novel is big and complex enough: the imagination demands a sequence of novels; or multiple narratives within a huge 'book-box', all calling one another in question. It was clearly right for Doris Lessing to leave Rhodesia in order to find herself as her kind of artist. Her fiction at its best can almost make Gordimer's seem provincial. Yet there is a price to pay – there always is. For the effort 'to get it all in' leads to unevenness of texture, lecturing, diffusiveness, over-elaboration. The intense concentration of 'The 'Ant-heap' can occur again, but episodically now and intermittently. Even *The Golden Notebook* has pits as well as peaks.

*July's People*, however, came after Nadine Gordimer's finest novel, and marks a turning point, beyond which the novelist faces increased difficulty and challenge. If my argument about the intrinsic nature of her imagination is just, it is not surprising that her finest, most concentrated, and most satisfying novels have been the ironic ones, the three 'plays unpleasant', where the novel is the ironic story writ large, and bigger scale offers greater scope for the things she does best. However, the extraordinary triumph of *The Conservationist* – as opposed to *The Late Bourgeois World* and *July's People* – is how her imagination grows to a new kind of involvement and a new kind of response. This comes partly from the marvellous formal invention which embodies the major irony that Mehring's 'present tense' has no future, and cannot cope with the past welling up; yet which is also made so present, as an experience of agonised consciousness and breakdown, as to disturb and complicate the usual ironic detachment. (Mehring breaks down because he is more sensitive and vulnerable than most white southern Africans.) Partly also the farm itself, originally used to locate the ironies of the title, seizes the imagination and draws it beyond its usual urban range. And partly it is because the bringing to bear of other cultures, though still held within the boundaries of 'third-person' narrative and thematic counterpoint, is also warmer and richer than before, though limited. On the other hand, the novels which attempt a non-ironic exploration seem much less satisfying. The effort to see a protagonist many-sidedly can seem rather laborious – apart from immediate sensual experience, always powerfully realised – and the tendency to typify is seldom overcome except at the centre. Even there, situation seems to define character rather than the other way round. In *Burger's Daughter* (1979), the nearest to a novel of character, Rosa exists in terms of, and to pose, her *problem* of judging between the personal and the political – a challenge also to her author who seems to me to fail it. For Gordimer proves unable to imagine a personal kind of life, or a fully loving relationship, or an experience of living culture, deep enough to mount a serious challenge to political commitment. In all these spheres the 'opposition' (when Rosa comes to Europe) is such straw that her decision to go back to South Africa is far less impressive than it should have been. Finally there is a suspect vagueness about and valuing of her significance in the struggle. Perhaps, for once, Gordimer was too personally involved. She was deeply disturbed by Biko's insistence that the fight for liberation had to be a black fight, in which whites had no real part; but her book, so powerful for most of its exploration, cooks its 'answer' in the end. Yet by *July's People* she seems to have swallowed the bitter pill. For corrosive irony returns precisely because the 'progressive' whites are indeed to be shown as finally irrelevant. Only where is the ironist to turn, then, if exposure of white inadequacy has reached its useful limit, and the real struggle is taking place elsewhere? Obviously imagination must reach out to the 'black' struggle and its implications – but for an essentially ironic imagination, and one whose power to 'know in togetherness' is limited both by its nature and its experience, how is that to contribute effectively? The two most recent novels seek new solutions, both interesting and capable as always, but also defining their limitations.[16] It seems likely, now, that the major exploration and illumination of the struggle will come from black writers, who know from the inside, themselves. Yet it was surely right for Gordimer's kind of imagination, essentially ironic and political, to stay in South Africa – as it was right for Doris Lessing to go. Only at the end of the day could there be any judging between them, and it would have to be a long, absorbing day.

## Notes

1. *The Essential Gesture*, ed. Stephen R. Clingman, London: Jonathan Cape, 1988.

2. Dan Jacobson, *The Confessions of Josef Baisz*, London: Secker and Warburg, 1977. To confirm the point, Jacobson's earlier South African fictions, *The Trap* (1955) and *A Dance in the Sun* (1956), written before he left, are still available in paperback.

3. *Some Monday for Sure*, London: Heinemann, 1976. *This Was the Old Chief's Country*, London: Panther, 1979. These collections are unfortunately limited to stories written before 1972 and 1953 respectively, but the Gordimer self-selection for the African Writers Series is particularly useful as representing how she wished to be seen as an African writer, and I think Lessing is right that date is of little significance for her African fiction.

4. 'My approach in these stories, as in very many others, is that of irony. In fact, I would say that in general, in my stories, my approach as a short story writer is the ironical one, and that it represents the writer's unconscious selection of the approach best suited to his material.' 'Introduction', *Some Monday for Sure* (1976), page unnumbered.

5. 'A Propos of Lady Chatterley's Lover' in *Sex, Literature and Censorship: Essays by D. H. Lawrence*, ed. Harry T. Moore, London: Heinemann, 1955, pp. 263–6.

6. Dennis Brutus, for example, reacted to 'the kind of impersonality you find in a microscope', and moreover saw in this a sign of 'how dehumanised South African society has become – that an artist like this lacks warmth, lacks feeling, but can observe with a detachment, with the coldness of a machine'. See 'Protest against Apartheid', in Cosmo Pieterse and Donald Munro (eds), *Protest and Conflict in South African Literature*, London: 1969, p. 97.

7. I argued this in 'This Old Maid: Jane Austen Replies to D. H. Lawrence and Charlotte Brontë', *Nineteenth Century Fiction* (Austen bicentenary number), December 1975, pp. 399–419.

8. *This Was the Old Chief's Country*, p. 10 – an introduction reprinted from the collection *African Stories* (London, 1964).

9. *This Was the Old Chief's Country*, p. 10.

10. An important but later exception would be 'Something Out There' from the collection of that title published in 1984. However, the extra length comes about because of the variety of situations ironically undermined, and set against the small group of saboteurs, rather than because of imaginative pressure to explore characters and relationships with greater complexity and fullness. In its selective ironic angling it is a multiple of connected 'short' stories. By contrast I take *The Late Bourgeois World* (1966) to be a novel (as indeed it is always listed), though a short one. The formal distinction ought to be qualitative not quantitative, a matter not of word-count but of the degree and nature of selectivity.

11. Gordimer makes this point herself in her introduction. It is also the theme of Stephen Clingman's *The Novels of Nadine Gordimer* (London: Allen & Unwin, 1986), subtitled 'History from the Inside', and a fine study from that angle.

12. Provided we define the word with care, hers is a definitively 'political' imagination. From this point of view, fiction concerned with the 'individual' rather than the 'representative' could be considered 'bourgeois'. I think, however, that both writers (albeit 'of the left') are so properly concerned with both imaginative concerns as to make such labels unhelpful in trying to understand the differing nature of their imaginations.

13. Women's participation has always been strong in the ANC. In 1955 2,000 women marched on the Union Buildings in Pretoria; in 1956 it was 20,000, led by Lilian Ngoyi and Rahima Moosa and Helen Joseph. Lilian Ngoyi was only the first of a number of remarkable African women leaders such as Josephine Sisulu, who headed the United Democratic Front after 1984; and Winnie Mandela, who, whatever the truth about the latest tragic affair, was for many years an extraordinarily courageous example and focus of resistance, to sustained and sometimes violent persecution.

14. See for example 'A City of the Dead and a City of the Living' in *Something Out There* (1984), and the remarkably passive wife of 'July', so different from the rural African women portrayed in the fiction of West and East African writers, and indeed in the first South African black novel in English, Sol Plaatje's *Mhudi* (1930), which has a heroine rather than a hero. It is only in her latest novel *My Son's Story* (1990) that Nadine Gordimer has built upon 'A Chip of Glass Ruby'

in identifying rather than opposing domestic womanhood with political activism in non-white women; but still without any exploration of how and why the quiet 'perfect wife' (or for that matter the 'good-time daughter') becomes active in the guerilla movement.

15. *The Grass Is Singing*, p. 26. This is particularly evident in two crucial scenes which show affinities with Lawrence: the scenes in which Moses is whipped across the face, and the counter-scene where Mary sees him washing himself and, in responding to him for the first time as a man, is also for the first time in touch with the earth she walks on. This imaginative affinity is perhaps even more important than the allusions to *The Waste Land*.

16. In *A Sport of Nature* (1987) the white girl Hillela is used like a mirror below whose surface we cannot see (apart from a few significant glimpses) but whose openness to others allows us to see them reflecting themselves, in the nature of their relationship with her, as she passes picaresquely (like 'Adventures of a Guinea') from one possession to another: from white suburbs, through a beach in Tanzania, and marriage to an Umkhonto leader, to a seat beside prime ministers at the independence celebrations of the new Azania. The trouble, however, is not only the forgoing of inward exploration of the white protagonist (now ironically 'irrelevant'), but also that effective exposure of the white world is succeeded by rather shallow imaging of the black ones into which Hillela moves. In *My Son's Story* Gordimer bravely determines to build on 'Some Monday' by occupying a wholly non-white world, in a third-person story of the rise and 'fall' of an ANC leader, counterpointed by the bitter first-person narrative of his son. One hesitates to criticise something as well done as Gordimer could do it, in terms of broadly human imagination, without being able to create the dense specificity of non-white experience under apartheid – and its impact on consciousness, which is the subject of Bessie Head. But this 'story' really needs a non-white to tell it as fully as it needs to be told, and to explore the stories of the wife and the daughter too.

# Allegiance and Alienation in the Novels of Bessie Head

## CRAIG MACKENZIE

Bessie Head is known primarily for her first three novels, *When Rain Clouds Gather* (1969), *Maru* (1971) and *A Question of Power* (1973).[1] These works diverge markedly from other African novels which address similar themes. In *When Rain Clouds Gather*, which deals with the conflict between modernity and tradition (a recurring theme in African fiction since the appearance of Achebe's classic *Things Fall Apart* in 1958), Head inverts the customary story line of this genre and eschews a simplistic paradigm of racial conflict by constructing, in fictional terms, the possibility of inter-racial co-operation and friendship. Her second novel *Maru* further establishes her uniqueness in Africa in its incisive probing into the racism that exists in traditional African societies and in its dramatic inversion of the social pyramid in Botswana: a despised Masarwa (Bushman) woman, considered the lowest of the low, marries a future paramount chief of the dominant tribe of the region and with this single act throws time-honoured prejudices into disarray. And, finally, in her concern with women and madness in *A Question of Power*, claims one critic, Bessie Head 'has almost single-handedly brought about the inward turning of the African novel.'[2]

Two influential critics have observed that the novels constitute a triology of sorts. In his seminal essay, Arthur Ravenscroft (1976)[3] argues that the novels reflect an increasing interiority of perspective, that each novel returns to the central issues of personal contentment and political power, and that each tries to resolve these issues in different ways. He discerns a pattern: the interior torments of the characters are set in a concrete, historically specific context; they work

111

through the psychological stress created by this disjunction to a reconciliation of interior and exterior, private and social.

Cherry Wilhelm (Clayton) (1983)[4] argues that the novels share a basic quest pattern in which the protagonist struggles to attain a sense of belonging in both a geographical as well as an existential sense. She observes in the novels a 'growing stress' on the 'psychic arena', and argues for a sequential movement away from the realism of *When Rain Clouds Gather*, through the allegorical mode of *Maru*, to the almost entirely inner, psychic struggle of Elizabeth in *A Question of Power*. Head thus becomes progressively more concerned with the 'symbolic and metaphysical significance' of personal events. Accordingly, the interest in each case is with smaller and smaller groups of people, ending with the narrating consciousness of a single protagonist.

This essay will consider some of the key issues and points of continuity in Head's first three novels. The tendency to think of these novels as a 'trilogy' has proved profitable. It produces readings in which the texts can be seen to engage and re-engage in a debate about personal imperatives and their articulation with political power and social commitment. Viewed in this way, the central characters of *Rain Clouds*, *Maru* and *A Question of Power* have structural and psychological correspondences with each other, despite the novels' divergent forms. The problems which are displayed on a flat Botswanan landscape in *Rain Clouds* are embodied by individual characters in *Maru* and are finally internalised completely in *A Question of Power*.

This essay will also identify certain structural weaknesses in the first two works of this 'trilogy'. Challenging and unusual though they are, these novels contain disjunctions and anomalies that threaten their internal coherence. This is especially the case with *Maru*, as Margaret Daymond has argued.[5] Although *A Question of Power* re-engages with the issues central to both *Rain Clouds* and *Maru*, and contains the same sorts of problems, the later novel is free of the strictures which apply to the other novels by virtue of its narrative strategy. Whereas the earlier novels attempt to contain potentially disruptive elements within an overarching narrative or fabular frame, in *A Question of Power* there is a liberating abandonment of any such totalising structure.

By locating the action of the novel within the consciousness of the protagonist, Head is free to explore to a greater extent the conscious and unconscious human mind – a dimension of human experience she demonstrates an extraordinary capacity to handle. At the same time, she is compelled to deal only obliquely with a discursive terrain she is least competent at: the conceptualisation of social process and the manner of its articulation with private life and personal imperatives. It is Head's treatment of this area that produces the discontinuities in her first two novels. *When Rain Clouds Gather* negotiates the conjunction of the private and social spheres very unsatisfactorily; and in *Maru*, the eponymous hero attempts to address the problem of racism in Batswana society while simultaneously seeking personal freedom and abdicating from political leadership of his tribe. In a *A Question of Power*, however, the connections between the inner life of the individual and the individual's engagement with the social and political sphere are severed, and the focus falls almost wholly on the inner world of the single protagonist. The text is therefore free to roam without restriction over the territory which surfaced in a fragmented and disrupted form in the two earlier novels.

When the novels are read as a trilogy, therefore, *Rain Clouds* can be seen to contain (and repress) the same disruptive forces at work in *Maru* and also those so dramatically foregrounded in *A Question of Power*. However, in *A Question of Power*, the absence of a totalising, meaning-yielding structure allows the reader both the freedom to interpolate meanings and the power to resist narrative closure. The process is encouraged by the text's gaps and disjunctions, as Head herself observed in an interview in 1983.[6] This is perhaps the reason *A Question of Power* has attracted more critical attention than any of Head's other works, and is now considered her major work.[7]

The dynamic of alienation and commitment, which galvanises the protagonists of all three novels, is only partially resolved in *Rain Clouds* and *Maru*. As the focus narrows from a broader, external view, to an inner, psychic one, so the issues themselves – existential alienation, the desire of the exile to belong, the struggle to unify the social and personal aspects of life – gain a greater emotional urgency. *A Question of Power* appears to represent the culmination of this process, and the success of this novel lies partly in its abandonment of the conventions that simultaneously underpin and hamper its predecessors.

*When Rain Clouds Gather* attempts to bring within a predominantly realistic frame elements of the romance and the African pastoral. For the psychologically dislocated Makhaya Maseko, rural Botswana promises reconstitution and a reintegration with the social world. The sterile, strife-torn urban ghetto of his native South Africa is about to be replaced by Golema Mmidi, a traditional African village, named, significantly, after the crop-growing activities of its inhabitants. His active involvement in the co-operative development of a tract of semi-desert rural Botswana promises to bring about the integration of the personal and social dimensions of his life.

His passage from the urban ghetto to the African countryside is therefore a reversal of the trend of the 'Jim-Comes-to-Jo-burg' genre which established itself in South African fiction in the wake of southern Africa's rapid industrialisation after the mineral discoveries of the late nineteenth century. A similar 'passage' can be discerned in the life of fellow-protagonist Gilbert Balfour, who escapes the stifling bourgeois orderliness of his life in England to help in turning the tide of desert encroachment in rural Botswana. Aided by a team of progress-minded villagers, Gilbert and Makhaya attempt to set the village on a path of self-sufficiency and self-respect.

Golema Mmidi is full of individuals who have fled there 'to escape the tragedies of life' (p. 22), people determined to make a fresh start in life and to survive. Their harsh circumstances and the lack of any traditionally acquired wealth have forced them to become progressive, to break with traditional tribal agriculture. The villagers – represented principally by Dinorego, the forward-looking Batswana pastoralist who first meets Makhaya and brings him to the village; Paulina Sebeso, a passionate and lonely widow exiled from her home in northern Botswana; Maria, Dinorego's daughter; and Mma-Millipede, with her eccentric blend of Christianity and Setswana custom – pose a threat to Matenge, their arch-conservative, tribalistic chief. Flanked by the semi-literate Pan-Africanist Joas Tsepe, Matenge becomes a force for evil in the novel. Modernity confronts tradition and the tendency in the novel is to favour the first: tradition no longer has answers to starvation, poverty and human misery, and the villagers of Golema Mmidi are prepared to explore the option of modernity. This, the text announces, represents 'the progress of mankind' (p. 145).

It is to the spirit of cautious reformism in the villagers of Golema Mmidi that Gilbert appeals. Joined by Makhaya, he works for the co-operative development of Botswana's resources. In this regard, Gilbert is the spokesman for small-scale capitalist development:

'Golema Mmidi has the exact amount of rainfall of a certain area in southern Africa where Turkish tobacco is grown very successfully. It's a very good cash crop too, and if everyone in Golema Mmidi grows a bit and we market it co-operatively – why, we'll all be rich in no time.' (p. 59)

The novel's tendency to valorise capitalist development is evident in this passage and, indeed, runs as a theme throughout the novel. In his discussion of the novel, Simon Simonse ascribes this to an authorial predilection:

> We might as well be frank about it from the start: Bessie Head does believe in the emancipatory potential of capitalist development. It is her contention that small-scale capitalism on a co-operative basis offers a realistic opportunity for revolutionising the stagnated relations of production in the countryside. *When Rain Clouds Gather* describes such a revolution.[8]

That there is an assertion of the necessity of 'small-scale capitalism on a co-operative basis' in the novel is undeniable. However, this does not necessarily constitute an endorsement of the process which will lead to exploitative social and economic relations. It is essential that the Batswana develop, yet this development is to be guarded by the proviso that all benefits accrue to the people themselves. Co-operative development, or communalism, is therefore the antithesis of rampant capitalism in *When Rain Clouds Gather*.

The precise nature of this development and path to general prosperity nevertheless remains a problematic area in the novel. Because Head does not conform to a recognised programme of political activity, her view of economic development is largely undefined. The key to this indeterminacy lies in her conceptual orientation: she does not work from a preconceived political ideology and apply it to the issue at hand. With Bessie Head, abstract moral principles have much more weight and are by their very nature less easily translated into practice. For her, generosity, courtesy and respect for the common person are the touchstones to positive social, political and economic strategies.

This orientation is what provokes Arthur Ravenscroft's reservations about the novels:

> The precise relationship between individual freedom and political independence, and between a guarded core of privacy and an unbudding towards others, may seem rather elusive, perhaps even mystical . . . and I see it as one of the weaknesses of *When Rain Clouds Gather*.[9]

Makhaya Maseko's quest in the novel is to find inner peace by an engagement with the social world. In Golema Mmidi he finds people willing to share their goods, both material and spiritual. The 'feeling of great goodness' (p. 184) that permeates the life of the village translates itself into both practical activity and human co-operation.

This 'feeling of goodness' is crucial in Bessie Head's fictive world. It is the unexamined 'given' from which she is able to construct a tenuous link between the public and the private. The weakness of this link is revealed in the attitudes that Paulina and Mma-Millipede have towards the co-operatives. They do not enter the project with an awareness of what it stands for – what it means to the economic life of the subsistence dwellers of Golema Mmidi. Their motivations are personal. When Gilbert anxiously asks Mma-Millipede to recommend a woman who will start co-operative tobacco farming under Makhaya's supervision she sees this as an opportunity for matching Paulina off with Makhaya. The link between the personal and the social thus becomes fortuitous, indeterminate.

This indeed is an example of the whole tone of the novel: everything positive develops by happy accident. This is why it has been accused of being excessively romantic.[10] The introduction of the 'God with no shoes' (p. 185) at the end of the novel is an attempt to make events less arbitrary – to compensate for the absence of a causal connection between events. On this reading, *Rain Clouds* can be seen to contain unresolved elements which can ultimately be traced to Head's uneasy blend of realism and idealism in the novel.

*Maru* belongs to a different order of fiction from *Rain Clouds*. The first few pages are an epilogue to the events which unfold through the rest of the novel. The linear progression of events in *Rain Clouds* is replaced by a circular pattern in *Maru* and our understanding of events throughout the novel is fashioned by our prior knowledge of their eventual outcome. The invitation, therefore, is to read more deeply into already-known events, to dwell longer on the wider social and metaphysical significance of the human drama.

*Maru* is at one level a story of rival lovers competing for the affections of the same woman. The drama is heightened by the fact that they are both in line for chieftaincy of their tribe and that the woman who commands their love is a Masarwa (Bushman) – a social outcast. The rivalry of Maru and Moleka is that of two powerful personalities vying for supremacy. Maru is portrayed as being manipulative and perceptive, Moleka as bright, passionate and energetic. Through most of the story it is Maru who has the upper hand; he has 'creative imagination' (p. 58) whereas Moleka has energy without the imagination to direct it: 'They were kings of opposing kingdoms. It was Moleka's kingdom that was unfathomable, as though shut behind a heavy iron door. There had been no such door for Maru. He dwelt everywhere' (p. 34).

Maru's god-like omniscience gives him ascendency, but this is threatened by the love which Margaret awakens in Moleka. Moleka's power is latent: it is an unknown quantity which Maru fears. With the awakening of his love for Margaret, Moleka's energy becomes channelled: he feels an indefinable surge of power. Maru's calculations are momentarily unbalanced, but he deftly averts this threat to his supremacy by engineering, firstly, the marriage of Moleka to his sister and, ultimately, his own marriage to Margaret. He abdicates political responsibility and moves away from Dilepe village, leaving tribal authority in the hands of Moleka. The social implications of Maru's marriage are profound: Margaret comes from a race of untouchables.

In addition to the complexity of the emotions of those acting out the drama, and the social implications of this drama, there lies another level of signification beyond the novel's surface realism. A single passage will demonstrate this: 'There had never been a time in his [Maru's] life when he had not thought a thought and felt it immediately bound to the deep centre of the earth, then bound back to his heart again – with a reply' (p. 7).

It is clear when reading *Maru* that individual characters are meant to stand for something else, that individual actions and events express things beyond the confines of narrative realism. There are two areas of significance prefigured by the text: the interior workings of the psyche and the creative activity of the artist. These run as the novel's sub-texts. Clearly the story line of *Maru*, the sequence of daily events, is simply a point of departure to other levels of meaning. What gives coherence to events in *Maru* are the inner workings of the minds of the characters.

The psychic plane – or in the terms used in the novel, the realm of the soul – is accessible only to Maru, Moleka and Margaret. The novel therefore becomes a three-sided struggle in the realm of the soul. All of these characters have dual identities, one applying to the real world, and the other a 'soul-identity'. The dynamic of alienation and commitment which is at work in all three novels is given a fresh direction in *Maru*. The movement of characters from alienation to commitment (a physical journey in the realism of *Rain Clouds*) is a journey of the soul in *Maru*. Maru's quest is to attain the realm of the inner self, the being in touch with the secret pulse of the universe. He moves from the alienation of his tribal, exterior identity to his inner identity as a 'king of heaven' (p. 35). Similarly, Margaret's journey from alienation to wholeness is a passage from her racially ascribed identity to her true inner identity. Head's contention is that socially ascribed identities are false, misleading, degrading to the true inner person. Through the union of two equal souls, Maru and Margaret defy the prejudiced world and point to a new world of true racial equality.

The second subtext that runs through the novel is a commentary on the nature of art and of the artist. When Margaret Cadmore senior (Margaret the protagonist's mother) comes across the dying Bushman woman, she discovers that her powers of artistic transformation are limited: something about the Bushman woman arrests her artistic impulse. Here she is presented with life that is too close to the bone for her satirical perspective. Yet she creates a person (Margaret, her adopted daughter) whose artistic powers enable her to penetrate to the heart of things, to understand the deepest motives in people. Maru has 'mastery over the universe', and Margaret gains access to this realm through her art. She is therefore his ideal partner. Maru remarks: 'If we have the same dreams, perhaps that means something' (p. 107). The two undercurrents in the novel – the exploration of the realm of the soul and the activity of the artist – meet at this point.

*Maru* is poised uneasily between the desire for personal fulfilment and the dictates of social conscience. The condemnation of race prejudice is unequivocally expressed through the novel. But what is not clear is the nature of the alternative to this, and the method of its implementation. *Maru* is offered on one level as a way to end racial antagonism: there is a concern to engage with the social world, institute change, put an end to prejudice and reactionary codes of behaviour, establish genuine equality between the races and the sexes. On another level one detects an implicit desire for the liberation of the pure, creative, individual soul. These ideals are in conflict in the novel: in his role as paramount chief-elect, Maru is ideally placed to institute reform, yet in doing so he alienates himself from the people of his society. He achieves change at the expense of leadership of his tribe.

As with *Rain Clouds*, the flaw in *Maru* arises from Head's inability to unite the public and the social with the inner life of the individual. The two dimensions of human experience are discontinuous in the novel. In order to salvage something of the novel from the tensions that threaten to pull it apart, the author does some special pleading on Maru's behalf. She attempts to persuade the reader to view Maru favourably because he is the embodiment of progressive social attitudes she wishes to endorse.[11] She justifies his manipulativeness, his lying, his half-truths and his scheming by pointing heavenward: Maru is in touch with the 'way things are' and his actions are thereby vindicated. He is amoral, but he moves in time with the inexorable pace of the universe.

A realist reading of *Maru* is unsatisfactory because the outcome of events thwarts the codes by which we judge behaviour. We are asked to judge Maru's manipulations not by human moral standards, but by the transcendental principles of destiny. Maru is not merely indulging his ego; he is obeying the 'gods in his heart'. He also deals racism a decisive blow and initiates a process of social reform that is going to be difficult to halt. However, racism is not solved by the exemplary behaviour of a single individual, however highly placed he may be. The author is forced to recognise this:

> When people of Dilepe village heard about the marriage of Maru, they began to talk about him as if he had died. A Dilepe diseased prostitute explained their attitude: 'Fancy,' she said. 'He has married a Masarwa. They have no standards.' (p. 126)

For the people of Dilepe, Maru has ceased to exist. This conclusion creates a disconcerting anomaly in the novel: Maru sets the tone for a new social order, but he then removes himself from the society and the people prove reluctant to follow his example. The people of Dilepe, we read, 'knew nothing about the standards of the soul, and since Maru only lived by those standards they had never been able to make a place for him in their society' (p. 126).

This is a recognition of Maru's political failure. Where he does succeed, however, is in his ambition to 'dream the true dreams, untainted by the clamour of the world' (p. 70), and this is the direction in which the novel has been straining all along: the liberation of the individual soul and the attainment of spiritual perfection. This preoccupation is carried to extremes in *A Question of Power*. The novel is a professedly autobiographical work which deals with Head's mental breakdown and subsequent recovery and renewal. Although all three of Head's novels have an autobiographical dimension, elements of *A Question of Power* are most conspicuously drawn from the life experience of the author. The central character takes the author's name – Elizabeth – and also shares her life story. She is born in a mental hospital after her mother is committed because of an affair with a black man. She is raised by a foster mother, and thereafter by a harsh missionary who 'came out to save the heathen'. Elizabeth then joins a political party, has the misfortune to marry a womaniser, bears his child, and after the inevitable breakup of the marriage, leaves on an exit permit for Motabeng village in Botswana, where she engages in co-operative gardening ventures with the local Batswana and an international group of volunteer workers.

According to the biographical record, then, it is clear that there is little attempt to disguise the fact that Head is telling – or more precisely, re-interpreting – her own life story in this novel. Fruitful though a biographical approach to the novel might be, this is not the approach I intend to take here. What is unusual about *A Question of Power* and what will ensure its place in future assessments of African literature is its decisive shift of attention to the psychic arena. And it achieves this on a formal level by resolutely denying traditional narrative conventions and, accordingly, the interpretative strategies traditionally employed by the reader.

Two worlds co-exist on different ontological planes in the novel: there is a recognisable, social world of co-operative gardening, human interaction, everyday events in the village; there is also an inner, psychologically constituted world, in which the logic of the nightmare, and of intuitive dream-association, predominates and the free play of ideas is allowed to proceed. Whereas the protagonists of the earlier novels were presented with rich interior lives which they attempted to integrate with an outer social world, a different balance is struck between these two dimensions in *A Question of Power*. Elizabeth's dreams possess a certain narratological authority: they are, in fact, the very 'stuff' of the text, the locus of the 'real life' of the novel.

In locating the action of the novel inside the mind of a character, Head seems to be adopting a distinctively modernist strategy: the 'outer' world bombards the sentient subject with a barrage of sensory impressions which must be configured by the subject's organising intellect; the subject's ordering gaze, in other words, imposes an interpretation on a seemingly random universe.

In a radical and idiosyncratic way, however, Head interrogates the notion of a centred, ordering subject. Instead of being the organising principle in a chaotic universe, Elizabeth's mind becomes the *site* of a monumental struggle between conflicting forces. This produces one of the central paradoxes of the novel. It professes itself to be autobiographical ('Elizabeth and I are one', Head remarks in the 1983 interview)[12] and yet, as Wilhelm has observed, 'the novel is the least documentary of the three: it has moved into the arena of psychic struggle'.[13]

Elizabeth is alienated from all of society's power structures: as a 'Coloured' she is denied full 'selfhood' in racist South Africa; as a 'half-caste' she is despised in traditional African society; and as a woman she bears the brunt of the patriarchal hierarchies in both societies. In a very real sense, Elizabeth 'creates' herself from the sketchy details supplied by the principal of the mission school in which she is placed as a young girl: ' "We have a full docket on you. You must be very careful. Your mother was insane. If you're not careful you'll get insane just like your mother. Your mother was a white woman. They had to lock her up, as she was having a child by the stable boy, who was a native" ' (p. 16).

Any sense of unity or coherence as a person has to be built up by Elizabeth through an act of will and, bereft of the usual social-support system of close friends and family, and under the pressure of extreme life experiences, this fragile sense of self fragments. Elizabeth's mind is then invaded by vertiginous nightmare sequences drawn from the deepest wells of her unconscious.

The way these dreams are presented in the novel, whether one construes this as the faithful record of the author's own descent into insanity or, alternatively, as a bold experiment in narrative technique, the reader is encouraged to be a producer rather than a passive consumer of meaning. In this Head is perhaps being no more adventurous than any number of contemporary writers with postmodernist tendencies. The intriguing thing about her own attitude to the novel, however, is how explicitly she articulates the gaps and discontinuities in the text, and how she actively encourages reader participation in the production of meaning. Consider what she says of the novel in the 1983 interview: 'It was like a book saying now, I'll tell you as much as I can, then you sort things out . . . it's a sort of book that's written in such a way that it invites people to fill in gaps and notes where the author has left blank spaces.'[14]

There is a palpable sense here that she is disavowing the traditional claims to authority: the author then becomes the conduit, so to speak, of a polyphony of discourses from outside herself. The notion of 'identity' which, ironically, usually provides the autobiography with a central, constitutive principle, is also undermined here. Indeed, throughout the novel there is a denial of the boundaries between what are conventionally conceptualised as 'the real' and 'the imaginary'. The catalyst for this is Elizabeth's insanity, which prompts a departure from societal norms of perception. Accordingly, the transposition of her dreams into fiction produces a form of narrative which similarly abrogates the usual norms and conventions.

It is therefore inappropriate to construct a logical, coherent way through the lurid dream sequences of the novel, but the issues which are foregrounded, and with which the dream personae Sello and Dan and other figures challenge Elizabeth, are those specifically related to her experiences as an underprivileged Coloured growing up in South Africa. These anxieties are common in the race-obsessed social system of South Africa: a sense of personal worth (a Coloured child as a product of an immoral alliance between black and white), an inability to identify with Black Consciousness and Pan-Africanist groups, and an anxiety that one is abandoning one's fellow downtrodden by elevating oneself socially and materially. In Elizabeth all of these anxieties combine with the universal subconscious fear of human depravities and aberrations. The issue which ultimately emerges from this disquiet is the question of personal power and how to use it for the betterment of humankind – hence of course the novel's title.

Elizabeth's inner struggle is induced, like Makhaya's and Margaret's, by her dual alienation from South Africa and from the Batswana. Thus Elizabeth's affirmation of good is not made on behalf of society in general. She is unable to assert, in a partisan way, the superiority of one culture, or society, or political system over another, and comes instead to ground her arguments upon the soul of the solitary individual, the basic unit of humankind.

In *Rain Clouds*, Makhaya's struggle is to reconcile his material existence with his inner life. His life is ordered by his experience in these two dimensions. He acts in the real world and the world in turn provokes an inner reaction. The two realms achieve a tenuous union in the end. With *Maru*, the focus has shifted to the inner lives of the central characters. Yet Maru succeeds in his ideals only when he has brought the outside world into harmony with his inward desires. In *A Question of Power* the relationship between inner and outer is at its most tenuous. There is virtually no causal connection between 'reality' and Elizabeth's nightmares. At one point in the novel she questions this disjunction: 'How did it all happen here, in so unsuspecting a climate, these silent, tortured, universal questions of power and love; of loss and sacrifice?' (pp. 97–8).

Elizabeth's struggle is entirely internal: she undergoes what she conceptualises as an experience of evil at its roots and emerges with an affirmation of 'good'. At the end of the novel, Elizabeth describes her 'journey into hell' in this way: 'Maybe, the work she and Sello had done together had introduced a softness and tenderness into mankind's history . . . They had perfected together the ideal of sharing everything and then perfectly shared everything with all mankind' (p. 202).

In broad terms this a similar kind of affirmation to that achieved somewhat less convincingly in the earlier novels. The 'ideal of sharing everything' is at the basis of Elizabeth's moral perspective. And she sees this principle as applying to every aspect of human life: thus in the economic sphere, for example, co-operatives are the expression of this communal spirit. Her mental breakdown occurs in the process of testing these ideals. But she has withstood the assaults upon her sense of human value and has emerged revitalised: 'from the degradation and destruction of her life had arisen a still, lofty serenity of soul nothing could shake' (p. 202).

The novels share a common concern with the theme of exile, and are deeply impregnated with the motifs of loneliness and alienation, but each novel engages with these concerns in significantly different ways. Head's attempt to resolve her protagonist's inner struggle in *Rain Clouds* by constructing an ideal world in which his innermost needs are met is ultimately unsatisfactory, and this is perhaps why the same themes are taken up again with greater urgency in *Maru*. The moral and existential complexity of Head's vision does not allow for a facile resolution, and thus *When Rain Clouds Gather* ends on a deeply ambivalent note: 'everything was uncertain, new and strange and beginning from scratch' (p. 188).

*Maru* resumes the earlier novel's debate about personal fulfilment and social commitment, but here the psycho-spiritual dimension of the material interaction between individuals is much more in evidence. Again, however, there is evidence of a bifurcation of thematic concerns that dilutes the novel's impact and occludes potentially fruitful avenues of interpretation.

*A Question of Power* foregrounds the deracination and alienation of the exile and, in turning inwards with greater conviction on the emotional and psychological anguish of its sole protagonist, the novel transcends the conceptual inconsistencies of its predecessors. Elizabeth's struggle becomes entirely internal, and the texture of the narrative adjusts accordingly: where the predominantly realistic texture of *Rain Clouds* is disrupted by elements of idealism, and where *Maru* attempts an uneasy blend of allegory and realism, *A Question of Power* abandons such narrative conventions and engages instead in a style and discourse utterly germane to psychological trauma. Its bold injunction to the reader is to abandon conventional expectations in order to strike directly towards the nightmare reality of Elizabeth's consciousness, to experience at a narrative level the monumental struggle of the protagonist and to emerge finally, with her, exhausted but spiritually renewed.

*Notes*

1. Editions of primary texts referred to are the following: *When Rain Clouds Gather* (1969), London: Heinemann, 1972; *Maru* (1971), London: Heinemann, 1972; *A Question of Power* (1973), London: Heinemann, 1974.

2. Charles R. Larson, 'Anglophone Writing from Africa', *Books Abroad* 48.3 (1974), p. 521.

3. Arthur Ravenscroft, 'The Novels of Bessie Head', *Aspects of South African Literature*, ed. Christopher Heywood, London: Heinemann, 1976, pp. 174–86.

4. Cherry Wilhelm (Clayton), 'Bessie Head: The Face of Africa', *English in Africa* 10.1 (1983), pp. 1–13.

5. M. J. Daymond, 'Bessie Head, *Maru*, and a Problem in Her Visionary Fable', *Short Fiction in the New Literatures in English*, ed. Jacqueline Bardolph, Nice: Faculté des Lettres et Sciences Humaines, 1989, pp. 247–52.

6. Bessie Head, 'Bessie Head interviewed by Michelle Adler, Susan Gardner, Tobeka Mda and Patricia Sandler, Serowe, 5 January 1983', *Between the Lines: Interviews with Bessie Head, Sheila Roberts, Ellen Kuzwayo, Miriam Tlali*, eds Craig MacKenzie and Cherry Clayton, Grahamstown: National English Literary Museum, 1989, pp. 5–30.

7. This tendency is reflected in the recently published *Bessie Head: A Bibliography* (comp. Craig MacKenzie and Catherine Woeber, Grahamstown: National English Literary Museum, 1992), which shows that a significantly greater number of articles have been written about *A Question of Power* than about any of Head's other works.

8. Simon Simonse, 'African Literature between Nostalgia and Utopia: African Novels since 1953 in the Light of the Modes-of-Production Approach', *Research in African Literatures* 13.4 (1982), p. 468.

9. Ravenscroft, 'The Novels of Bessie Head', pp. 178–9.

10. Ibid, p. 179.

11. *Maru* always occupied a special place in the author's estimation of her own work. In the interview included in *Between the Lines* (see above) Head made the following remark with respect to *Maru*: 'it's the book that I regard as my most beautiful' (pp. 11–12). Throughout the interview she defends the book against her interviewers' objections regarding Maru's duplicitousness and Margaret's passivity.

12. *Between the Lines*, p. 25.

13. Cherry Wilhelm, 'Bessie Head: The Face of Africa', p. 3.

14. *Between the Lines*, p. 27.

# Jean-Baptiste Tati Loutard: Death and Identity

## BELINDA JACK

The title of Jean-Baptiste Tati Loutard's recent prose text, *Le Récit de la mort*, foregrounds what has always been an important element in the dense fabric of his writing: death.[1] But nowhere is its role easy to characterise as it is rarely a detachable theme or subject. Rather it is a nexus establishing connections amid a diverse range of concerns. To some extent, both the coherence of his writing in terms of its social, political and philosophical correlatives and its *poetic* coherence (the relationship between types of imagery and the function of certain poetic figures, metonymy, for example), relate to an understanding of death. Of all the recurrent elements in his writing – River Congo, water, the sea, movement, light and darkness, birds, dream, slavery, time and history, legend, social and political concern – death holds a privileged position as a point of interchange among them. Death has to do not only with certain themes (slavery, time, memory, for example), but also to do with his metaphysics or world-view, his notion of individual identity and, at a wider level, nationalism, and his relationship with both the *vili* tradition and European traditions. These are to some extent discrete areas but death can be regarded as a point of contact bringing these into relationship. As Tati Loutard says in one of the aphorisms of *La Vie poétique [Poetic Life]*, part of *Les Racines congolaises [Congolese Roots]*, death, for all its obscurity, can be peculiarly illuminating in certain contexts:

> La mort est un corps obscur par nature; placée près de l'art elle devient, exceptionellement, une source lumineuse.

126

[Death is by nature an obscure body; in rare cases, as when placed next to art, it becomes a source of light.]²

In Tati Loutard's tales, *Chroniques congolaises* and *Nouvelles chroniques congolaises*,³ death frequently functions not as a convenient *conclusion* to the narrative but as a pre-text or presence. 'Le Secret d'un homme' ['One Man's Secret'], from the latter collection, *begins*, 'Ta Tchicaya était mort à Bacongo' [Ta Tchicaya had died in Bacongo] (p. 149). His death is set up as a pre-text for a story about his life of apparent celibacy: 'De son vivant, personne parmi son entourage n'avait pu percer le mystère qui enveloppait sa vie sentimentale' [During his lifetime no one in his circle had been able to solve the mystery which surrounded his private life] (p. 149). It is when he dies that his life will be explained: 'Le corps était là, comme une lettre cachetée' [The body was there, like a sealed letter] (p. 151). Then Old Tchibangou speaks: 'Avec la complicité d'un matelot, nous nous sommes embarqués à Pointe-Noire pour Dakar, en 1928 . . .' [With the complicity of sailors we embarked at Pointe-Noire for Dakar, in 1928 . . .]. The old man tells of his friend's passionate love of a Senegalese girl whose parents initially rejected him for reasons of ethnic and religious difference, of their subsequent marriage, of his sudden and inexplicable disappointment, of the death of his wife and infant in childbirth, and of his disappearance. Tchibangou recounts how they met many years later and emphasises the burden of his friend's guilt. It is throughout the night, as the mourners watch over the body, that the story is told. Then day comes: 'Le jour commençait à s'ouvrir . . . La fraîcheur de l'aube pénétrait les corps subrepticement . . . Le matin annonçait le séparation, l'enterrement' [Day was beginning to break . . . Imperceptibly, the freshness of dawn entered their bodies . . . The arrival of morning announced the moment of separation, the burial]. Although the burial is thus described, the members of the community know Ta Tchicaya very much better than they knew him when he was alive; they now understand him, he has been resurrected and lives on in the collective memory. As Tati Loutard writes elsewhere: 'La mémoire collective nous console du tombeau: l'humiliation ultime' [The collective memory consoles us in the face of the tomb: our ultimate humiliation].⁴

Death is equally revelatory in 'Hé', from the *Nouvelles chroniques* (pp. 25–38). Rather than functioning as a pre-text, here death serves as a 'presence'. Death does not occur as an event in the narrative but recurrent references to death interspersed in the narrative are of crucial importance: 'Car l'être humain vient par l'eau et s'en va par le sang' [Because human beings come by water and go by blood], for example (p. 31).

'Hé' is about a mad woman, 'De Tchipiara', wife of Lalonzi. She wanders aimlessly, having abandoned her husband and child, seemingly never sleeping, attracting fascinated attention and commotion wherever she finds herself. Near the beginning of the story her constant wakefulness is described:

> Où passait-elle ses nuits? Personne ne l'avait surprise quelque part, dormant ou même somnolant. Ses yeux s'étaient ouverts pour de bon. La folie les avait dilatés. Même la mort, disait-on, ne les fermerait pas.

> [Where did she spend her nights? No one had surprised her somewhere, asleep or even dozing. Her eyes had opened for good. Madness had dilated them. Even death, it was said, would not close them.] (p. 28)

Towards the end of the story an explanation of De Tchipiara's madness is offered by an old man:

> Lalonzi la martyrisait, l'enfermait parfois toute une journée dans la chambre à coucher, par jalousie, pour l'avoir simplement entendue répondre au salut d'un passant. Après le déjeuner, il avait l'habitude de dénombrer les morceaux de poisson ou de viande qui restaient dans la marmite. Le soir, c'était une scène de ménage, si le compte n'y était pas. Et la nuit, il la privait de sommeil par toutes sortes de honteuses manies . . . Je ne suis pas surpris qu'elle soit devenue folle.

> [Lalonzi martyred her, sometimes locked her up all day in the bedroom out of jealousy simply because he had heard her reply to the greeting of a passer-by. After lunch, he would count out the pieces of fish or meat which were left in the pot. In the evening there would be a scene if the count was out. And at night he would deprive her of sleep by all kinds of shameful practices . . . I'm not surprised she went mad.] (p. 36)

The narrative functions of the old men in 'Le Secret d'un homme' and 'Hé' are superficially the same: they offer, because of their privileged knowledge, insights into unusual behaviour. In the first case apparent and unexplained celibacy, and in the second, madness. They propose psychological explanations for what is seen as abnormal living. The old man in 'Hé', however, also functions as an interpreter of *vili* tradition. His narrative is, in effect, a gloss on the succinct reference to De Tchipiara's open-eyed death. Within the local tradition, this manner of death has great significance:

> The 'fetish *chibinga*'\* sometimes will not allow the corpse to close its eyes. This is a sure sign that the deceased is annoyed about something, and does not wish to be buried.
>
> (\**Chibinga*' is the state of a corpse which remains with its eyes open, and is also the power *nkissi*, that is the cause of this affliction.)[5]

The reader familiar with the tradition would assume that De Tchipiara's open-eyed death pointed to an injustice in her life and might well associate this story with other stories of jealousy ('The Jealous Wife', Dennet, p. 46) and maltreatment of wives ('The Wicked Husband', Dennet, p. 54). As the cause of death is always divined, the reader familiar with the tradition might well assume that Lalonzi's cruelty will be discovered.

Neither of these stories is 'about' a single theme. 'Le Secret d'un homme' is at once about celibacy, the secrecy of marriage, guilt, the social, financial and ritual consequences of death, and individuals' connections with the wider community. It is the event of death which draws these ideas into relationship. 'Hé' equally is about marriage and men's power; it is also about madness. It is death which is projected as a point where these separate questions will be focused.

In Tati Loutard's poetry death belongs within a dense poetic fabric. Certain titles set the poem up as memorial or epitaph 'Mort d'un héros ['Death of a hero'], 'Mort d'une héroïne' ['Death of a heroine'] from *La Tradition du songe*, 'Le cancer d'un jeune artiste' ['The cancer of a young artist'],[6] 'La mort du poète (pour Langston Hughes')'] ['Death of the Poet (for Langston Hughes)'] from *Les Racines congolaises*. One of the functions of death in poems such as these is relatively straightforward: death acts as a *pre-text* (real or imagined) for the poem. The same had been true of 'Le Secret d'un homme'.

Facile reference to certain titles accounts for death only in its most obvious and unoriginal poetic relation. More often in Tati Loutard's poetry death appears unexpectedly or, if presaged, realised only in retrospect. For example, on re-reading 'Les voix' ['The Voices'], a memorial to those who have died at sea, presumably slaves who lived during the 'siècles de mépris' [centuries of contempt], the title refers to the voices *of the dead*.[7] Like the 'souillures' [impurities], the 'os/Sous les croix des polypiers' [bones/Under the polyps' crosses], 'leur noir sommeil marin' [their dark ocean sleep], and 'le lourd cercueil du silence des fonds' [the heavy shroud of the silent deep], the 'voices' of the title also functions metonymically.

The abstraction that is death suggests poetic treatment dependent on metaphor. But metaphor, working by *substitution*, would not allow for the accumulation which metonymy allows. Just as 'La mer a rassemblé tous leur os' [The sea has collected together all their bones], so the poem collects together voices, bones, the heavy coffin of the silent deep, and a moan. These are not metaphors for death or the dead, they do not stand *in their place*, they are sensorily perceptible attributes of the dead. Exploitation of this kind of linguistic figure articulates, at the same time, a particular metaphysics: the dead are always present *in some form*. An example of this can be seen in the lines from 'Village disparu' (*La Tradition du songe*):

> Par temps chaud se montrent des tombes
> Où l'histoire toute veuve s'est enfoncée.
>
> [During the hot weather tombs appear
> Where history totally widowed has gone deep.]

But the dead have to be *made visible* through the poet's language: 'Mais j'ai l'oeil qui perce les profondeurs; et l'oreille qui écoute' ('Les voix') [But I have eyes which penetrate the depths; and ears which listen ('The Voices')]. The poet's assertions may be extravagant, his eye 'perce les profondeurs/*Plus que les doigts fins du soleil* [pierces the depths/*More than the thin fingers of the sun* (my emphasis)]. Here it is metaphor that describes the poet's ability to gain access to the dark regions of human experience in history, and though his claims seem bold, the poem fulfils them; those who died at sea are made present in the poem and the poem guarantees them continued presence. This idea is made explicit in 'L'Arbre et l'amour' ['The Tree and Love'] from *La Tradition du songe*:

> Tu survivras en émigrant de livre en livre
> Ainsi ton immortalité est-elle mieux protégée
> Que celle des enfants du Levant
> Jadis inhumés dans les poteries d'argile.

> [You will survive by emigrating from book to book
> Thus your immortality is better protected
> Than that of the children of the Levant
> Buried long ago in clay pottery.]

Reference has already been made to *vili* tradition in connection with Tati Loutard's *chroniques*. Here and there in his poetry are lines which are translations of *vili* sayings, a number concerning death. His line 'Amère est la bouche le jour de la mort' [Bitter is the mouth the day one dies] is a direct translation of the *vili: cilunmbu ci kofwa munu nduli*. The exclamation 'Dieu n'a point pitié! Dieu n'a point pitié!' [God has no pity! God has no pity!], which occurs in one of the poems in the *Poèmes de la mer* collection, is part of a *vili* chant sung at wakes.[8] It is no coincidence that it is in relation to death that Tati Loutard draws most directly (and perhaps reverently) on the indigenous tradition. He does this not simply to enrich the poetic fabric, to add 'cultural resonance', but to restate particular ideas about death, ideas which belong to, and sustain, the 'collective memory'.

But the relationship between the oral *vili* tradition and a written tradition in French is a complex one. The former articulates a particular vision which depends for its validity on coherence. The danger is that the *vili* saying, when translated into French and transplanted into a hermeneutically more complex context, becomes philosophically gratuitous and functions only as a sign of 'cultural eclecticism' for its own sake. Tati Loutard's poetry avoids this. Firstly he does not footnote the *vili* and thus prevents its foregrounding. Secondly, the *vili* saying is fully integrated into the poetic fabric. As he himself states:

> Il existe un logique poétique si rigoureuse qu'elle fait apparaître à celui qui la possède la gratuité de certains vers. Un bon poète corrige son

poème comme un bon logicien redresse un raisonnement boîteux. (*La
Vie poétique*, p. 16)

[There is a poetic logic so rigorous that it reveals, to those who possess
it, the gratuitousness of certain poetic lines. The good poet corrects his
poem in the same way as a good logician corrects faulty reasoning.]

The logic referred to here is not the logic of the philosopher. Tati
Loutard distinguishes very clearly between the two: 'Le poète et le
philosophe sont deux passionnés de la vie; mais le philosophe est plus
facilement sûr de lui que le poète: il se ferme vite; le poète reste plus
longtemps ouvert face au monde' (*La Vie poétique*, p. 18) [Both the poet
and philosopher are passionate about life; but the philosopher is more
readily sure of himself than the poet; he closes up quickly; the poet
remains open before the world for longer].

Tati Loutard's poetry is rich in responses to death. Two extremes are
presented within *Les Racines congolaises*. In 'L'Appel de la mer' ['The
Call of the Sea'], a death-wish:

> Et c'est la naissance d'un immense désir
> D'enfouissemment dans les remous obscurs
>
> [And it is the birth of an immense desire
> To be smothered by the dark currents]

is replaced by light and renewed hope:

> Mais la lampe d'un pêcheur qui aborde au loin
> Brise l'appel de la mer . . .
> Et le feu jaillit pour une nouvelle invite
> A l'espoir.
>
> [But the lamp of a fisherman coming ashore in the distance
> Shatters the call of the sea . . .
> And fire bursts forth
> Inviting hope once again.]

Important parallels with Valéry's *Le Cimetière marin [The Graveyard by
the Sea]* and *La Jeune Parque [The Young Parque]* will be explored later.

'Baobab', on the other hand, in the 'Retour au Congo' section, begins with a projection of self-planting and ends with a projection of something closer to self-burial. Thus the lack of ambiguity of the first lines:

> Baobab! je suis venue replanter mon être près de toi
> et mêler mes racines à tes racines d'ancêtre
>
> [Baobab! I have come to plant my being close to you
> And to entwine my roots with your ancestral roots]

are replaced in the final three lines by:

> Et quand faiblira le sol sous mes pas
> Laisse-moi remuer la terre à ton pied: Que doucement sur moi elle se
> retourne!
>
> [And when the soil weakens under my feet
> Let me stir the soil at your foot: That gently it would fall back on me!].

Here the active first person at the beginning of the poem looks to a time when the earth will act *on him*. This longed-for renunciation of life is far from maudlin: the poet knows that ultimately he will become part of something more substantial, more permanent and, most importantly, immutable. The concrete imagery associated with this is geological. In 'Mort d'une héroïne', the heroine's life has guaranteed her the protection of a 'gîte minéral [mineral shelter]. In 'Le dernier du village' ['The Last One of the Village'] from *La Tradition du songe*, the 'spéléologue' is addressed in this way:

> Spéléologue des profondeurs d'un grand siècle
> Tu peux ouvrir aujourd'hui ton musée
> D'ossements pour tes contemporains enfouis
> Comme un gisement de calcaire coquillier.
>
> [Caver of the depths of a great century
> Today you can open your museum
> Of bones for your buried contemporaries
> Like a stratum of shelly limestone.]

Continued existence is also guaranteed through memory, which is often described as physical rather than intellectual: 'Je m'en souviens par le nombril' [I remember through my navel]. Legend, history and dream also preserve life: 'Nous croisons nos morts dans les songes' [We meet our dead in dreams]. In 'Village ancestral' (*La Tradition du songe*) the *griots* are dead:

Toi [village ancestral] qui fus riche en conteurs de légendes
Il te reste une cigale récitant
D'une voix monocorde
L'hymne au soleil de midi.

[Oh you, (ancestral village) who were so rich in story-tellers
All that you have now is a cicada reciting in a monochord voice
The hymn to the midday sun.]

There is also the life afforded by poetry which is often described using a geological vocabulary, as in these examples from *Eléments de la vie poétique*: 'Les sentiments participent de notre nature végétale. C'est dans la poésie qu'ils se minéralisent' [Our feelings are part of our vegetal side. It is in poetry that they mineralise]; 'La poésie a ses galeries souterraines comme certaines rivières. Mais sa source est toujours vive' [Poetry has its underground caverns like certain rivers. But its source is always living]; 'L'esprit poétique est répandu dans le nature qui en use pour quelques-unes de ses créations: grottes, cheminées de fée, formations géologiques' [The poetic cast of mind is scattered throughout nature which she exploits for certain creations: caves, rock chimneys, geological formations]; 'Entre la forêt et la ville, il y a eu la savane et en contrebas la grotte: notre espace paléo-poétique' [Between the forest and the town, there had been the savannah and below, caves: our palaeo-poetic space].

These antitheses – vegetal/mineral, surface/subterranean – recur throughout Tati Loutard's writing. They constitute part of a visual three-dimensional landscape/cave-scape, and one which often bears similarities with the Congo. The opposition between the geomorphic (concerned with the earth's crust) and the geophysical (concerned with the properties of the earth's substance, i.e. seismological, meteorological, oceanographical) is also a metaphor for the oppositions between what is visible and invisible, known and unknown, living and comprehensible, and dead and mysterious. Some of the most striking lines in his poetry are the point of interchange between the two. This is frequently a moment which is not clearly perceived. In the following example, it is 'Dans le lointain des flots' that 'l'aile du goéland/Evente la mer' [In the distant waves, the sea-gull's wing fans the sea], the gull's wing fans the sea, exposing its depths. The poem thereby enters the realms of the oceanographical.

One of the most unexpected features of Tati Loutard's focus on death is the degree to which it is *prospective* rather than simply retrospective. Sartre identifies a similar paradox in Baudelaire's vision:

C'est cette détermination du présent par le futur, de l'existant par ce qu'il n'est pas encore, qu'il nommera 'insatisfaction' . . . et que les philosophes appellent aujourd'hui transcendance. Personne n'a compris comme lui que l'homme est un 'être des lointains' qui se définit beaucoup plus par sa fin et le terme de ses projets que par ce qu'on peut connaître de lui si on se limite au moment qui passe.

[It is this recognition of the present by means of the future, of that which exists by that which is not yet, that he terms 'dissatisfaction' . . . and which today's philosophers call transcendence. No one has understood as he has that man is a 'being of the distance' who defines himself more by the end and term of his projects than by what one can know of him if one limits oneself to the fleeting moment.][9]

Tati Loutard's 'insatisfaction' is both philosophical and political. So too, of course, was Baudelaire's. Walter Benjamin had described him in the title of his book as 'a lyric poet in the era of high capitalism'[10], and Mallarmé (whose texts also exhibit an obsession with death) is equally, 'an observer of capitalism in spate'.[11] Mallarmé's 'Quand l'ombre menaça' [When the Shadow Threatened] refers to the 'siècles hideux' [the hideous procession of human epochs] and this is Historical Time, as opposed to an abstract and infinite time. Tati Loutard's reference to the 'siècles de mépris' ('Les voix'), on the other hand, while historical, is also historically specific.

Baudelaire and Mallarmé are not the only writers with whom Tati Loutard's poetry establishes intertextual relationships. Fragments from the Bible and writers as diverse as Chekhov, Shakespeare, Ibsen, Valéry, Jean-Joseph Rabearivelo, Saint-John Perse, Aimé Césaire and Eluard are also part of the fabric of Tati Loutard's writing. The way in which other (often dead) poets 'live on' in Tati-Loutard's texts and are echoed and confronted in the latter's work varies. His lines 'Et la porte ouverte sur le fleuve/Sur les rives astrées de la nuit' [And the door open on the river/On night's starry banks] concerns a landscape which is *home*. It relates directly to Saint-John Perse's lines at the beginning of his epic *Exil*: 'Porte ouverte sur le sable, porte ouverte sur l'exil' [Door open on the sand/Door open on exile].[12] Here the relationship is based on opposition. This relationship is suggested in Tati Loutard's *Eléments de la vie poétique*: 'Nous imitons d'abord. Nous travaillons ensuite sur un refus' (p. 61) [First we imitate. Then we work on a refusal]. But the relationship is not always one of opposition or refusal. A comparison of lines from Césaire and Tati Loutard underlines a parentage, a similarity of vision. In the *Cahier d'un retour au pays natal*, Césaire writes at a point of climax: 'lie ma noire vibration au nombril même du monde' [bind my black vibration to the very navel of the earth].[13] Tati Loutard's lines in 'Les voix', 'Je m'en souviens par le nombril/Qui me noue aux siècles de mépris' [I remember by the navel/Which binds me to the centuries of contempt], also posits a deeply physical relationship with history, nature and the world. But there are refusals of Césaire too. The latter's famous lines describing Négritude:

> elle (ma négritude) plonge dans le chair rouge du sol
> elle plonge dans la chair ardente du ciel
> elle troue l'accablement opaque de sa droite patience
>
> [it thrusts into the red flesh of the soil
> it thrusts into the burning flesh of the sky
> it digs under the opaque dejection of its rightful patience]

are rewritten and the process fails in Tati Loutard's lines in 'Une femme parle' (*Les Racines congolaises*):

> Et la vie de l'homme plonger dans la terre
> Sans jamais plus germer
>
> [And the life of man thrusting into the soil
> Without ever again germinating].

Mention was made earlier of important parallels between Valéry and Tati Loutard. Here there is a strong sense of shared vision but the *loci* of the poems are very different. The intertextuality is most explicit in the title of Tati Loutard's 'L'Appel de la mer'. At the beginning, the sea offers the comfort of death, but the coming of light brings hope, as quoted above, 'Et le feu jaillit pour une nouvelle invite/A l'espoir'. The heroine of *La Jeune Parque* is facing the sea: 'L'être contre le vent, dans le plus vif de l'air/Recevant au visage un appel de la mer' [Her being against the wind, in the most invigorating air/Her face receiving the call of the sea].[14] The light which brings hope in Tati Loutard's poem functions in very much the same way as the wind in Valéry's famous line 'Le vent se lève! . . . il faut tenter de vivre' [The wind rises! . . . Life calls to be attempted!] as the poet receives the creative stimulus of the sea breeze blowing over the cemetery where the poet stands in *Le Cimetière marin*.[15] But Tati Loutard's poetry is both firmly anchored and deeply rooted in the Congo, that is to say in the river and the territory. References to the Congo are numerous throughout his oeuvre as are references to major historical events of the history of the République Populaire du Congo.

Valéry's own understanding of the way in which poetic influence functions may offer more insights into Tati Loutard's writing and its relationship with other works than his own aphoristic statements. Valéry writes:

Nous disons qu'un auteur est *original* quand nous sommes dans l'ignorance des transformations cachées qui changèrent les autres en lui; nous voulons dire que la dépendance de *ce qu'il fait* à l'égard de *ce qui fut fait* est excessivement complexe et irrégulière. Il y a des oeuvres qui sont les semblabes d'autres oeuvres; il en est qui n'en sont que les inverses; il en est d'une relation si composée avec les productions antérieures, que nous nous y perdons et les faisons venir directement des dieux.

[We say that an author is *original* when we are ignorant of the hidden transformations which changed others into him; that is the dependency of *what he does* in relation to *what has been done* is excessively complex and irregular. There are works which are like other works; there are those that are simply the opposite; there are those whose relationship with earlier productions is so complex, that we lose the thread and make them the result of the direct intervention of the gods.][16]

In the case of the relationship between Tati Loutard's writing and the oral tradition the notion of intertextuality opens up new dimensions. Oral tradition depends on constant restatement, and each articulation is also a modification. What matters in Tati Loutard's poetry is that, as Valéry suggests, the relationship with earlier productions (whether French, francophone African, Malagasy, West Indian, Russian, or *vili*) is so complex that 'we attribute his works to the direct intervention of the gods' – but which 'gods'?

Like Valéry's, there is an extraordinary intellectual coherence about his oeuvre. Tati Loutard rejected the easy coherence offered by the Négritude doctrine with its prescriptions for black writing. As he explained in his post-face to *Poèmes de la mer* and in various articles published in the *Annales de l'Université de Brazzaville*, there are two main counts on which he takes issue with Négritude. Firstly on the grounds that it limits the writer's freedom, the 'libre expression des tempéraments' [free expression of temperaments]. He compares the 'retour aux sources' of Négritude with that of the German philosopher Herder in the eighteenth century. Négritude is a literary movement in the same way and not a black cosmology or metaphysics. His other major criticism was related to what he saw as a spurious cultural homogeneity. That anglophone African writers on the whole rejected Négritude seemed to point to a difficulty. As far as 'l'âme noire' was concerned Tati Loutard pointed out that dance, the cult of the dead and communion with cosmic forces were all important to the Romans and Etruscans, for example, and that 'la poétique de l'émotion' had been characteristic of the Romantic Movement.

Tati Loutard's culturally comparatist perspective serves as a warning to those who might be tempted to locate his vision, its cosmology and metaphysics, exclusively within the *vili* tradition. He is a poet who displays a wonderful contempt for what Harold Bloom calls 'The Anxiety of Influence'. Commenting on younger writers he declared:

Dans leur phobie de ne pas pouvoir dire autrement que l'Européen ou l'Asiatique . . . [les jeunes Africains] usent leurs forces à cultiver une différence convenue, alors qu'il suffirait d'ôter l'écran de la race pour libérer leur tempérament d'écrivain.

[Such is their fear of not being able to speak differently from the European or the Asian . . . that (young Africans) waste their energies cultivating a conventional difference when it would be sufficient to lift the screen of race to liberate their true writerly selves.][17]

However formative other texts may be (written or oral), Tati Loutard describes the Congo as his poetic source:

Terre riche en ressources poétiques. Tout ici exalte le coeur et l'imagination, les paysages les plus divers, les événements les plus bouleversants des sociétés modernes.

[A land rich in poetic resources. Everything here exalts the heart and imagination, the most diverse landscapes, the most staggering events of modern societies.][18]

In Tati Loutard's poetry it is often death which is the nexus positing relationships between these diverse 'resources'.

Death is, of course, a phenomenon which has to do with Time, and as the social anthropologist J. Davis has recently argued, the way Time (or as he says 'Times'), is understood has to do with Identity. As the titles of many of Tati Loutard's works suggest, in particular his *Anthologie de la littérature congolaise d'expression française [An Anthology of Congolese Literature of French Expression]*, he is deeply committed to a *national* literature.[19] But an easy and spurious national identity will not do. In its obsession with death, his poetry, in particular, exemplifies the complexities of the relationships between Times and Identity. Davis holds:

Times are not all the same, and . . . therefore our consequential pasts (what we take into account when we take decisions) are different . . . These differences are in turn consequential: it is all very well to show that in another country, another time, people construed the world differently . . . But we also have to show . . . that the differences make a difference.[20]

Davis shows this very convincingly in his paper 'Times and Identities' (1991). Two distinct conclusions follow. Firstly his approach 'brings history into relation with myth' (p. 18). These are both, Davis argues, 'kinds of thought about the past but (among other differences) use different kinds of time to place personal experience in the world. The old division into just two bags – untrue myth, true history – really won't do' (p. 18). His other important conclusion is that 'the themes of times and identities are related, at any rate in the sense that time is a central ingredient of identity' (p. 7).

In an analogous way then, Tati Loutard's exploitation of death as a nexus proposes – abiding by poetic logic rather than the logic of social anthropology – fundamental relationships between the world, times and, most importantly, identity. This may in part explain his subtle, allusive but utterly persuasive and profoundly rooted nationalism.

### Notes

1. Jean-Baptiste Tati Loutard, *Le Récit de la mort [Tale of Death]*, Paris: Présence Africaine, 1987. All translations are my own unless otherwise stated.

2. J.-B. Tati Loutard, *Les Racines congolaises précédé de La Vie poétique*, Paris: L'Harmattan, 1978, p. 15.

3. J.-B. Tati Loutard, *Chroniques congolaises [Congolese Chronicles]*, Paris: Editions Oswald, 1974; *Nouvelles chroniques congolaises [New Congolese Chronicles]*, Paris: Présence Africaine, 1980, pp. 149–62 (p. 149).

4. J.-B. Tati Loutard, 'Eléments de la vie poétique', *La Tradition du songe*, Paris: Présence Africaine, 1985.

5. R. E. Dennett, *Notes on the Folklore of the Fjort*, London: Folklore Society, 1898, p. 115. For an account of current research on Congolese oral material see Auguste Miabeto, 'Etat de la recherche sur la littérature orale', *Notre Librairie*, 92–3, March–May, 1988, pp. 56–61.

6. J.-B. Tati Loutard, *L'Envers du soleil*, Paris: L'Harmattan, 1978.

7. 'Les voix' is from J.-B. Tati Loutard, *Poèmes de la mer*, Yaoundé: Editions Clé, 1968. See also Gerald Moore's bilingual edition with introduction, *Poèmes de la mer/Poems of the Sea*, Ibadan: New Horn Press, 1990.

8. Gervais Boungou-Poati, 'Apports de la tradition orale à la littérature d'expression française', *Notre Librairie*, 92–3, March–May, 1988, pp. 65–8 (p. 68).

9. Jean-Paul Sartre, *Baudelaire*, Paris: Gallimard, 1947, 1975 reprint, p. 37.

10. Walter Benjamin, *Charles Baudelaire: a lyric poet in the era of high capitalism*, London: Verso, 1983, translated from the German by Harry Zohn.

11. Malcolm Bowie, *Mallarmé and the Art of Being Difficult*, Cambridge: CUP, 1988.

12. Saint-John Perse, *Eloges suivi de La Gloire des rois, Annabase, Exil*, Paris: Gallimard, 1960, p. 150.

13. Aimé Césaire, *Cahier d'un retour au pays natal/Return to My Native Land*, bilingual edition, Paris: Présence Africaine, 1971, pp. 154–5.

14. Paul Valéry, *La Jeune Parque, Oeuvres I* (Pléiade), Paris: Gallimard, 1957, pp. 96–110 (p. 110).

15. P. Valéry, *Le Cimetière marin*, bilingual edition. Edinburgh University Press, 1971, pp. 20–1; translations from this text.

16. P. Valéry, 'Lettre su Mallarmé', *Oeuvres I*, pp.633–43 (pp. 634–5).

17. J.-B. Tati Loutard, quoted by R. Chemain and A. Chemain-Degrange, *Panorama critique de la littérature congolaise contemporaine*, Paris: Présence Africaine, 1979, p. 19.

18. J.-B. Tati Loutard, quoted by Chemain and Chemain-Degrange, p. 146.

19. J.-B. Tati Loutard, *Anthologie de la littérature congolaise d'expression française*, Yaoundé: Editions Clé, 1976.

20. J. Davis, *Times and Identities*, Inaugural Lecture, University of Oxford, Clarendon Press, Oxford, 1991, p. 4.

# Transformative Strategies in the Fiction of Ngũgĩ wa Thiong'o

## ABDULRAZAK GURNAH

Ngũgĩ's fiction relies on allegorical formations whose narratives are constructed into apparently self-evident paradigms. This is not inconsistent with the tendency of allegory to seem to be articulating a higher level of truth, separating out paradigmatic analogies from a tangle of minor and competing ones. These prime analogies, in other words, appear to utter a collective truth which transcends the disabling complexities of parochial realities. Such an approach need not imply a tendency to focus on the general rather than particular experience, but it does suggest that the latter has the capacity to reveal the former.

In Ngũgĩ's fiction, these paradigmatic analogies include: expropriation of African land and the subsequent rupture of 'whole' ways of life; the inhumanity or 'unnaturalness' of the European settler; the cynicism of 'neocolonial' capital and the grotesque complicity of African élites. The discourse is dominated by its transformative 'text' in which the captive nation, overcome in recent history, awaits its desired redemption. The nation is debilitated by its captivity, of course, and its condition is portrayed as having physical and figurative dimensions, as we shall see later. Its transformation out of this state, which is an advance towards a lost plenitude despite its language of radical change, is outlined in the allegory that the narrative plays out. History here is the enabling code of recognition, allowing complex, or even conflicting, 'national' experiences and their narrativisations to merge under a dominant discourse. Its implications are to bring forth a physical and historical unity, a vision of collective origin which is legitimised by common space and experience. ('Hail, the splendour of this land!/Hail, the land ringed round with deep lakes,/Turkana to Naivasha,/Nam-Lolwe to Mombasa!/Hail, this necklace of blue waters!')[1] In a real sense, this discourse constructs Ngũgĩ's 'Kenya', which like all 'nations' in Africa and elsewhere has plural existences in the imagination.[2]

In this discourse, for example, both expropriation of land for European settlement, and the expulsion of Africans who lived on it but were surplus to labour needs (coyly coded as 'land alienation' in the narrative of imperialism) are portrayed as paradigms of colonial experience, or national persecutions under which everyone suffered. But land expropriation was not a universal experience in colonial Kenya, and where it occurred it was not on the scale in which it befell the Gikuyus and their neighbours. Nor has it come to signify rupture in the same charged way Ngũgĩ so consistently demonstrates in his fiction. In Ngũgĩ's writing, land has come to acquire a metonymic function, signifying a wholesome mythic past whose retrieval is paralleled by the desire for the lost land.

Also, the intensity with which European settlers are demonised in the fiction reflects and enacts a degree of interaction and conflict which was distinct in the 'national experience' of colonial Kenya, where in some cases Europeans were a distant though nonetheless profound influence. The loathing with which children of African mothers and Italian prisoners-of-war are spoken of in *Weep Not, Child* (1964), for example, portrays such marginal relations as utterly unwholesome. Indeed, if this area of contact represents 'the margin' where hybridity begins, here it is seen as an unstable and treacherous terrain. But it is not that all marginality is seen as disabling. Njoroge, the central boy-child figure in the novel, enters a marginal space by going to the mission school, and the whole dilemma he dramatises centres on his occupation of that space. Although the novel's outcome is ambivalent in this respect, Njoroge's marginal position contains unrealised and dynamic potential. The text valorises this potential as the source of Njoroge's transformative fantasies, and maintains an adequate distance to suggest their naivety.

Also, the city might be cited as another, though much more complex, example of marginal space in the way that it draws the young men to it. (It also draws young women to it but with unambivalent outcomes – they are corrupted into some form of prostitution.) Its attraction is described as 'the call of the city', suggesting a mysterious and unknowable compulsion, which transforms the young men into intractable contestants against the colonial order.

On the other hand, the children of the black women who have sexual relations with the Italian prisoners-of-war are rejected as grotesque and degenerate. The children are described as not ' "white" ' in the 'usual' way. They are not black in any way at all, and ' "white" ' only in the degenerate fashion suggested below:

> They were ugly and some grew up to have small wounds all over the body and especially around the mouth so that flies followed them all the time and at all places. Some people said that this was a punishment. Black people should not sleep with white men who ruled them and treated them badly.[3]

'Black people' in the above refers to women, of course, for later the barber talks of African men having sex with European women during their travels in the service of the imperial army. In the men's case the experience is treated as a traveller's tale of daring and exotic knowledge, given extra relish in that it describes the conquest of the oppressor's women, but in this description of the men's sexual relations with Europeans there is no outrage. When asked what the European women were like, the barber says 'Not different' (*Weep Not, Child*, p. 9). They were thin, and they took money, and were disappointing despite the initial attraction of being European – 'Who could believe that a white woman like Mrs Howlands could make herself cheap enough to go with black men for money?' (p. 11) – but there is no suggestion that the men deserve 'punishment' for seeking such women out.

What the barber and his listeners comment on is that white women for all their grandness will still sleep with black men, a response which implies both self-contempt and deference, the triumph of the discourse of conquest. The black women having babies which are not ' "white" in the usual way', on the other hand, offends a deeper sense of what is moral and clean. Underlying it is the assumption that for women sex is equivalent to submission, which is itself the bedrock of patriarchal authority. The 'white' oppressor is indistinct and undifferentiated in this case, different and same: Italian or English, prisoner or settler. And since it was 'the whites' who brought calamity on the people, for African women to submit to them is abject.

The 'calamity which has befallen the people' forms the landscape of Ngũgĩ's fiction. It is a characteristically bleak landscape – a dystopia –

rendered in metaphors of varying complexity but linked, as was suggested earlier, to the loss of the land. These dystopic metaphors range from crises within individuals, conflicts in social relations and relations within families, to a figuration of the land itself as demoralised and enveloped in gloom. In *Weep Not, Child*, the crisis for Ngotho, Njoroge's father, arises from his landlessness, which leads to loss of esteem for himself as an individual as well as for the generation which had 'done nothing' while the land was taken away. 'A man who went with tattered clothes but had at least an acre of red earth was better off than the man with money' (p. 19). The subsequent desire of his son Boro to 'kill the whites', rendered in disturbingly amoral terms in the conversation with his lieutenant, expresses the disruption that has taken place among the people. Boro and his brother Mwangi had both gone to fight in the imperial armies during the 1939–45 war. Mwangi had been killed, and Boro had returned to unemployment and bitterness, before 'the call of the city' politicised him. In the conversation referred to, the lieutenant asks:

> 'But don't you think there's something wrong in fighting and killing unless you're doing so for a great cause like ours?'
> 'What great cause is ours?'
> 'Why, Freedom and the return of our lost heritage.'
> 'Maybe there's something in that. But for me freedom is meaningless unless it can bring back a brother I lost. Because it can't do that, the only thing left to me is to fight, to kill and rejoice at any who falls under my sword.' (pp. 102–3)

The despair suggested by Boro's words here is reiterated in the recurring references to 'the sun going down' and the growing 'darkness in the land', references which increase in frequency as the fighting escalates. The bleak image of the landscape figures the decline of the community, a loss initiated by the rupture of its 'wholeness'. In *Matigari*, Ngũgĩ's latest novel, where a similar analogy is employed, 'the land is cloaked in fog' and is oppressively and inexplicably hot.[4] These images of a demoralised land prefigure Matigari's discovery that the settler, Settler Williams, is still in occupation, abetted in this neocolonial era by the comprador African John Boy Junior. In an important sense, Matigari's sensitivity to the land legitimises his connection to it, as it does for Ngotho's claim to the farm which 'belongs' to the European settler Howlands. Both express this affiliation beyond their individual claims, and refer to a collective and mystical ownership which is above dispute.

Ngũgĩ's fiction uses the substance and symbols of Gikuyu creation myth repeatedly, and does so with ceremony and solemnity. The creation myth reiterates and legitimises the claim to ownership. In the early novels, *Weep Not, Child* (1964) and *The River Between* (1965), the recounting of the myth of Gikuyu and Mumbi is a kind of initiation for Njoroge and Waiyaki respectively, a metaphorical handing over of the deeds of the land. 'This land I hand over to you . . . It is yours to rule and till in serenity' (*Weep Not, Child*, p. 24). In *The River Between*, Chege takes his son Waiyaki to the shrine at the top of the hill and, standing under the sacred Mugumo tree, he solemnly describes how the first ancestors, Mumbi and Gikuyu, were granted the land: '[God] gave the country to them and their children, and the children of their children.'[5] The land was not just a gift, of course, but a 'covenant'. In return Mumbi and Gikuyu were to 'hold' the land and sacrifice only to Murungu. It was a failure to keep vigilant to this covenant which brought 'the white man' and cataclysmic rupture, as foretold by the outcast seer Mugo wa Kibiro. (In addition to being an 'initiation', the ceremony at the top of the hill is also to tell Waiyaki that he is in a direct blood-line from Mugo wa Kibiro, and to lay on him the task of fulfilling the seer's prophecy of a descendant who would come to lead the people out of captivity. The redeemer who would transform captivity into fulfilment is a familiar ruse in Ngũgĩ's fiction, as we shall see later.)

Ironically, the European settler figure, Howlands, in *Weep Not, Child* also has a mystical attachment to the land. In his case, the mysticism is informed by the hard-edged narrative of imperialism, the taming of empty and disorderly lands: 'Here was a big trace of wild country to conquer' (p. 30). Whereas for Ngotho the land is his 'heritage' and its loss the source of profound alienation, for Howlands it is an expression of his resourcefulness and virility. Howlands's greedy pleasure in the land is privileged over all his other relationships, with his wife, his children, the settler community, England. His avarice for its possession has replaced all other affections. The irony of this shared, though contrasted, attachment is further intensified in the way Howlands is unaware of Ngotho's true ownership, and misreads his loving nurture of the farm.

Howlands is, of course, figured critically, especially in the later parts of the novel when he becomes the sadistic District Officer who tortures Njoroge and Ngotho, the latter almost to the point of death. The critical traces are there from the start, in the description we are given of him. The description pointedly insists that his appearance is representative: 'Mr Howlands was tall, heavily built with an oval-shaped face that ended in a double chin and a big stomach. In physical appearance at least, he was a typical Kenya settler' (p. 30). The representation here suggests intimidating size and greed, a grossness of morphology indicative of the inner state. His ferocity not only commands obedience but silence around him, even from his own family. It is, significantly, only at Siriana High School that Howlands's son and Njoroge can talk. This is the marginal space between the two cultures, where the hierarchical system remains intact but where the Africans acquire the right to renegotiate their relationship by accepting their subjecthood to colonial knowledge. Despite such ambivalence the school is a space of dynamic possibility for Njoroge, who valorises colonial education for its transformative potential with the same zeal as Waiyaki does in *The River Between*. Siriana, for example, is described as: 'an adobe [sic] of peace in a turbulent land' (*Weep Not, Child*, p. 108). It is also suggested here for the first time, although of course it had already been apparent by implication for a while, that Njoroge's vision is escapist: 'He did not know that this faith in the future could be a form of escape from the reality of the present' (p. 111). Siriana, which 'seemed a little paradise' (p. 115), is soon to be followed by the hell of the interrogation room. The climax of Howlands's desire for possession is suggested by the threat to castrate Njoroge with a pair of pliers during the interrogation, looking to deprive the younger generation of 'manhood' as he had deprived Ngotho's. Howlands had castrated Ngotho (taking his 'manhood' away with the land, defeating him in every 'essence'), and now he seeks to perform the same act on Njoroge in order to take full possession of the future as well as the present.

There are a number of elements in this representation of Europeans as demons: their eyes redden in moments of anger, marking their excessive anger and cruelty, and their 'unnatural' appearance; their voices are cold; the wives are bored and beat the servants, perhaps as a result of perverted or jaded appetites; they take sadistic pleasure in inflicting excessive pain – 'they laughed derisively' as Njoroge passed out (p. 118). In the end Howlands confirms his position as the ruthless imperialist by playing out the slave-plantation-owner role to the full: authoritarian, sadistic, and then he 'takes' black women for relief. Not only do these strategies turn the Europeans into monsters, but they casually reduce the tragedies of the Howlands family to a melodramatic farce. 'The daughter had turned missionary after Peter's death' (p. 31). The description allows us to dismiss both events as of only minor account, more so since we are doubtful of the full humanity of the subjects.

By the appearance of *Devil on the Cross* (published in English in 1982, but appearing first in Gikuyu in 1980) the representation of Europeans has hardened considerably: 'Even the hair on their arms and necks stood out stiff and straight like the bristles of an ageing hog' (p. 91). Here too the European is physically marked by excess and greed, but the hint of brutishness in the earlier description has now become grotesque, a transformation apparent also in the intensification of the cynical self-awareness with which they are consistently characterised.

Where Europeans are figured as capable of human warmth, it is to show how inevitably they decline to cynicism and authoritarianism. The decline suggested here ironically reprises another enduring trope of the imperialist narrative, that however liberal the European is when he sets out, Africa (or it could be Asia or anywhere else where 'the silent sullen peoples' are found) will require that he or she act with greater sternness. In the imperialist narrative this is both a comment on the African's unknowability (indolent, infantile, strange) and also a comment on the nature of empire (austere, lonely, an unrewardable burden). The 'anti-imperialist' argument of Conrad's *Heart of Darkness* (1899) is a critical elaboration of this, for as 'the wilderness' finds Kurtz out, it turns him into a greedy and sadistic monster, and exposes to him the only possible relationship the European can have with the native. The Thompson figure in *A Grain of Wheat*, like Kurtz a man who apparently had started out with liberal sympathies, echoes Kurtz's 'Exterminate the brutes' with his own 'Eliminate the vermin', in both cases an expression of the European's descent into barbarism.[6]

These representations affirm Europeans as a malady, sickening and declining in an environment which rejects them and is hostile to them.

Above all, they naturalise the African and figure the European as unnatural in that land, not simply by right of prior occupation but in 'essence'.

The tendency to treat complexity as if it had 'manageable parts' is often present in Ngũgĩ's fiction, growing more pronounced in the later novels. By particularising the parts, transformative strategies can be undertaken. In the example we have been discussing, the figures of the landless African and the heartless European describe both the problem and the transformative potential. The return of the 'lost heritage' would also be a return to plenitude.

In this respect, the fiction of competing languages, at its best in *A Grain of Wheat*, changes over six novels to one of a privileged voice. The growing dominance of the patriarchal figure is allied to and complements this change, implying the roots of the 'heritage' and therefore the source of authority. In the early fiction, the figure of the father arouses an unnamed fear, which is also an aspect of his aura. 'Njoroge feared his father. But it always made him feel good to listen to him' (*Weep Not, Child*, p. 23). In *The River Between* we find: 'Waiyaki kept quiet. He was never at ease in front of his father' (p. 10); and 'Waiyaki entered very quietly, because he was always uneasy in the presence of his father' (p. 16). The family of Ngotho, though polygamous and likely (by implication in the text) to be unstable, holds together because of the patriarch's particular qualities of tolerance: 'The feeling of oneness was a thing that most distinguished Ngotho's household from many other polygamous families . . . This was attributable to Ngotho, the centre of the home' (*Weep Not, Child*, p. 40). Later Ngotho refuses to take the Mau Mau oath because of the impropriety of having it administered to him by his son (p. 74).

Howlands too feared and revered his father, in precisely the same representational terms as Waiyaki and, more pronouncedly, Njoroge: 'The little quarrels he had had; the father whom he had feared and revered; the gentle mother in whose arms he could always find solace – all these at times assaulted his memory, especially in these troubled times' (p. 76). His final thoughts, just before his murder by Boro, are recollections of a youthful vision prompted by a sight of Njoroge's eyes:

> He did not know what had happened to him since he saw something in the eyes of Ngotho's son. He had remembered himself as a boy, that day

so long ago when he had sat outside his parents' home and dreamt of a world that needed him, only to be brought face to face with the harsh reality of life in the First World War. (p. 127)

The idealisation of youthful vision is also testimony to the mysterious potency of the father. Njoroge and Waiyaki are ceremonially given the task of carrying on the obligations of the father. 'Njoroge listened to his father. He instinctively knew that an indefinable demand was being made on him' (*Weep Not, Child*, p. 39). In Waiyaki's case, as we saw earlier, his father shows him the extent of the lands Murungu had given to Mumbi and Gikuyu, and also tells him of the prophecy of the leader who would come to save the people: 'Arise. Heed the prophecy . . . Be true to your people and the ancient rites' (*The River Between*, p. 24). Not surprisingly, both Njoroge and Waiyaki have a vision of themselves as chosen to fulfil a task. Waiyaki in *The River Between* is described in this way: 'Waiyaki was made to serve the tribe, living day by day with no thoughts of self but always of others. He had now for many seasons been trying to drain himself dry, for the people' (p. 85). Mugo too, in *A Grain of Wheat*, though without a living father to lay the burden on him, nonetheless recognises himself as chosen: 'He, an only son, was born to save' (p. 118). That the burden is seen in these indefinable terms enhances its mysterious authority and also confirms that it is not a matter the individual can renegotiate. The patriarch has the right to make these demands for the same mysterious reasons. It is only in *Matigari* that the authority of the visionary figure derives from past individual action. Matigari had been a fighter in the forest and now gathers a following because his words carry conviction but also because his individual history gives him authority. But he expresses this authority in patriarchal terms. He is acknowledged as father and husband by the boy and the young woman he redeems from ruin, two figures which in the allegorical structure of the novel represent youth and woman.

Matigari is also different from Waiyaki, Njoroge and Mugo in that he is able to articulate his vision (as is Mūturi in *Devil on the Cross* and, in a more ambivalent way, Kihika in *A Grain of Wheat*). In the earlier fiction, *vision* is unstable, ground for hubris or madness. The fullness of vision, and the burden of selection, are only articulated in solitary reflection, 'walking alone in the fields' and 'finding companionship with the nights'.

The heroic privileged voice of the visionary in the later fiction is handled with suspicion in the earlier novels, where the telling of stories, recounted by both mothers and fathers, is a more potent expression of the communal vision. Njoroge is deeply distressed when he is asked to tell a story in class and freezes, for he has begun to grasp that the stories are the 'heritage' of the people (p. 17). Also his brother Boro, 'who had been to the war', did not know stories. Boro has lost his affiliation to the ways of his father's generation, has lost wholeness and completeness. This alienation is expressed not only in his lack of stories, but in his drunkenness and resentment, and finally in choosing to fight in the forest for the expulsion of the European settlers (p. 21). If Boro's bitterness has a histrionic quality, it is because this is part of the ambivalence about the portrayal of the heroic voice. The suspicion of the fanatically heroic fighter begins to diminish after *The Trial of Dedan Kimathi* (1976),[7] but in both *Weep Not, Child* and *A Grain of Wheat*, Boro and Kihika are shown with some ambivalence. In the former, we are told: 'Njoroge thought Boro was mad' (p. 70). In *A Grain of Wheat*, Mugo too describes Kihika as mad: 'Each word confirmed Mugo's suspicion that the man was mad . . . Kihika was mad, mad' (pp. 166–7). When we discover that the substance of Boro's 'philosophy' turns out to be: 'Unless you kill, you'll be killed' (p. 102), then it is clear that he is to be taken critically. The intensity of Kihika's self-conviction is also so like hubris that Mugo's horror at the potential of his fanaticism is unsurprising.

Both the voice and the imaging of the fiction harden in the later novels. The mode of the early novels is tentative and self-doubting; its effect is to reflect not so much an uncertainty of tone or method (though it may well be both at times) but an aspiration to self-knowledge, a modesty about motivations and ends which is dynamic because it acknowledges the potentialities of this reflection. In *Devil on the Cross* the voice is confident and worldly, and the frequent appeal to proverbs and a stylised language of thought asserts a consensual wisdom which the voice is party to. Clearly the voice aspires to speak as if from inside its proposed audience, albeit that its tone is firm and hectoring. The privilege the voice is accorded here, and more especially in *Matigari*, does not invite negotiation or dialogue. It has assumed the trappings of patriarchal authority, setting out the obligations of the people.

The dominance of the patriarchy in the fiction is most evident, predictably enough, in the way women are figured. When Waiyaki receives from his father the 'heritage' of Gikuyu and Mumbi, he also learns how women have fallen:

> Long ago women used to rule this land and its men. They were harsh and men began to resent their hard hand. So when all the women were pregnant, men came together and overthrew them. Before this, women owned everything. The animal you saw was their goat. But because the women could not manage them, the goats ran away. They knew women to be weak. So why should they fear them? (*The River Between*, p. 18)

In this figuration, women are both capriciously cruel and weak, and require to be kept under firm control. It is significant that pregnancy is the condition of their greatest vulnerability, and it is this condition, or the fear of it, which more often than not exposes the moment of crisis for women in the fiction. Their inability to resist granting men access to their bodies brings about their first crisis.

Kareendi's story in *Devil on the Cross* is told as a parable of exploitation. She is a mythical victim of sexual oppression. Here, very briefly, is her story. Kareendi becomes pregnant while still at school. Her lover might have been a fellow student, a village 'loafer' with a job in the city, or a rich man. Whoever it is he refuses to accept responsibility: 'Kareendi of the easy thighs, ten cent Kareendi . . . you can't collect pregnancies wherever you may and then lay them at my door just because one day I happened to tease you' (p. 18). Kareendi has the child and leaves it with her grandmother. Through enormous sacrifice she completes her education and trains as a secretary. In her search for a job, she is forced to reject a string of predatory bosses until eventually she does find a job where she does not also 'have to make a bed'. At about the same time she also meets a new lover to whom she devotes herself and all her earnings. One day the boss does make his unsurprising demand, which Kareendi resolutely rejects and is fired. When she tells her lover how she lost her job, instead of sympathy he accuses her of being 'Kareendi of easy thighs' and rejects her. The only prospect ahead of her, it is firmly implied, is becoming a prostitute.

'What will prevent Kareendi from walking the streets' (p. 25). 'For the day on which they [Kareendis] are born is the very day on which every part of their body is buried except one – they are left with a single organ' (p. 26).

Her experience, or a variation of it, also befalls Warĩĩnga in *Devil on the Cross*, Mumbi in *A Grain of Wheat*, Wanja in *Petals of Blood* (1977), Gũthera in *Matigari* and so on. All these women grant access to their bodies out of confused motives and are disgraced. Indeed the Kareendi story is constructed as a resonant prelude to stories of other women whose oppression comes about through their need to fulfil naive desires. The misuse of women is, of course, posed as criticism of men – particularly rich or treacherous men – but women's consistent inability to resist this misuse expresses their weakness. It becomes a precondition of their later redemption to a more 'committed' stance that they first suffer such squalid failures.

If women's most dramatic failure is often figured as their inability to avoid the consequences of bad sex, their weakness is also expressed in other ways. Mwihaki, the central girl-child figure in *Weep Not, Child*, is not only distanced from the turmoil of the village but is actually unable to grasp crucial and primary distinctions on the matter which lies at the heart of the conflict – land ownership. She is moved by the 'dumb consolation' Njoroge had offered her when they were children, but 'the declaration of the emergency had not meant much to her' (p. 89) – never mind that her father is the leader of the Home Guard, and is daily involved in arrests, tortures and killings. In the conversation she has with Njoroge soon after this we see her whimpering and whining about a teacher's predictions of the world's end, while Njoroge 'indulgently' reassures her that they were safe for a few more years yet (p. 93). In the same novel, Mwihaki's father Jacobo is not only the figure of the traitor, but a man who takes the advice of his wife, and lives long enough to regret it. Both Ngotho and Howlands specifically reject the advice of their wives. If this portrayal changes in the later fiction, it is because the later women have been 'politicised' by their errors.

We saw earlier that Ngũgĩ's method is increasingly to treat complexity as if it had 'manageable parts', and by particularising these to suggest transformative strategies. The 'role of women' is one such part, as is the location of both the rupture and the originary plenitude in mysticism about land. In *Devil on the Cross* and *Matigari*, the latest novels, this method finds form in the set-piece allegory. In *Devil on the Cross*, the bus represents the state and the passengers are obviously representative figures whose stories reveal the oppressions under which the nation lives. Jameson's argument that Third World writing functions as national allegory – 'where the telling of the individual story . . . cannot but ultimately involve the whole laborious telling of the experience of the collectivity itself' – an argument hard to justify beyond a handful of examples similar to those Jameson chose to discuss in his article, receives full vindication here.[8]

Mūturi, the man in blue overalls, turns out to be a worker, a former Mau Mau, and now secretly working to end 'neocolonialism'. Wangarī, who had boarded the bus without paying, begins another version of oppressed womanhood. (Mūturi pays her fare when she is threatened with eviction, instinctively recognising her integrity and, incidentally, confirming that he is a man of compassion.) It turns out that Wangarī had 'worked for the land', carrying guns to the fighters in the forest. The loss of her farm and her arrest describe the complicity of the police with neocolonial capital (p. 43). Warīīnga is the more familiar representation of women in the fiction, the Kareendi figure: made pregnant while still at school by a rich old man, pursued by her boss, rejected by her lover. She does not pay attention while the crucial discussion about political choices takes place on the bus, distracted by the events which have brought her here – her seductions.

Another passenger is Gatuīria, a young man with a suitcase and a book. He turns out to be an academic – hence the book – unable to prevent himself from speaking a mixture of Gikuyu and English (rather than just Gikuyu). He is also the African artist in the process of rediscovering his Africanness, which the others had never lost (p. 58). The extent of his alienation becomes clear when we discover that he had spent 15 years out of the country – hence the suitcase – studying European music before he returned to write music that will express something of his own culture. He idealises the desire for national unity in a metaphor of a many-voiced 'voice', 'bringing together the many different peoples of Kenya'. He falls in love with Warīīnga, but it turns out later that he is the estranged son of the rich man who had seduced Warīīnga while she was a schoolgirl.

The man in dark glasses, Mwīreri was Mūkiraaī, is a businessman – in this context a composite representative of neocolonial capital and the complicit comprador élite. His furtive and frightened manner implies his guilt, but after he loses his apprehensions he speaks the 'neocolonial' ethos he is there to represent. Finally there is the owner/driver of the bus, a man for whom duplicity is a guiding principle (p. 50), and who before the end of the novel murders Mwĩreri wa Mũkiraaĩ for money. The debate the driver and Mũturi engage in during the journey constructs a didactic discourse on the choices available to the people. The explanation of how 'workers' are oppressed through 'ideology' and socialisation is made crushingly explicit. By the end of the novel, the debate is resolved in these terms: 'And there is only one cure: a strong organisation of the workers and peasants of the land, together with those whose eyes and ears are now open and alert' (p. 205).

The set-piece allegorisation here, and later in *Matigari*, has a declamatory project which announces itself unmistakably. The peasant/worker with his/her regalia (in the case of Mũturi a boiler suit and history of political involvement, in the case of Matigari a gun buried under a Mugumo tree) is the upright hero. The woman Wangarĩ is also of this breed, fierce and committed, with the aggressively defiant language of 'the patriot'. Warĩĩnga, who is more typical of the naive and distracted configuration of woman, is later also transformed into 'a patriot' (p. 132). The same transformation befalls Gũthera in *Matigari*, under the protective tutelage of Matigari. Both Warĩĩnga and Gũthera adopt the aggressive language of 'the patriot' after their redemption.

'The patriot' more often than not is given macho trappings: aggressive language, blind courage, weapons which in the end have to be used despite the moral reluctance to do so, and a vision of 'self-reliance' which is unwilling to be discouraged by 'pragmatic' caution (p. 219). There is also a firm connection between patriots and patriarchs. It is to the patriarchs that patriotic feelings come most naturally. This is more clearly expressed in *Matigari* than in *Devil on the Cross*, but it is present in the latter too. The earlier 'heritage' expressed with some ambivalence in *Weep Not, Child* as the desire for restitution of the stolen lands and thus a return to the time before the rupture, now appears quite bluntly as 'the heritage of our founding patriarchs and patriots' (*Devil on the Cross*, p. 197).

For women like Warĩĩnga and Gũthera, deliverance into 'the patriot' state arrives as a mystical experience, a sudden burst of irresistible knowledge under the agency of an appropriate man.[9] In the case of Gūthera, we have already observed, it is Matigari who enables it. For Warīīnga, a voice overwhelms her on the golf course:

> Warīīnga was afraid. She tried to stand up, but she felt tied to the ground and to the tree by invisible wires of fatigue. She gave up the attempt. And suddenly she felt herself completely free of fear, and she said to herself: Come what may, I'm going to stop running away from life's struggles. (p. 184)

She later recognises the voice as belonging to a radical student who is already 'a patriot'.

If 'the patriot' is valorised in this way in *Devil on the Cross* and *Matigari*, 'the traitor' is figured as a stark antithesis. By contrast, the 'traitor' Karanja in *A Grain of Wheat* is given room to agonise over his treachery, and by the small acts of generosity he performs, some uncertainty in the judgement he invites is suggested. He protests to Mumbi, the woman he had always desired and whom he had once asked to be his wife:

> 'Take this maize flour and bread, or else you will die. I did not betray Kihika, I did not. As for carrying the gun for the whiteman, well, a time will come when you too will know that every man in the world is alone, and fights alone, to live.' (p. 146)

His position is rejected, of course. It was always going to be. What befalls him is to be seen as an example – the self-seeking opportunist who betrays the interests of the community will always end up alone and alien, rejected by his own people and rejected by their oppressor. A sense of community strengthens the individual, aloneness diminishes him or her, because it takes away the context in which actions have meaning. But by allowing the Karanja-position to offer a kind of defence, this becomes a means of contrasting more tellingly the network of obligations between individual and community. The 'defence' is thus not only a means of probing the motivation behind such actions, but a narrative technique of exposure.

One of the ways fiction convinces is by suggesting that behind the surface lies an imaginatively more complex world which its construction in the narrative approaches but does not quite convey. Thus the narrative is able to hint at and release what it is not possible to reveal fully, and to liberate the reader into seeing affiliated networks of knowledge and meaning. In these later fictions of Ngũgĩ such possibilities are absent. The strategies which transform Ngũgĩ's narratives into national allegories also work against such liberating potential. The novels are excessively indicative. They lean too obviously on an inflexibly allegorical method, and construct a polemic which is bluntly authoritarian: listen and obey. Also, because their analyses of social problems are dramatised as unproblematic, their protagonists are merely the grim-jawed figures of the poster or comic strip. The blunt method and its instrumental ends produce artefacts which intimidate with their self-righteousness, and provoke resistance to such heavy-handed persuasion.

## Notes

1. Ngũgĩ wa Thiong'o, *Devil on the Cross*, Heinemann: London, 1982, p. 128. First published in Gikuyu by Heinemann Educational Books (East Africa), 1980. The verse quoted here is spoken by Warĩĩnga as part of 'an incantation' of outrage against the nation's oppression.

2. For more detailed discussion of 'the nation' see, for example: Benedict Anderson, *Imagined Communities: Reflections on the Origins and Spread of Nationalism*, London: NLB, 1983; and *Nation and Narration*, ed. Homi K. Bhabha, London: Routledge, 1990.

3. Ngũgĩ wa Thiong'o, *Weep Not, Child*, London: Heinemann, 1964, p. 6. 'Some people' might suggest that this is a received opinion from an extreme point of view, but the children's description in the narrative is unambiguous.

4. Ngũgĩ wa Thiong'o, *Matigari*, London: Heinemann, 1989. First published in Gikuyu by Heinemann Kenya Ltd, 1987. The English translation is by Wangui wa Goro. For a discussion of the sources of *Matigari* and the problems which arise out of its translation from Gikuyu see Simon Gikandi, 'The Epistemology of Translation: Ngũgĩ, *Matigari*, and the Politics of Language', *Research in African Literatures*, Vol. 22, No. 4 (Winter 1991), pp. 161–8.

5. Ngũgĩ wa Thiong'o, *The River Between*, London: Heinemann, 1965, p. 19.

6. Ngũgĩ wa Thiong'o, *A Grain of Wheat*, London: Heinemann, 1967.

7. Ngũgĩ wa Thiong'o and Micere Githae Mugo, *The Trial of Dedan Kimathi*,

London: Heinemann, 1976. In their Preface the two playwrights describe how determined they were to write of Kimathi's 'heroic deeds of resistance', and how their research for the play educated them about 'the continuing struggle against oppression'. The play marks the point in Ngũgĩ's writing where discussion of choices between political actions becomes overt and direct, and introduces the aggressive agit-prop which has become characteristic of the later writing.

8. Frederic Jameson, 'Third World Literature in the Era of Multinational Capitalism', *Social Text*, Fall 1986, pp. 85–6.

9. For a more detailed discussion of Ngũgĩ's representation of women 'patriots', see Elleke Boehmer, 'The Master's Dance to the Master's Voice: Revolutionary Nationalism and the Representation of Women in the Writing of Ngũgĩ wa Thiong'o', *Journal of Commonwealth Literature*, Vol. XXVI, No. 1, 1991, pp. 188–97.

# Wole Soyinka and the Federal Road Safety Commission

## GABRIEL GBADAMOSI

Even when it is conceded that a nation is not merely what it is at a given moment but in its entire potential, a danger remains for all who sometimes wonder, as I often do, if the nation they know is not simply one of their imagining.[1]

When Wole Soyinka was awarded the 1986 Nobel Prize for literature, the Swedish Academy's citation described him as a writer who 'fashions the drama of existence'. Reporting the award, a British newspaper, *The Times*, put its own gloss on Soyinka's achievement, describing him as the first African and first black to have received it, and as a writer obsessed 'by his tragic vision of his native land'.[2] What these plaudits fail to address are the genuinely unique and distinct features of this work. Soyinka *does* have a 'tragic vision', but not a western one; he *is* fashioning a 'drama of existence', but an African one. How many have taken these claims seriously? He has a vision of the roads in Nigeria, as they criss-cross its tropical rain-forests in the south and sub-Saharan desert in the north, as sites of a new drama of existence on the African continent. With their plangent, vigorous human and ecomonic life, and their spectacles of road-death, they are metaphors of historical destiny. They are, moreover, the sites of a tragic experience which issues not in the passive acceptance widely diagnosed of western tragedy, but in a recourse to his culture's own 'deepest mythopoeic resources', an act of self-retrieval, a newly articulated African identity.[3] Soyinka has made possible a vibrant African tragic art, notably in his play *The Road*, which serves as a key to much of his work, and this is rooted in an engagement with the upheavals in Africa of the postcolonial period.

Less well known about Soyinka is his presidency of the Nigerian Federal Road Safety Commission. In *The Road*, Soyinka has, with a touch of self-parody, created a character known as the Professor, who presides rather magisterially over the 'AKSIDENT STORE'. The world of the play, with its 'motor park' passenger touts, drivers and drifting unemployed, is recognisably Soyinka's native Nigeria – a teeming, chaotic, inescapably hybrid, post-Independence West African state. Re-created in an accident junk-yard, it has spawned an eclectic, scavenger culture in which there are – a continuation of the 'aksident store' sign – 'ALL PART AVAILEBUL'. Shifting the debris of this semi-mechanised monster is the inscrutable figure of the Professor, in his messianic search for an elusive 'Word'.

The Nigerian critic, Biodun Jeyifo, has commented on the play's portrayal of 'the adaptive anarchy of our neocolonial peripheral capitalist society'.[4] Both Jeyifo and Soyinka are part of a generation of Nigerians who came of age in and around the time of Independence in 1960, and took upon themselves the task of interrogating the new state. The tone they take is often one of scourging irony. Figured and parodied in the person of the Professor, theirs is the interrogation of a monster – recalling the casting out of unclean spirits by Christ into the Gadarene swine (St Mark 5:9) – one whose name is *Legion*, incorrigibly plural:

> PROFESSOR: Come out of there. I can see you. How many of you are there? Come out come out. You may be the devil's own army but my arm is powered with the unbroken Word![5]

Among the many voices and tones that Soyinka adopts there runs a subtle thread of the messianic, whether coupled with parody as in *The Jero Plays*, or satire as in *Madmen and Specialists* and *Kongi's Harvest*. It is also present in those plays which enact a logic of ritual sacrifice, in the lyrically intense *Death and the King's Horseman* and the violent foreboding of *The Strong Breed*. In *The Road*, it is one of many ways of voicing the crises of an emergent nation state. The potential dangers of that messianic strain are clearly wrestled with, and ironised, in the figure of the Professor.

It is difficult to make out the Professor's many-sided, authoritarian character. Although a presiding oracular presence within the play, his pronouncements obscure rather than clarify what is happening. They are borrowed idioms, ranging from the portentous hints of dire biblical warning to a sly legalese. His language is riddled with the eclectic, half-digested scraps of disparate information he might be expected to pick up in his rubbish trawl for the 'Word'. So, too, in the genesis of his character, he comes across as a patchwork of different cultural influences. In the stiff dignity of his Victorian top-hat and threadbare, shiny lapels, a chair-stick hanging at his elbow and bundles of old newspaper under his arm, he is traceable to the tramp figures of Samuel Beckett's *Waiting for Godot* – a cast-off, a pathetic vessel for the detritus of human community. As a version of the White Man – *Oyinbo* – he belongs to the satirical stock characters in the *onidan*, a dramatic version of the Yoruba *egungun* masquerades. For the speakers of tonal Yoruba, who include Soyinka, this character speaks unintelligibly through his nose.[6] However, neither the Professor as a character nor his meanings seem quite yet formed, strewn as they are between different cultural idioms. Fragmentary, incomplete, he seems a contingent figure, waiting for something to happen. Yet his vatic certainty, a visionary blindness, makes him a brooding presence that stands across our apprehension of what is emerging from the play's tensions.

The Professor first enters clutching a road sign with the word 'BEND', which he claims to have found growing miraculously from the road, and plucked. Only later do we hear of a spot where a car went off at a bend, smashing into a tree:

> PROFESSOR: Gbram! And showers of crystal flying on broken souls . . .
> Oh there was such an angry buzz but the matter was beyond repair.
> They died, all three of them crucified on rigid branches. I found this
> word growing where their blood had spread . . . (p. 159)

In coupling a Christian image of crucifixion with death on the road, Soyinka melds them in the presence, and figured absence, of a word, 'BEND', a contingent version of the 'Word'. This word is both present on stage and absent at the site of the crash. It is the beginning of the kind of wordplay that is a fascinating linguistic – and visual – substructure in *The Road*, issuing in the multiple, stunning image pile-ups, mirages and sign-post miracles which shimmer on its surface. Whether a reason for the crash is that the sign was absent, or was perhaps obscured by a mirage (whether, in fact, the absent-minded Professor plucked the sign before or after the crash), there remains a shimmering doubt about causality. Next to it, in the moral spectacle of the Passion, the crucifixion and death of the incarnate Word, is the question, Why? How do we explain these senseless deaths?

In engaging with the underworld of road culture among Nigeria's rootless, makeshift populations and sprawling shanty-towns, Soyinka conjures a notorious paradigm of indiscipline and chaos in the society. More than this, his play is scattered with images of many different road-deaths such as the one above. In the wreckage of fatal accidents left to rust along the arterial roads of Nigerian life, a further significance becomes balefully clear. What the Professor obscures in the play is death, a modern Nigerian one, on the road. What he presides over is an 'aksident store' which, with the ghoulish dynamism of Nigerians, cannibalises the wreckage of those accidents to create the dented *molue* and battered *bolekaja* mammy wagons still coughing fumes into a collapsed infrastructure. Soyinka explores, in those attitudes to death by which a society glimpses itself, a traumatic self-image forming out of the collision of disparate influences.

The question for a dramatist is first of all how these complex image and wordplays begin to meld with a visual, dramatic language. In *The Road*, Soyinka's use of a Yoruba mask-idiom forges from a fragmented consciousness of the meanings of death a newly vibrant, ironic art. In Yoruba, the word *oro* literally means *the word*, but is also the spirit of death which 'flows' along the road.[7] *Oro* is, furthermore, the presiding spirit of the Agemo cult in Soyinka's native Ijebuland, and the Agemo masked dance is used in the play to enact, as Soyinka puts it in a note for the producer, 'the movement of transition . . . a visual suspension of death'. He goes on in the note to describe Murano, the character in the play who is possessed by the Agemo spirit (and is, ironically, both lame and mute), as a dramatic embodiment of this suspension: 'He functions as an arrest of time, or death, since it was in his 'agemo' phase that the lorry knocked him down' (*The Road*, Author's note for the Producer, p. 149). To use a crippled mute, knocked down by a lorry, as a visual suspension of death is a bold, polemical stroke. The deformation of the Agemo masked dance is to be imagined. But to erect a metaphysics of the 'Word' around the mute victim, is, to say the least, ironic. As described by the Professor, Murano has a foot in each world: one in this world, on the road, and one resting 'on the slumbering chrysalis of the

Word. When that crust cracks . . . that is the moment we await' (p. 187).

Murano and the paraplegic dance of the Agemo are only one strand in this visual suspension of time, or death. So, too is the 'Victorian' figure of the Professor. It should be noted that 'an arrest of time' is also an arrest of causality. This is something we meet throughout the work of Soyinka, part of his technical tool-box. As seen with the 'BEND' road-sign and its related crash, images and events are decoupled from their immediate causes and relocated, in a pause of reason, as spectacles of wonder and inexplicable road-death. Even the explicit images of death in the play are contingent, visual suspensions concealing some further dynamic. In the resumption of reasoning that follows can be found what Soyinka calls, above, 'the movement of transition'.

This can be seen most clearly in the case of the traumatised driver Kotonu, who has seen one too many accidents to be able to drive again, and his despairingly loyal tout, Samson. For them, separate past events are wrested out of their time frames, merged and re-enacted in the forward movement of the action as one continuous, ongoing accident. Half-way through the play, which spans the period of one day, from morning to evening, Kotonu and Samson narrate the death of Kotonu's father at which they were both present. Also a driver, he died when his lorry with its load of stockfish went into his back and broke his spine, leading Kotonu to remark that torn bodies on the road all have the smell of stockfish (p. 190). Meanwhile, bodies from an accident on the bridge are heard being brought in for a mass burial. Although Kotonu and Samson have been more or less continuously on stage – and off the road – since the opening of the play, it seems that they were also present at this accident, the accident-too-many which has put Kotonu off driving. With the sense that this accident has only just happened, our grasp on time as it unfolds in the play is broken. There is then an interval in the play. In the second half, described as happening about an hour later, this fracturing of time is made explicit. It opens with Samson reasoning with Kotonu over what they saw on the build-up to the accident on the bridge, as they were being overtaken on the road by a doomed lorry:

KOTONU: I swear it was what I saw. The lorry was filled with people but there was not one face among them . . .
SAMSON: Because they had rags on their faces. It was only a kola nut

lorry from the North and the rear half was filled with people. The truck was top-heavy as always. And they had cloth on their faces to keep out the dust.

KOTONU: Oh yes the dust. The wraith of dust which pursued them.

SAMSON: There you are, you admit it – the dust. How could you see anything for dust? Only vague shapes . . .

KOTONU: But it cleared I tell you. Before my eyes it cleared and I saw I was mistaken. It was an open truck and it carried nothing but stacks and stacks of beheaded fish, and oh God the smell of stockfish! But we caught up with them finally . . . at the broken bridge, and you shouted –

SAMSON: Look out Kotonu! [*A violent screech of brakes.*]

KOTONU: It's all right. I've seen it.

[*They walk forward, skirt an area carefully and peer down a hole in the ground.*] (p. 196)

In the unfolding transitions, from a lorry full of people with no faces, or with rags across their faces, pursued by a wraith of dust, to stacks of beheaded stockfish, Soyinka captures an African animist outlook. These are African eyes, and in the eyes of Kotonu the wraith of dust is alive, just as, earlier, Say Tokyo Kid, the timber lorry driver, describes having to wrestle at the wheel with the spirits of the timber (p. 171). But the vengeful coherence of the wraith is dispersed by Samson's idiomatic rationalisation of not seeing anything for dust. As each of the images is pulled into coherence, there is a fragmentation in the ways of looking. In Samson's holding off, the animist sensibility is scattered among other ways of apprehending the events at the bridge. It is, moreover, a sensibility suspended above terrible possibility: the traumatic realisation that it might have been their lorry, Samson and Kotonu's, which went over the edge. A final shock comes with the sight of stockfish – smelling of torn bodies on the road – in an image of doomed souls thundering towards an abyss. It is an image informed by the fundamentalist Christian revivalism, tinged with animism, of such African versions of Christianity as Nigeria's Aladura Church. At this point, time is telescoped and we are thrown forward into a present suspended above that traumatic event.

In his essay, 'The Fourth Stage' (1973), Soyinka speaks of tragedy as a wrench within the human psyche, returning us to our own sources.[8] The pleading of Samson, on the edge of the broken bridge, for Kotonu to kill them a dog for the god Ogun, marks a decisive shift into a re-integrative metaphysics of transition, beyond the disintegration of the abyss, into what is described by Soyinka as 'the heart of Yoruba tragic art . . . the Mysteries of Ogun':

> Yoruba tragedy plunges straight into the 'chthonic realm', the seething cauldron of the dark world will and psyche, the transitional yet inchoate matrix of death and becoming. Into this universal womb once plunged and emerged Ogun, the first actor, disintegrating within the abyss. (p. 22)

The dense, ironic, rather difficult style of this essay is worth persisting with. In it Soyinka consciously lays out, in contradistinction to Nietzsche's *Birth of Tragedy*, his ideas for an African tragedy drawn from Yoruba cosmology. Taking Dionysos and Apollo, elaborated by Nietzsche as paradigms of destructive and creative potentials in tragic experience, Soyinka considers the Yoruba gods, or *orisas*, and, brushing aside Obatala, tackling Sango, inserts Ogun in the place of Nietzsche's deities. To these qualities in Ogun, he adds those of Prometheus: a constructive defiance, a refusal to despair. Ogun is central to Soyinka, being as he is an ironic over-reacher, who, though brought up as a Christian, has espoused Him as his personal deity.

Ogun is the god of war and of iron. His is a creative–destructive dualism, implicit in his being both iron-worker and warmonger. Both these subsidiary arts are regrouped into the greater art of political protagonist in Soyinka's long poem, *Ogun Abibiman*, the tensed blood and forged conscience of his race yearning for liberation in South Africa:

> In time of strife, none vies with Him
> Of seven paths, Ogun, who to right a wrong
> Emptied reservoirs of blood in heaven
> Yet raged with thirst – I read
> His savage beauty on black brows,
> In depths of molten bronze aflame.[9]

As well as the god of iron, Ogun is god of the roads and the iron that travels them: he is the patron of drivers and their touts. For Soyinka, he represents a vitality in Nigerians – even in their road culture – a 'savage beauty', which is his answer to senseless death, and the central, pessimistic axiom of Nietzsche's tragic sage, Silenius, that it is an act of hubris ever to have been born. For the Yoruba, Soyinka insists, it is no less an act of hubris to die ('The Fourth Stage', p. 32).

This is Soyinka's essentially humanist philosophy, underlying his engagement with the Road Safety Commission as much as with the politics of the new Nigerian state. The incident, for which he was tried and acquitted, of holding up of a radio station to protest at corrupt elections in Nigeria's Western Region in 1965 (the same year as the first production of *The Road*), suggests the tenor of that engagement. It is not a quietist position. Rather, it articulates an optimism for the potential of Africa and Africans to tackle, in their own way, the large questions looming over them in the postcolonial situation.

The use of indigenous categories of thought and being to confront contemporary experience is a lesson that has not been lost on subsequent writers. Ben Okri, in his novel, *The Famished Road*, has taken the Yoruba concept of the *abiku* – a spirit-child in a constant, fated cycle of early death and rebirth – and with it located a Nigerian idea of historical destiny. Like its central character, the spirit-child, Nigeria is itself an *abiku* country which can choose between dying or holding on to stay the course of Independence.[10] In *The Road*, Samson's concluding prayer at the broken bridge is, 'May we never walk when the road waits, famished' (p. 199).

There are, of course, dangers in what may seem like the obscurantism of Soyinka's thought. Much of it was originally generated in opposition to the ideas of Negritude. Coming from the francophone African world, this was a reaction against the integrationist colonial practice of France, and became state ideology in the newly 'independent' Senegal. It proposed a radical separation of black African identity from what it perceived as white European rationalism. As such it was an avowedly irrationalist, intuitive creed, instituting a continuing and widely disseminated aesthetic which Soyinka has elsewhere attacked as 'neo-Tarzanism' in a 'zoo-o-platonic republic'.[11] For Soyinka, it was an irritating, racist, neo-pastoralist fiction of the African's self-involved, passionate, pre-logical existence. (Note that his Ogun is a technocrat, not a pastoralist.) In an early, polemical essay, 'The Future of West African Writing', Soyinka compared Negritude, unfavourably, with an aesthetic based on indifferent self-acceptance of Africanness.[12] It is an early statement of his later dictum that a tiger does not shout its tigritude, it *acts*. However, from his critics on the Left, and sometime allies such as Biodun Jeyifo,[13] his own mythopaeic reformulations of African identity remain open to accusations of being obscure and misleading idealisations of Yoruba thought and historical experience.

In his play, *Madmen and Specialists*, a brutal satire on the Nigeria of the civil war, Soyinka elaborates just such an obscurantist philosophy – the murderous chimera of 'As'. First taking form as a cannibalistic grace over a meal of human flesh: 'As Was the Beginning, As is, Now, As Ever shall be . . .'[14] – a perversion brought on by engagement with the war – it becomes a paean to the worship of power released from any moral compunction. Thought up by the supposedly insane character of the Old Man, Bero's father, 'As' bears some darker resemblance to Soyinka's re-integrative metaphysics of Ogun:

> BERO: Father's assignment was to help the wounded readjust to the pieces and remnants of their bodies. Physically. Teach them to make baskets if they still had fingers. To use their mouths to ply needles if they had none, or use it to sing if their vocal cords had not been shot away. Teach them to amuse themselves, make something of themselves. Instead he began to teach them to think, think, THINK! Can you picture a more treacherous deed than to place a working mind in a mangled body? (p. 242)

Taught by the Old Man, four beggars, maimed victims of war, act as a terrible chorus of the violent, cannibalistic ethos of As, taking its half-comprehended injunction to 'THINK!' as a tool, a torturer's needle, with which to become specialists in 'THE TRUTH!' (p. 223).

With its metaphor of the infliction of pain, a savage interrogation of the mysteries of 'As', *Madmen and Specialists* subsumes, darkens and transforms the interrogations of tragic experience in *The Road*. This reflects a darker moment in the writing of Soyinka following the disillusionment of the 1967–9 civil war. In the notes of his imprisonment for opposition to that war, *The Man Died*, Soyinka reflected on his own uncompromising search for 'the truth', and the possibility of having deceived himself about the potential of Nigeria as a nation (see the quotation at the start of this essay). In this case, his satire in *Madmen and Specialists* on the genocidal demagogy of the forces behind the civil war must also be seen as self-satire. Nevertheless, Soyinka still retained his faith in the people, as opposed to the nation or state, of Nigeria: 'In moments of grave doubts it is essential to cling to the reality of peoples; these cannot vanish, they have no questionable *a priori* – they exist' (*The Man Died*, p. 175). Soyinka's satire, his voice, did not become bleakly destructive or disillusioned. Rather, he burrowed more deeply within the resources of his own culture and people, and committed himself to his own reading of Yoruba metaphysics as it confronts 'tragic' experience.

In his 1975 play, *Death and the King's Horseman*, Soyinka takes a story, based on an historical incident in the Yoruba town of Oyo, in which the Elesin, or king's horseman, is prevented by the British District Officer from committing ritual suicide to follow his king into death. The play dramatises a conflict of world views, 'the universe of the Yoruba mind'[15] against British colonial interventionism, but focuses that conflict on the Elesin himself, who is held responsible by his people for a loss of will:

> PRAISE-SINGER: Elesin, we placed the reins of the world in your hands yet you watched it plunge over the edge of the bitter precipice. You sat with folded arms while evil strangers tilted the world from its course and crashed it beyond the edge of emptiness – you muttered, there is little that one man can do, you left us floundering in a blind future . . . Our world is tumbling in the void of strangers, Elesin. (p. 75)

The question here is, what is this 'world' in the play?

*Death and the King's Horseman* is, as Soyinka himself has said of one of his plays, *The Swamp Dwellers*, a 'play of mood'.[16] Its mood is created by an intense lyric beauty as the action drifts towards a moment, the 'gateway' (p. 62) of Elesin's transition from this world to the next in response to the summons of his king:

> PRAISE-SINGER:   If you cannot come Elesin, tell my dog.
> I cannot stay the keeper too long
> At the gate.
> ELESIN:   A dog does not outrun the hand
> That feeds it meat. A horse that throws

|  | its rider |
|---|---|
|  | Slows down to a stop. Elesin Alafin |
|  | Trusts no beasts with messages between |
|  | A king and his companion. |
| PRAISE-SINGER: | If you get lost my dog will track |
|  | The hidden path to me. |
| ELESIN: | The seven-way crossroads confuses |
|  | Only the stranger. The Horseman of the King |
|  | Was born in the recesses of the house. (p. 42) |

With this we are back on the terrain of Ogun, of seven paths, and the dog which is Ogun's favourite sacrifice. Though the play has satirical episodes, and its final action is aborted into a blood ritual of death, its main thrust is in this lyrical bringing to birth through, in the words of Soyinka which preface the play, 'an evocation of music from the abyss of transition' (Author's Note, p. 7).

To understand more of what is happening here, it is useful to refer to the wider background of Yoruba theatre. Among the phenomena of Nigerian culture in the period leading up to and following Independence were the hugely successful Yoruba Popular Travelling Theatres which evolved a style of folk opera. The single largest figure to loom in this tradition was that of Hubert Ogunde.[17] The operatic structure of his plays involved an 'opening glee' of music, dance and invocation to settle audiences into the drama. The invocations involved a call to the good graces and attention of the audience and also a propitiation of the 'world', as in Ogunde's 1964 play, *Yoruba Ronu*:

| CHORUS: | The one who knows the World will inherit the World. |
|---|---|
|  | You who do not know the World accept my |
|  | condolences on your suffering . . . |
|  | We do not know whither the World is going |
|  | No one knows from where the World is coming. |
|  | But we know from where we set out.[18] |

The 'world', or *aiye*, is part of the three-tier universe of Yoruba cosmology, along with *ile* (earth) and *orun* (heaven). Any performance in the open space of theatre encounters, and is a potential disruption of, this 'world' with its structure of spiritual forces as well as the human presence of an audience. It has been argued by the Yoruba scholar, J. Adedeji, that the dramatists of the Popular Travelling Theatres still entertained a nagging fear of *aiye* and possible retribution for its balance having been disturbed. He traces this back to the traditional Alarinjo theatre which used satire, carefully, to perform a re-integrative social function: 'The traditional Yoruba dramatist uses his art to explain his knowledge of the world through satirical representations. In this act he needs a sensitive participation of his spectators in the reality of his art.'[19] To achieve this, the dramatist creates a 'mood', a sense of beauty which looks to find an echo in the mind and sensibility of an audience. The bleak, harsh voice of satire is a discordant ugliness which disrupts the balance of forces in this 'world'. It is this discordance which is heard in the accusations against Elesin in Soyinka's play, whose failure to listen to the voices of his own world has ruptured that balance and his own will to act:

> IYALOJA: No, you said, I am the hunter's dog and I shall eat the entrails of the game and the faeces of the hunter . . . You said No, I shall step in the vomit of cats and the droppings of mice; I shall fight them for the left-overs of the world. (p. 68)

In *Death and the King's Horseman* the dark period of Soyinka's satire has given way to a balance, a lyric beauty which insists on a redemptive will even while acknowledging defeat and despair.

Throughout Soyinka's work there exists this enigma of 'will' in the hero, or 'Protagonist Ego',[20] who emerges out of, but is in conflict with, the totalising concept of a Yoruba world view. It lies at the heart of a contradiction in Soyinka's syncretic version of tragedy: between a dynamic reassertion of will in the figure of Ogun, and an enervation or paralysis of the will implicit in the Aristotelian catharsis of western tragedy. In Soyinka's play *The Road*, the Professor shows how contingent this wilful protagonist can be, poised on the edge of a strange kind of being. Taken up in *Madmen and Specialists*, the messianic, visionary ego acquires a voice of dark satire, a strain which broods on the redemptive possibilities of violence. In *Death and the King's Horseman*, the problem is focused in the character of Elesin, whose 'will' is at odds with the context of a 'world' of Yoruba forces and their implicit harmony. Soyinka struggles with this dilemma in his work. Even at the level of his dramaturgy, he wrestles with conflicting idioms in giving shape to what is a syncretic drama. For this reason his plays, as distinct from his poetry or prose works, are often seen as obscure and difficult to stage. In them can be seen a current of thought which resists a totalising, dramatic language of explanation. They are still open to irresolvable challenges of 'tragic' experience, notably in their treatment of time, which can leave audiences bewildered, and their evocation of 'world', with its multiple tensions, in a self-actualising drama of becoming.

The Yoruba concept of man's relation to the *orisa*, the possibility of man's participation in a divine, heroic, protagonist essence, is central to Soyinka's idea of choric revelry and tragic art. It is a vital key to any production of Soyinka's work. Anyone who knows the Yoruba people and the extraordinary *presence* of their music and dancing, sees a wilful, explosive drama of drunken euphoria, and catches new rhythms in the seemingly disconnected *moments* of ecstatic and profligate abandon. Out of this can be recognised Soyinka's articulation of will. But the quality of that Yoruba will is sometimes very dark, very bleak.

Soyinka has held to his 'tragic vision' drawn from a Yoruba world view, and has created a drama of existence out of its confrontation with events in its own, often disastrous, history. In so doing he has entered into a dialogue with his own culture, and ranged outward from it to look at a world perceived through its eyes. In standing up to take his Nobel prize, he indeed faced a world of his own imagining, as a Nigerian, and should be applauded for it.

## Notes

1. Wole Soyinka, *The Man Died – prison notes of Wole Soyinka*, London: Rex Collins, 1972, p. 174.

2. *The Times*, London: 17 October 1986.

3. Wole Soyinka, *Who's Afraid of Elesin Oba?* (1979) in *Art, Dialogue and Outrage*, Ibadan: New Horn Press, 1988, p. 129. See also, Andrew Gurr, *Third World Drama: Soyinka and Tragedy*, in *Critical Perspectives on Wole Soyinka*, London: Heinemann, 1981, pp. 139–45.

4. Biodun Jeyifo, *The Truthful Lie: Essays in a Sociology of African Drama*, London: New Beacon Books, 1985, p. 14.

5. Wole Soyinka, *The Road* in *Collected Plays 1*, London: Oxford University Press, 1973, p. 157.

6. Oludare Olajubu, in *Critical Perspectives on Nigerian Literatures*, ed. Bernth Lindfors, Washington, DC: Three Continents Press, 1976, p. 5.

7. See Oyin Ogunba, *The Movement of Transition*, Ibadan: Ibadan University Press, 1975, p. 132. And J. Omosade Awolalu, *Yoruba Beliefs and Sacrificial Rites*, London: Longman, 1979, p. 72.

8. Wole Soyinka, 'The Fourth Stage', *Art, Dialogue and Outrage* (1988), p. 21.

9. Wole Soyinka, *Ogun Abibiman*, London: Rex Collins, 1976, p. 7.

10. Ben Okri, *The Famished Road*, London: Jonathan Cape, 1991, p. 478.

11. Wole Soyinka, 'Neo-Tarzanism' in *Art, Dialogue and Outrage* (1988). And, unpublished lecture, delivered in the English Faculty, Cambridge University, 12 March 1990.

12. Wole Soyinka, 'The Future of West African Writing', *The Horn*, Vol. IV, No. 1, 1960, Ibadan: University of Ibadan.

13. Biodun Jeyifo (1985), p. 35.

14. Wole Soyinka, *Madmen and Specialists* in *Collected Plays 2*, London: Oxford University Press, 1974, p. 241.

15. Wole Soyinka, *Death and the King's Horseman*, London: Methuen, 1975, Author's Note, p. 7.

16. *Critical Perspectives on Nigerian Literatures* (1976), p. 188.

17. See Ebun Clark, *Hubert Ogunde and the Making of the Nigerian Theatre*, London: Oxford University Press, 1979.

18. Hubert Ogunde, *Yoruba Ronu*, trans. J. Adedeji, in *Critical Perspectives on Nigerian Literatures* (1976), pp. 51–2.

19. Adedeji, *Critical Perspectives on Nigerian Literatures*, p. 53.

20. 'Who's Afraid of Elesin Oba?' in *Art, Dialogue and Outrage*, p. 118.

# Biographical Notes

SIMON GIKANDI is Associate Professor of English Language and Literature at the University of Michigan, Ann Arbor. He studied at Nairobi, Edinburgh and Northwestern Universities. He is the author of *Writing in Limbo: Modernism and Caribbean Literature* (Cornell University Press, 1992), *Reading Chinua Achebe: Language and Ideology in Fiction* (James Currey and Heinemann USA, 1991) and *Reading the African Novel* (James Currey and Heinemann USA, 1987). He is currently working on *Maps of Englishness: Postcolonial Theory and the Politics of Identity* and *In Search of Hidden Knowledge: Culture and Nationalism in Central Kenya*.

ADEWALE MAJA-PEARCE was born in London in 1953 and grew up in Lagos, Nigeria. He returned to Britain to complete his studies and obtained an MA from the School of Oriental and African Studies, University of London. His publications include *Loyalties and Other Stories* (Longman, 1986); *In My Father's Country* (William Heinemann, 1987); *How many miles to Babylon?* (William Heinemann, 1990); *Who's afraid of Wole Soyinka?* (Heinemann, 1991); and *A Mask Dancing: Nigerian Novelists of the Eighties* (Hans Zell, 1992). He has edited *Christopher Okigbo: Collected Poems* (Heinemann, 1986), and *The Heinemann Book of African Poetry in English* (1990). He currently works as Africa editor of *Index on Censorship* magazine, and is Series Editor of the Heinemann African Writers Series.

RASHIDAH ISMAILI ABUBAKR was born in Dahomey and spent many of her early years in Nigeria. Later she went to France and Italy, and then the United States where she did her PhD. She says of herself: 'My earliest teachers were the illiterate women of my family; aunts, cousins, older women, but especially my grandmother and my mother. The men in my family have been the "educated" ones.' She now lives in New York and teaches at Rutgers University, New Jersey. She is also a playwright and a poet, and often works in collaboration with musicians like Abdullah Ibrahim. Her second volume of poetry *Missing in Action and Presumed Dead* (Africa World Press Inc, Trenton, New Jersey) was published in 1992.

FRANK M. CHIPASULA is currently an Associate Professor of Black Literature at the University of Nebraska at Omaha, in the USA. He earned his

BA from the University of Zambia, two MAs in Creative Writing and Afro-American Literature and a PhD in English Literature from Brown and Yale Universities. His first book of poems, *Visions and Reflections* (NECZAM, Lusaka, 1972) is a pioneer work in English by a Malawian poet. Since 1984 he has published *O Earth, Wait for Me* (Ravan Press, Johannesburg, 1984), which received an Honourable Mention in the 1985 Noma Award for Publishing in Africa, *Nightwatcher, Nightsong* (Paul Green, Peterborough, 1986), and *Whispers in the Wings* (Heinemann, 1991). He is also the editor of *When My Brothers Come Home: Poems from Central and Southern Africa* (Wesleyan University Press, 1985). His novel, *In A Dark Season*, will soon be published in the Heinemann African Writers Series.

TERESA DOVEY was born in South Africa, and has studied and worked in France, England, the USA and Australia. Her PhD on J. M. Coetzee was obtained at the University of Melbourne. She has published a book, *The Novels of J. M. Coetzee: Lacanian Allegories* (Johannesburg: Ad Donker, 1988), and has published articles on contemporary Australian and South African writers. She assisted in the compilation of the J. M. Coetzee Bibliography published by the National English Literary Museum in Grahamstown, South Africa, and also wrote the Introduction. Currently she is a lecturer in the English Department at Rhodes University in South Africa.

DEREK WRIGHT has taught at universities in Africa and Australia and is currently Senior Lecturer in English at the Northern Territory University in Darwin, Australia. He is the author of over 60 articles in the areas of African, American and postcolonial literatures, including articles on Wole Soyinka, J. M. Coetzee, Ayi Kwei Armah, Chinua Achebe, Nuruddin Farah, John Updike, Doris Lessing and Randolph Stow. He has also published three books on African writing: *Ayi Kwei Armah's Africa: The Sources of His Fiction* (Zell, 1989); *Critical Perspectives on Ayi Kwei Armah* (edited, Three Continents Press, 1992); and *Wole Soyinka Revisited* (Twayne, 1993). His poems have appeared in various Australian journals.

MARK KINKEAD-WEEKES, born and brought up in South Africa, is Emeritus Professor of English at the University of Kent at Canterbury, England, having retired early to work on the new Cambridge biography on D. H. Lawrence. He has written books on Samuel Richardson (*Samuel Richardson: Dramatic Novelist*, Methuen, 1973) and Golding (*William Golding: A Critical Study*, Faber & Faber, 1961; re-issued 1984), and many articles on English, American, African and Caribbean literature. He is also the editor of the scholarly Cambridge edition of D. H. Lawrence's *The Rainbow*.

CRAIG MACKENZIE was awarded an MA by the University of Natal for a study on the works of Bessie Head. Until 1991 a researcher at the National English Literary Museum in Grahamstown, he now teaches in the English Department at the Rand Afrikaans University, Johannesburg. His publications include *Bessie Head: An Introduction* (1989), *Between the Lines: Interviews with*

*Bessie Head, Sheila Roberts, Ellen Kuzwayo, Miriam Tlali* (1989) co-edited with Cherry Clayton, and a posthumously published collection of Bessie Head's autobiographical writings in the Heinemann African Writers Series, *A Woman Alone* (1990). His articles on South African literature have appeared in *World Literature Written in English*, *English in Africa*, and various other South African literary journals, as well as in the recent Garland critical anthology *International Literature in English* (1991). He is currently doing research on South African short fiction.

BELINDA JACK is Lecturer in French at Christ Church, University of Oxford. Born in the United Kingdom, she read for her first degree in French with African and Caribbean Studies at the University of Kent, England. She took her doctorate at the University of Oxford. Her book on francophone literatures worldwide is to be published by Oxford University Press. She has contributed several articles on African and Indian Ocean writing in French for the forthcoming *Oxford Companion to Literature in French*. She is also working on a book on black and white feminist theory and the readings they generate of black women's writing.

ABDULRAZAK GURNAH was born in Zanzibar, Tanzania. He was educated there and in England and now teaches literature at the University of Kent at Canterbury, England. He is the author of three novels: *Memory of Departure* (1987), *Pilgrims Way* (1988), and *Dottie* (1990). All three novels were published by Jonathan Cape, London. His new novel, *Paradise*, will be published later in 1993 by Hamish Hamilton. He is also an Associate Editor of the journal *Wasafiri*.

GABRIEL GBADAMOSI, born in 1961 in London of Irish/Nigerian parents, studied literature at Cambridge University. He now works as a poet and playwright. He lived in North Africa and took up a Winston Churchill Fellowship to travel across West Africa looking at theatre. He was awarded an Arts Council Arts Bursary in 1987, and was writer-in-residence at the Manchester Royal Exchange Theatre. Most recently he worked with the European Theatre Convention in Portugal, and is presently a Judith E. Wilson Fellow in Cambridge University. His plays include *No Blacks, No Irish*; *Shango*; *Abolition*; and *Eshu's Faust*, and a play for BBC television, *Friday's Daughter*. His poetry has been published in *The New British Poetry 1968–1988* (Paladin, 1988), and *The Heinemann Book of African Poetry in English* (Heinemann, 1990).

# Index